Joshua's Spiritual Warfare

Understanding the Chiasms of Joshua

Thomas B. Clarke

Bible Discernments
Publishing Division of Prayer Gardeners
Syracuse, NY USA

Cover: Petrus Comestor's *"Bible Historale"*, France, 1372
Courtesy of Museum Meermanno Westreenianum, The Hague

Joshua's Spiritual Warfare: Understanding the Chiasms of Joshua
Copyright © 2008 by Thomas B. Clarke

Bible Discernments
Publishing Division of Prayer Gardeners
4113 W. Seneca Turnpike
Syracuse, NY 13215

Printed in the United States of America

ISBN 978-0-9816213-0-2

All rights reserved. No part of this publication may be reproduced, stored in a retrieval system, or transmitted in any form or by any means – electronic, mechanical, photocopy, recording, or any other – except for brief quotations in printed reviews, without the permission of the author.

Unless otherwise stated, Bible quotations are taken from *The Holy Bible, New International Version*, Copyright © 1973, 1978, 1984 by The Zondervan Corporation.

Bible quotations identified KJV are from *King James Version*.

Bible quotations marked NKJV are from *New King James Version* of the Bible. Copyright © 1979, 1980, 1982 by Thomas Nelson Inc., Publisher.

www.Bible-Discernments.com

To Nancy, my faithful wife and best friend –

Dear, you have been so faithful and supportive during this writing, and I truly honor you for that. Your steadfast zeal for more of the Lord is a constant encouragement to me. You seek His presence in your daily life and anxiously wait to hear His voice. I am so blessed that you are my wife.

As I write this dedication, I know you are sleeping, having gone to bed hours before. Sleep well, my dear; you will need your energy in this spiritual battle.

> *A chord of three strands is not quickly broken* (Eccl 4:12).

> *Glorify the LORD with me; let us exalt his name together* (Ps 34:3).

To Pastor J. Lee Simmons –

Your constant encouragement brings tears to my eyes. Thank you for your great support and tremendous insight.

Contents

Foreword

Introduction — 1 —

Part One – Background — 5 —
   Who was Joshua? — 5 —
   Introduction to the Chiastic Approach — 23 —
   Structure of the Book of Joshua — 35 —

Part Two – The Battle — 41 —
   First Outer Tier Chiasm — 41 —
   Chapter 1 – The Lord Assures Joshua — 43 —
   Chapter 2 – The Lord Has Given the Whole Land — 51 —
   Chapters 3 and 4 – Transformed at the Jordan — 65 —
   Chapter 5 – Sins of the Fathers — 83 —
   Chapter 6 – The Deliverance of Jericho — 101 —
   Chapter 7 – Achan's Sin — 121 —
   Chapter 8 – Achan's Sin is Resolved — 131 —
   Chapter 9 – Gibeonites are Grafted-In to God's Community — 145 —
   Chapter 10 – The Sun Stands Still — 153 —
   Chapters 11 and 12 – More Kings are Defeated — 161 —

Part Three – The Allotments — 169 —
   Second Outer Tier Chiasm — 169 —
   Chapters 13 to 21 – Allotments of the Land — 171 —
   Chapter 22 – An Altar to Remember Us By — 181 —
   Chapters 23 and 24 – Love the Lord, Serving Him Faithfully — 193 —
   Concluding Remarks — 207 —

Spiritual Principles — 211 —

Foreword

In an age where the church is characterized by lethargy and indifference; where sexual deviation is epidemic and divorce seems more common that true conversions and holiness has become an archaic word; it is more than obvious that this generation has wandered in the wilderness of spiritual carnality. Spiritual defeat is common, accepted, and excused.

A new generation needs to be raised up and equipped to defeat spiritual giants and possess what God has given as our inheritance. The eternal lessons of Joshua and his new generation of people of faith model for us the path to spiritual victory through spiritual warfare.

In Thomas Clarke's book *Joshua's Spiritual Warfare,* the author clearly demonstrates God's plan for spiritual victory. Clarke's unique style, using the chiastic approach, greatly assists in gleaning spiritual warfare principles from Joshua. I have found the book not only intriguing and highly interesting, but most vitally a significant weapon to fight the good fight of faith and enter into all of God's good and wonderful provisions and promises. Such work is desperately needed in such spiritually desolate times.

Dr. J. Lee Simmons, Senior Pastor, Faith Chapel

Introduction

The story of Joshua, his life and accomplishments, is a story of liberation. Most frequently, people think of Joshua as the great commander that led Israel in the conquest of the Promised Land. The liberation of the Promised Land was accomplished through a man who was willing to listen to the Lord's voice and to act on it.

This book is more about spiritual warfare than it is the liberation of the Promised Land. Effective spiritual warfare should be based on lifestyle rather than just intercession; it is the battle in our minds between the powers of Good and evil. The Lord is attempting to pull us to Him, and the devil is attempting to manipulate and deceive us so that we are pulled to him. The devil can attempt to addict us (spirit of obsession), oppress us (spirit of oppression), make us feel unworthy (spirit of worthlessness) and depress us (spirit of depression). The purpose of this book is to help free us and to keep us free from whatever spirits the devil attempts to send our way.

Much has been written about spiritual warfare by people well known in Christian circles: Charles Stanley, Chip Ingram, Derek Prince and Neil Anderson, to name just a few. Most books on spiritual warfare focus on what the New Testament says about spiritual warfare. Yes, there may be some references to the Psalms, Genesis (especially chapter 3), Proverbs, or other Old Testament books; but the predominant emphasis in most spiritual warfare books is on the New Testament.

Please think about this regarding the life of Joshua: when the Israelite army went up against the nations in the Promised Land, was that in any way similar to spiritual warfare? [I hope you said Yes!] Clearly Joshua was dedicated to freeing the people of Israel from the forces that would try to defeat them. Just as armies prepare themselves for physical warfare, we too should prepare ourselves for dealing with spiritual warfare.

This book is unique in several ways:

- A linguistic style called the "chiastic approach" is used to analyze the Book of Joshua. The lessons from these "chiasms" are applied to spiritual warfare and victorious Christian living. It is a premise of this book that by analyzing the chiasms of the Book of Joshua, we can uncover key principles of spiritual warfare.

- This "chiastic approach" also opens a fresh understanding of the events in the Book of Joshua.

- Regarding spiritual warfare, the emphasis is on the events during Joshua's lifetime, but is applied to today's readers.

This book will be a new teaching for many people. As Christians mature in their faith, they sometimes wonder "Is there more?" This book opens a new way of looking at the writings in the Bible by looking at the chiastic approach and then applying it in the area of spiritual warfare. The chiastic approach has been hidden from many Bible scholars, yet it is offers a profound understanding of the Bible.

I thank the Lord for the many revelations that the Holy Spirit has provided in the writing of this book. Just the events of Joshua 5 and 6 continue to cause me to bow down in reverence to Him. My prayer for the readers of this book is that, in the same way, each person catches a fresh revelation from the Lord. As with any new idea, it is important to submit these ideas to the Holy Spirit for clarification, direction and application.

Approach

In this book, there are three interwoven themes:

- **The life, times and faith of Joshua** – We will look at the events that Joshua witnessed from his first battle in Exodus through his death at the end of the Book of Joshua. In many cases, the events are interpreted in non-traditional ways because the associated chiasm provides a deeper meaning. Geography lessons will be used to help understand the times that Joshua lived in. In the first and last chapters of this book, we will review those attributes that made Joshua a great man in the Lord.
- **The chiasms in the Book of Joshua** – You may ask **"What is a chiasm?"** A chiasm **(ky'-az-um)** represents a writing style that – once understood – clarifies, emphasizes and reveals deeper meaning in the Scriptures than is revealed in just a surface reading of these same verses. When we get to the Book of Joshua, I frequently refer to chiasms. A chiasm is an example of the linguistic style called the "chiastic **(ky'-az-tic)** approach." Many Bible scholars have never heard of this, yet it was identified over two hundred years ago. Once you understand how the chiastic approach works, it can dramatically enhance your understanding of those verses in the New and Old Testament where a chiasm appears.

  Some people do not initially grasp the idea behind the chiastic approach. If that is you, do not be dismayed. The second

Introduction

chapter of this book is devoted to understanding this writing style. If that is not enough, there are numerous sites on the Internet that attempt to explain it even further. Some of these sites are secular because this writing style was not limited to the Bible.

- **The application to today's spiritual warfare** - In my opinion, good Bible study should provide a way to apply what is learned. At the end of many sections, we will look at 'Spiritual Principles' that provide an application of what has been discussed. These Spiritual Principles are repeated at the end of this book where they are organized into various categories.

In addition to the 'Spiritual Principles', there is an analogous comparison of the physical battle that Joshua faced with the spiritual battle that each of us face today. The analogy compares the destruction of kings and kingdoms with the deliverance of individuals today. In this way, we will look at examples of spiritual warfare that Joshua encountered.

Content

This book has three parts:

Part One	Background information: who was Joshua and what are chiasms?
Part Two	The invasion into Israel and the total destruction of thirty-one cities in the Promised Land (Joshua 1 – 12).
Part Three	The distribution of the land with an emphasis on loving and serving the Lord (Joshua 13 – 24).

In this book, I pay a good deal of attention to Hebrew words and how they are used. This book presents the Hebrew based on the Interlinear Bible, which was used to determine patterns and derive meanings. [1] I also make use of the many other reference materials in the PC Study Bible. [2]

---

[1] Biblesoft, Inc., *"Interlinear Transliterated Bible"*, Copyright © 1994, 2003, 2006, All Rights Reserved
[2] Jim Gilbertson, "PC Study Bible V5.0C for Windows", (Biblesoft, Inc., Copyright © 1988-2006, All Rights Reserved)

Contribution to Biblical Understanding

This book is a new teaching in several respects:

- The study of the chiastic approach has largely been confined to an academic audience. The attempt is made in this book to make chiasms understandable to a broad range of people.
- Previous identification of chiasms within the Book of Joshua has come up with no more than a handful. This book identifies sixty-seven chiasms in Joshua alone. Often, one chiasm stops and another immediately begins.
- This book directly relates chiasms to spiritual warfare within the Book of Joshua. This is the first work to make this association.
- The chiasms in this book are presented as an arrangement of circles within circles within a circle. This helps explain the overall structure of Joshua.
- Many events in Joshua are presented in a fresh way, often because a chiasm reveals a new understanding.
- The many chiasms are applied in such a way that we can understand how to become more Christ-like in our daily walk.

Your Preparation

If you have not read Exodus through Joshua recently, you may benefit by reading three chapters per day, which should adequately prepare you for this book:

Books	Chapters	Number of Chapters
Exodus	1 - 20, 23 - 24, 31 - 34	26
Leviticus	8 - 10, 16, 23 - 24, 26	7
Numbers	9 - 14, 16 - 17, 20 - 27, 31 - 32	18
Deuteronomy	1 - 11, 16, 20, 27 - 32, 34	20
Joshua	1 - 24	24
	Total	95

Understanding the book that you are about to read should be within the capabilities of a broad range of Bible believing people. Inadequate preparation, however, is possibly the largest reason for struggling with this book. If that is you, are you prepared for this challenge?

Part One – Background

Who was Joshua?

> *Moses and Aaron, Nadab and Abihu, and the seventy elders of Israel went up and saw the God of Israel. Under his feet was something like a pavement made of sapphire, clear as the sky itself. But God did not raise his hand against these leaders of the Israelites; they saw God, and they ate and drank.*
>
> *The LORD said to Moses, "Come up to me on the mountain and stay here, and I will give you the tablets of stone, with the law and commands I have written for their instruction."*
>
> *Then Moses set out with **Joshua** his aide, and Moses went up on the mountain of God* (Ex 24:9-13).

What a phenomenal experience. On the way up Mount Sinai, Moses, Aaron, his sons and seventy elders had an encounter with God. The stone underneath God's feet, translated here as sapphire, was a deeply intense blue rock that can be highly polished. God was revealing himself to them. Not only did they see God, but they also ate and drank with Him.

The Lord then told Moses to go to the top of the mountain. So Moses set out with Joshua. Who? Who was going towards the top?

Aaron was possibly the most surprised with the appointment of Joshua to go up the mountain. Aaron was the older brother of Moses, had personally witnessed the Lord perform ten plagues simply by the movement of their hands, and had seen the God of Israel firsthand. To his mind, Aaron was certainly the second in command to Moses. Joshua was only the captain of an army of Israelites.

Let us look at three ways that the Lord had used Aaron prior to taking Joshua up the mountain of God: during the plagues, in the defeat of the Amalekites, and in meeting the Lord.

During the plagues, Aaron knew the key role that he played in getting the Israelites out of Egypt. Twice Moses questioned the Lord because of his faltering lips (Ex 4:10-13; 6:12). On the third time, the Lord gave Aaron the responsibility to talk to Pharaoh instead of Moses (Ex 7:1,2). Then in the first four miracles, the Lord spoke to Moses but it was Aaron that performed the miracles instead of Moses:

- Aaron used his staff and his hand so that the Lord could turn his staff into a snake (Ex 7:10).
- Aaron stretched his hand and the Nile was changed into a river of blood (Ex 7:19,20).
- Aaron stretched his hand and more frogs came into Egypt than anyone could possibly imagine (Ex 8:6).
- Aaron stretched his staff and there were gnats everywhere (Ex 8:17).

In the second plague, after the frogs were covering the land and after Moses spoke to Pharaoh for the first time, Moses did command the frogs to go away (Ex 8:10-12). It was not until the sixth plague that Moses himself performed one of the ten plagues by tossing soot into the air (Ex 9:10). Moses was initially so unsure of himself that Aaron had to first demonstrate the technique of miracles.

Aaron and Moses were the ones used by the Lord to perform the ten plagues; Joshua was not even a part of this. In fact, the first mention of Joshua in the Bible was thirty days or so after they crossed the Red Sea, and that was the defeat of the Amalekites (Ex 17:8-16).

The second way the Lord used Aaron was in the defeat of the Amalekites (Ex 17:8-16). Aaron might have thought something like: "I remember the battle that you, Joshua, fought against the Amalekites. Joshua, it was not your prowess that won that battle, but it was because Hur and I helped hold up the hands of Moses. You were loosing that battle but we stepped in to help." Aaron knew the key role that he had played in that battle and he knew that Joshua would have been defeated without their help.

The third way was immediately before the Ten Commandments were spoken; the Lord instructed Moses to bring Aaron with him to the top of the mountain (Ex 19:24). Aaron had been chosen by the Lord.

Prior to Exodus 24:9-13, Aaron had the position of second in command to Moses. Joshua had only commanded the army to defeat the Amalekites. Joshua is described as the aide to Moses (Ex 24:13), but notice the order of presentation in Exodus 24:9: Moses, Aaron, Aaron's sons Nadab and Abihu, and seventy elders. Even if Joshua was one of the seventy elders, he was not mentioned by name.

I can imagine Aaron asking "Why, then, dear brother Moses, have you selected Joshua to go up the mountain with you?" Aaron was likely expecting to be selected once again to accompany his brother. Why then did Moses select Joshua to go up on the mountain of God? What was it that placed Joshua in this second in command position? Why not Aaron?

Moses stayed on top of that mountain for forty days with Joshua nearby, and the Lord gave instructions that are documented in Exodus 25 - 31. At the end of that time, Aaron yielded to the beckoning of the people and made an idol out of gold in the shape of a calf (Ex 32:1-5). Aaron showed himself to be weak in the site of his fellow Israelites, but why was he so weak? It appears that Aaron yielded to the people's wishes to "make gods" because a **spirit of jealousy** came upon him over the appointment of Joshua. We may never know if that is so, but there may be no better explanation of Aaron's behavior.

Who was this man Joshua that potentially got Aaron so upset? After a brief geography lesson on Mount Sinai, we will look at some of his characteristics.

Geography: Mount Sinai

As we go through this book, geographic details are provided from which spiritual implications are drawn where appropriate. Few Christians have traveled to Mount Sinai and many have not traveled to Israel. For those that have traveled to Israel on a tour, Jericho is typically the only place along the tour which was a significant part of Joshua's conquest. Tour buses normally do not travel to cities like Shechem (modern day Nablus), Gibeon (modern day el-Jib) or Ai in the West Bank, or to the country of Jordan. The intent of these geography lessons is to help you visualize the setting, giving insight into the events and times of Joshua from a non-traditional standpoint.

If you have a newer model computer with an Internet connection, I invite you download *Google Earth*. [3] This totally free software from Google, Inc. allows you to look at the geography of any area on the earth using 3D imaging. It's phenomenal!! Based on satellite imagery, maps and aerial photographs, you can see the farm land of the Jordan Valley, the extensive winding of the Jordan River, the oasis near Jericho and any other location on this planet.

---

[3] I use Google Earth on my home computer using a dial-up modem. A high speed Internet connection is faster but not a requirement. Rather that provide a reference like www.google.com which is subject to change, I recommend you type "Google Earth Download" in your Internet search engine and then locate it from there. You should also find the "minimum and recommended configuration" which can be used to determine if the computer will be able to operate Google Earth properly. If you download other free software that is offered from Google, that is up to you. As a computer professional, I recommend downloading just Google Earth, assuming you have adequate resources on your PC or Mac. YOU ONLY NEED "GOOGLE EARTH" to see these locations.

As we progress through this book, I will invite you to enter the longitude and latitude of nine Biblical locations using Google Earth. As you do this, I also encourage you to explore the land of Israel and Jordan using this software. For example, one of the first things I did with Google Earth was to position myself on the largest mountain in Jordan near where Moses died; I was curious how much of Canaan that Moses would have been able to see (Deut 34:1-3).

Tradition has placed Mount Sinai on the southern end of the Sinai Peninsula. In some places in the Bible, Mount Sinai is identified as Mount Horeb, but they are the same location. Once you have installed Google Earth, type the following longitude and latitude which will take you to the traditional location of Mount Sinai:
   28 32.38'N, 33 58.4'E
You probably will have to adjust the controls in the top right portion of your screen to bring the image into focus. Using these controls, you can tilt your viewpoint so you can see the size of the mountains.

While there are mountains nearby that are higher, Mount Sinai is over 7,000 feet high and is barren. Trees and brush cannot be seen anywhere on this mountain – only barren rock. The Lord took Moses and Joshua to a place where not only was His presence to be known, but dependence on the Lord was to be experienced. While they were on that mountain, they could not eat or drink because there was nothing to eat and nothing to drink (Deut 9:9,18). That is dependence on the Lord.

Joshua's Holiness

> *But as for me and my household, we will serve the LORD* (Josh 24:15).

There is no record in the Bible of Joshua's height or weight, the color of his hair or his complexion. We do not know what he ate or drank or how long his hair was. From the above verse, we can see that he had a household at the end of his life. The *Midrash*, which is a collection of Jewish oral teachings and tradition from as long ago as the 2nd and 3rd century AD, states that Joshua eventually married Rahab, had daughters but no sons, and many prophets including Jeremiah were his descendents. [4] This writing in the *Midrash* can be questioned, however, because the Bible states that Rahab married Salmon (Matt 1:5).

Whether or not Joshua married Rahab, it really doesn't matter. What is important is to understand his relationship with the Lord by

---

[4] *Jewish Encyclopedia*, Online:
http://www.jewishencyclopedia.com/view.jsp?artid=71&letter=R&search=rahab
, 6 April 2007

trying to get a measure on his holiness. Holiness is described in the Bible as something from God, not from ourselves:

> *Keep my commands and follow them. I am the LORD. Do not profane my holy name. I must be acknowledged as holy by the Israelites. I am the LORD, who **makes you holy*** (Lev 22:31,32).

Understand this: in order for the Lord to speak to Joshua as he did, he must have had a strong anointing of holiness about him. I cannot make myself holy and you cannot make yourself holy. We can present our offerings in the proper manner, we can keep ourselves sexually and physically pure, we can eat the proper foods, and we can try to keep ourselves from sin. The Lord is the one who fills our spirit when He sees a properly prepared vessel. Through his Holy Spirit, we receive His presence within us, and that is what makes us holy.

How was Joshua holy? He was not a priest. Only Levites could be priests, and Joshua was from the tribe of Ephraim (Num 13:8). Yet holiness was not limited to just one tribe. All Israelites were called to live a life of purity in the presence of God.

The power of God was certainly evident in Joshua's presence: the Jordan River stopped flowing (Josh 3:16), the walls of Jericho fell down (Josh 6:20), and the sun stood still for 24 hours (Josh 10:13). Holiness does not require the presence of power; the presence of power is not evidence of holiness. Holiness does require intimacy with the Lord, and Joshua heard the voice of the Lord on many occasions.

Was Joshua without sin? Moses sinned when he hit the rock with his staff by not honoring the Lord (Num 20:11), which was why he was not allowed into the land of Canaan. Joshua stepped ahead of the Lord in going to Ai (Josh 7:2), and he failed to seek the Lord during the Gibeonite deception (Josh 9:14), both of which might be considered sin. Holiness is not the complete absence of sin, but it requires a conscious and regular path of purity. Moses, Aaron and Joshua all achieved a high level of holiness because they learned from their sins and dealt with them properly.

Francis Frangipane wrote this about holiness:

> "...holiness begins the moment we seek God for Himself. A touch from God is wonderful but we are in pursuit of more than just experience – more than 'goose bumps and tears.' We are seeking to abide with Christ, where

we are continually aware of His fulness (*sic*) within us,
where His presence dwells in us in glory." [5]

Joshua was such a man, seeking to hear God's voice and being in His presence. Because of his training and his anointing, Joshua followed the example set by Moses. He was trained by the most holy of the men at that time:

> *Since then, no prophet has risen in Israel like Moses, whom the LORD knew face to face, who did all those miraculous signs and wonders the LORD sent him to do* (Deut 34:10,11).

Joshua had many encounters with spiritual warfare and we will review these in detail throughout the remainder of this book. More important than the many miracles that were performed under Joshua's covering are how these lessons are applied in our own lives. None can be more important than receiving His glory because of our holiness.

An important prerequisite for holiness is humility. Joshua learned from the most humble of men:

> *Now Moses was a very humble man,* **more humble** *than anyone else on the face of the earth* (Num 12:3).

When Ai was defeated, Joshua demonstrated the characteristic of humility: he *"tore his clothes and fell facedown to the ground before the Ark of the Lord, remaining there till evening"* (Josh 7:6). An arrogant or prideful man might have gathered a lot more soldiers and charged back up the hill in revenge. This was not how Joshua behaved and it is not how we should behave. If we fall at the feet of our Lord when things don't go well, we are assuming the correct posture for the restoration of holiness.

The Book of Joshua concludes by stating that Joshua died at the age of one hundred and ten (Josh 24:29). Joshua assembled all of the tribes of Israel at Shechem shortly before he died and said:

> *Now fear the LORD and serve him with all faithfulness. Throw away the gods your forefathers worshiped beyond the River and in Egypt, and serve the LORD. But if serving the LORD seems undesirable to you, then choose for yourselves this day whom you will serve, whether the gods your forefathers served beyond the River, or the gods of the Amorites, in whose land you*

---

[5] Francis Frangipane, *Holiness, Truth and the Presence of God* (Cedar Rapids, IA: Arrow Publications, 1986), 17-18.

> are living. But as for me and my household, we will serve the LORD *(Josh 24:14,15).*

These are not the words of a failing, faltering or defeated man; they are the words of a man who lived a fruitful life, dwelled with the Lord, walked with God, and spoke life into a nation that was naturally rebellious. This was Joshua's holiness.

> **In our pursuit for increased holiness, we must be successful at spiritual warfare.**

The War Between the Powers of Good and Evil

Joshua had to fight the battles of spiritual warfare just like the rest of us. This is a war between the powers of Good and the powers of evil, and this war is in very close proximity. Satan rules as the prince of the world, and our physical bodies must reside in this world. The battle is for our very own soul; it is Satan's plan to defeat us and take our soul with him. The battle line where spiritual warfare takes place may not be physically seen, but the evidence of this battle can be very apparent:

> *For we wrestle not against flesh and blood, but against principalities, against powers, against the rulers of the darkness of this world, against spiritual wickedness in high places (Eph 6:12 KJV).*

We must understand that for any person, there are both Good and evil spirits that are at war. The battle is for the control of our minds. With regard to Ephesians 6:12 (above), Joyce Meyer stated:

> "From this Scripture we see that we are in a war. A careful study of this verse informs us that our warfare is not with other human beings but with the devil and his demons. Our enemy, Satan, attempts to defeat us with strategy and deceit, through well-laid plans and deliberate deception." [6]

Joshua was just as much a target of this spiritual warfare as anyone else, yet he would be considered successful. As we will see, his teachable spirit allowed him to use the spirits of authority and wisdom to overcome the enemy's attacks and strongholds.

---

[6] Joyce Meyer, *Battlefield of the Mind*, (Fenton, MO: Life In The Word, Inc., 1995), 15.

Joshua's Teachable Spirit

Joshua's name was originally Hoshea, but Moses gave him the new name Joshua (Num 13:16). The name Hoshea means 'salvation', and the name Joshua means 'the Lord saves'. In other words, his very own purpose was to save the people from the powers of darkness and evil through the power of the Lord. Joshua's new name reflects his ability to be taught the greater things of the Lord:

> *The LORD would speak to Moses face to face, as a man speaks with his friend. Then Moses would return to the camp, but his young aide Joshua son of Nun **did not leave the tent*** [of meeting] (Ex 33:11).

My children are probably average compared to yours, but to me they are very unique and special. My older daughter Laurel was the apple of my eye for many years; my younger daughter, Becky, was born 5 years later. Laurel had a strong ear for music, so I taught her what I could on the piano. She knew reading was important to her parents, so she learned how to read at a very early age. Wherever we went, Laurel would tag along, mimicking the actions of her mother or father.

Joshua, like my daughter Laurel, had a very teachable spirit. In Exodus 33:11 (above), we see that Joshua was so zealous for the Lord that he did not leave the tent of meeting. His zeal made him very teachable.

As Moses came down off the mountain after having been there for forty days, Joshua told Moses *"There is the sound of war in the camp"* (Ex 32:17). Where had Joshua been for the forty days prior? Both of them had gone to the top of the mountain (Ex 24:13). The Bible does not state whether Joshua had the same encounter with the Lord that Moses did, but we can be sure that Joshua did not go to the base of the mountain where Aaron was. Because Joshua had a teachable spirit, he wanted to take in everything that he could.

When Joshua identified the *"sound of war in the camp,"* Moses had to teach discernment to Joshua's new ears. Moses responded to Joshua *"It is not the sound of victory, it is not the sound of defeat, it is the sound of singing that I hear"* (Ex 32:18). Both Joshua and Moses heard the sound, but Moses had understanding. Joshua thought it was the sound of war but Moses heard singing. The Lord had told Moses in Exodus 32:7 that his people had become corrupt. In Exodus 32:18, Moses was teaching Joshua how to discern properly because Joshua had a teachable spirit.

Another sign of a teachable spirit is how Joshua handled correction. In Numbers 11:26-28, Joshua witnessed two men who were prophesying like the seventy elders but were outside the Tent. Joshua went to Moses with the false assumption that prophesying should be limited to the Tent of Meeting. Moses had to correct Joshua by rebuking a spirit of jealousy: *"Are you jealous for my sake? I wish that all the LORD's people were prophets and that the LORD would put his Spirit on them"* (Num 11:29). Joshua had nothing to say, which shows his teachable spirit because he received the admonition from his mentor.

Just the fact that Joshua sat at Moses' feet for forty years indicates his teachable spirit:

> *Hear now, O Israel, the decrees and laws I am about to* **teach** *you. Follow them so that you may live and may go in and take possession of the land that the LORD, the God of your fathers, is giving you* (Deut 4:1).

At the end of this book, we will review how well Joshua performed as a leader of Israel and as a lover and servant of the Lord.

> **To become better at spiritual warfare, be eager to be taught and be receptive to correction.**

Joshua's Spirit of Authority

Some people think that because the Holy Spirit did not come in power until the day of Pentecost, that the Holy Spirit was not a significant player in the Old Testament. Others have suggested that it was the Holy Spirit that came upon Joshua based on Numbers 27:15-20 (below). I suggest that neither interpretation is exactly correct.

The word *"spirit"* that is used in these verses is the Aramaic word **ruwach** (roo'-akh) which means 'wind' (such as in Exodus 14:21 where the Lord blew a strong east wind which opened the sea) or 'spirit' (when related to a person). Remember: **ruwach** can mean wind or spirit, not necessarily the Holy Spirit.

Joshua was given a spirit of authority when Moses laid his hands on him:

> *Moses said to the LORD, "May the LORD, the God of the* **spirits** *of all mankind, appoint a man over this community ... So the LORD said to Moses, "Take Joshua son of Nun, a* **man in whom is the spirit**, *and lay your hand on him. ... Give him some of your* **authority** *so the whole Israelite community will obey him"* (Num 27:15-20).

Note the order of presentation. First, the Lord is the God of the spirits of all mankind. Secondly, we see that this spirit **(ruwach)** was in Joshua. Then, Moses was instructed to lay hands on him. The laying on of hands was necessary to pass on the spirit of **authority**. As a result, Joshua carried the respect of the people, the Lord and the demons.

When Joshua spoke to the people, they not only listened, but for the most part, they followed his directions. When the sun stood still, it was because Joshua spoke to the Lord with spiritual authority. When the kings were defeated in the Promised Land, the success was in part due to the authority that Joshua had over the spirits.

Moses demonstrated this spirit of authority in the defeat of the Amalekites:

> *So Joshua fought the Amalekites as Moses had ordered, and Moses, Aaron and Hur went to the top of the hill. As long as Moses held up his hands, the Israelites were winning, but whenever he lowered his hands, the Amalekites were winning. When Moses' hands grew tired, they took a stone and put it under him and he sat on it. Aaron and Hur held his hands up — one on one side, one on the other — so that his hands remained steady till sunset. So Joshua overcame the Amalekite army with the sword* (Ex 17:10-13).

Joshua's army fought the physical battle, but there was a much stronger spiritual battle taking place. By the authority of the hands that Moses held up (with the help of Aaron and Hur), the spiritual forces behind the Amalekites were defeated – by defeating these evil spiritual forces, the army under the direction of Joshua was able to defeat the people known as the Amalekites.

Moses passed the authority on to Joshua. Elijah passed the authority on to Elisha. Christ, through his death and resurrection, passed that authority on to us, if we are willing to obey His commands. Jesus also transferred His power: *"All authority in heaven and on earth has been given to me. Therefore go ..."* (Matt 28:18). In the parallel verses in Mark 16:15-18, the authority is over all sorts of spirits: demons, snakes, poisons and sicknesses.

Shortly after our church moved into its new building several years ago, we invited a spirit-filled preacher and evangelist to speak at a two day seminar. This man spoke Friday night and Saturday morning. After lunch on Saturday, he asked our church secretary why she was wearing a very elaborate breathing mask. She explained that the new carpets emitted a chemical that was toxic to her body. Taking the authority that Christ had placed in him, he cast that spirit out of her. Immediately she was healed; the remainder of that day and following weeks, she went without that breathing apparatus. This authority is available to each one of us if we are willing to use it.

Spiritual warfare includes taking authority over those demonic spirits in the name of Christ, and speaking those words that need to be said. Do not let the deceiver steal our ability to win the battle. Don't let the devil trick us!!

> Christ provides the spirit of authority to believers; authority includes the ability to encounter the evil spirits and defeat them.

Joshua's Spirit of Wisdom

Joshua also had a spirit **(ruwach)** of **wisdom** just after the death of Moses:

> *Now Joshua son of Nun was filled with the spirit of **wisdom** because Moses had laid his hands on him. So the Israelites listened to him and did what the LORD had commanded Moses* (Deut 34:9).

Joshua did not have the strength that was in Gideon, nor did he have the spirit of prophecy that was in Samuel, nor the spirit of power that Elijah or Elisha had. No, it was wisdom. Wisdom was necessary so that, when the Lord spoke, he knew when and how to cross the Jordan, how to conquer Jericho, who had brought the sin into the camp, and how to destroy Ai. Wisdom, which is the Hebrew word **chokmah** (khok-maw'), was given to:

- Aaron to perform his duties as a priest (Num 28:3).
- Bezaleel as master builder to construct the tabernacle and its elements (Num 31:3).
- Aholiab and all workers as craftsmen for their portions of the tabernacle (Num 31:6).
- For all of Israel, that by observing all that Moses commanded, they would demonstrate their wisdom (Deut 4:6).

Solomon, in the Book of Proverbs, described how a person with the spirit of knowledge and the spirit of understanding was of an excellent **ruwach** (spirit):

> *He who has knowledge spares his words,*
> *And a man of understanding is of a calm **spirit** (Prov*
> *17:27 NKJV).*

Such was the spirit of wisdom that Joshua was blessed with. When the waters parted the Jordan River, it was the presence of the ark of the Testimony that caused the waters to stop, not the power that was upon Joshua. The walls of Jericho did not fall because of Joshua's strength; however, the Lord told Joshua when and how often to blast the trumpet and shout. Clearly, a spirit of wisdom had to be upon Joshua to even think of saying to the Lord that the sun was to stand still!

I am always enamored by the snow geese when they visit our area. In our area of upstate New York, the snow geese can often be seen migrating between somewhere in southern USA and northern Canada. In late March, my wife and I will drive to a hillside overlooking one of the Finger Lakes. About 6:00pm, if they are in the area, they start coming in from the surrounding hillside. The snow geese are beautiful, gracious, almost completely white, somewhat smaller than the Canada goose, and with a more delicate sound. Masses and masses of these geese fly in a loosely formed cluster (not a V shaped formation) towards the water to spend the night. If you have ever seen snow geese in a field where corn has been harvested, they cover the barren ground to give the appearance that the whole field is covered with snow. It would not be unusual to see twenty thousand or even fifty thousand of these birds on the lake, but only for a week or so.

Then I ponder to myself: "What causes these beautiful birds to migrate?" We may never know such mysteries while here on earth, but I wonder if a spirit of wisdom, knowledge and understanding is given to these snow geese specifically for the purpose of migration. That is their calling; to go from south to north, and then in the fall to go from north to the south. The Lord provides.

> **If we are called by the Lord to a particular ministry, the Lord will provide the necessary spirit(s) to supplement our needs.**

Joshua and the Sword

The Lord spoke the following words about the sword to Moses – but it was Joshua, not Moses, who received the benefit from these words:

> *If you follow my decrees and are careful to obey my commands, I will send you rain in its season, and the ground will yield its crops and the trees of the field their fruit. Your threshing will continue until grape harvest and the grape harvest will continue until planting, and you will eat all the food you want and live in safety in your land.*
>
> *I will grant peace in the land, and you will lie down and no one will make you afraid. I will remove savage beasts from the land, and the **sword** will not pass through your country. You will pursue your enemies, and they will fall by the **sword** before you. Five of you will chase a hundred, and a hundred of you will chase ten thousand, and your enemies will fall by the **sword** before you* (Lev 26:3-8).

By far, the most widely sold book in the world is the Bible. Unfortunately, many people take this book that they have heard so much about and start reading at the beginning: Genesis, Exodus, but stop soon thereafter. Many never get to the Book of Joshua because they lose interest somewhere in Exodus and Leviticus. Usually they do not get to Numbers or Deuteronomy, or the more readable story about Joshua and his triumphs. The details for the tabernacle and how to live a life of righteousness seem to weigh the person down and they put the Bible down in discouragement.

For those that do press in to read these books, the blessings and curses described in Deuteronomy 28:1-68 is among the most impressive to many people. The above verses from Leviticus offer an abbreviated version of the blessings from Deuteronomy. These verses, however, mention the **sword**, which is one of the armaments of spiritual warfare.

The word *"sword"* is identified as the Hebrew word **chereb** (kheh'-reb), which means "drought; also a cutting instrument (from its destructive effect), as a knife, sword, or other sharp implement: axe, dagger, knife, mattock, sword, tool." [7] Thus, in Leviticus 26:7,8 (above), the sword was used to cut out and destroy that which does not belong among holy people.

While my wife was still practicing nursing at a local hospital, she would take twenty minutes cleansing her hands and arms for surgery. She used soap, a scrub brush and a dagger-like instrument to clean everything, particularly her fingernails. This 4" long "weapon" **(chereb)**

---

[7] "Biblesoft's New Exhaustive Strong's Numbers and Concordance with Expanded Greek-Hebrew Dictionary", Biblesoft and International Bible Translators, Inc., 1994

was stainless steel, had a file along the flat edge, and had an impressive point on the end. Her objective was to completely remove all forms of contamination that might infect the patient's body. Her **chereb** cleansed her hands and arms along with the soap and scrub brush because purity in surgery is of utmost importance.

Joshua, the assistant to Moses, both observed and used the power of the sword during their forty years in the desert:

- Joshua overcame the Amalekite army with the **sword** (Ex 17:13).
- After the twelve spies returned to the camp, a plague killed the ten men that gave a bad report. Then many of the Israelites wanted to go up to the Promised Land, but Moses warned them that if they do, they will fall by the **sword**. Yet they went up and they were defeated just as Moses warned (Num 14:36-45).
- The Israelites were able to defeat the Amorites under king Sihon (that is, the hill country east of the Jordan River) with the edge of the **sword** (Num 21:24).
- Balaam's donkey saw the **sword** held by the angel of the Lord (Num 22:21-31). Later, Balaam (who practiced divination), was also put to death by the same **sword** (Num 31:7,8).
- Moses gave instructions to destroy with a **sword** any towns in the Promised Land where wicked men are leading them astray (Deut 13:15).
- When battling nations outside of the land of Canaan, Moses gave instructions to kill all men who do not submit to peace with a **sword** (Deut 20:13).

After Joshua took over the leadership of the Israelites, he encountered the Commander of the Army of the Lord, who was wielding a sword (Josh 5:13). Joshua went on to use the **chereb** during the invasion of Canaan:

- After the fall of Jericho, everything that remained in Jericho was destroyed by the **sword** (Josh 6:21).
- During the second invasion of Ai, all of the inhabitants were slain by the edge of the **sword** (Josh 8:24).
- Joshua took the community of Makkedah by totally destroying everyone with the **sword** (Josh 10:28).
- The southern cities were put to the **sword** and totally destroyed (Josh 10:29-39).
- The northern cities and kings were put to the **sword** (Josh 11:10-14).

As we work through the Book of Joshua, we will see that the sword (**chereb**) was used by the Lord to remove evil spirits from the Promised Land. This same sword is available today to come into our lives, ferreting out what does not belong.

> **Do not fear the sword, but welcome its ability to remove causes of disobedience, thereby bringing greater holiness in our lives.**

Joshua Heard From the Lord

*Take the helmet of salvation and the sword of the Spirit, which is the **word** of God* (Eph 6:17).

This verse is part of the larger set of verses that are most commonly quoted about spiritual warfare, namely Ephesians 6:10-18. In these verses, various armors of God are described; the sword of the Spirit is one of those armors.

When Paul wrote the "word of God" (above), he was stating in Greek the **rhema** of God. The word **rhema** (hray'-mah) is an utterance either individually or collectively. *Vines Expository Dictionary* states that **rhema** refers to "that which is spoken, what is uttered in speech or in writing."[8] More than that, it is the revelation of God.

The Lord spoke these words to Moses while they were in the Plains of Moab east of the Jordan:

> *Be careful to follow every command I am giving you today, so that you may live and increase and may enter and possess the land that the LORD promised on oath to your forefathers. Remember how the LORD your God led you all the way in the desert these forty years, to humble you and to test you in order to know what was in your heart, whether or not you would keep his commands. He humbled you, causing you to hunger and then feeding you with manna, which neither you nor your fathers had known, to teach you that man does not live on bread alone but on every **word** that comes from the mouth of the LORD* (Deut 8:1-3).

---

[8] W. E. Vine, *Vine's Expository Dictionary of Biblical Words*, (Nashville: Thomas Nelson Publishers, 1985), 683.

Jesus condenses these same verses in the New Testament: *"It is written: 'Man does not live on bread alone, but on every **word** that comes from the mouth of God.'"* Here, the Greek word **rhema** is translated into the word "word." **Rhema** is not Bible knowledge; it is a word that comes directly from the Lord. So Deuteronomy 8:3 and Matthew 4:4 are stating that we are to live on the revelation that is provided by the Lord.

There is a "word of God" which is what comes from the Bible. That type of word is called **logos**. We can and should memorize Bible Scriptures, be able to recount Biblical stories, and understand how to apply God's word. For example, when *"The word of the Lord spread through the entire region"* (Acts 13:49), this was similar to the knowledge one receives when one opens the Bible. Both logos and rhema are translated into English as the "word of God", yet they do not have the same meaning.

Rhema occurs when the Lord speaks, and this is what both Moses and Joshua heard. According to Exodus 3:4, Moses had an encounter with God on Mount Horeb. Moses hid because he was afraid to look at God. Then the Lord spoke to him. Notice the transition: first it was God who spoke, and then it was the Lord who spoke. God is the Hebrew word **Elohim**, and Lord is the Hebrew word **YHWH**. The author of Exodus uses the word God (Elohim) a few more times after that, but primarily it was the Lord (YHWH) that spoke to Moses.

Christians believe that God and Lord are one, and Elohim and YHWH are two different names for the same spiritual entity. God (Elohim) is His formal name and LORD (YHWH) is His personal name. In the same way, the formal name for first President of the United States was President Washington and his personal name was George. Martha Washington spoke to George the person.

When the Bible states "The LORD said to Joshua" or "Joshua said to the LORD," this is being spoken through the intimacy of relationship. It was not God, but the LORD, who is referred to. The LORD spoke to Joshua out of his close and personal walk with him. This is what makes the **rhema** possible. Today, if we don't have the sense that the LORD is dwelling within us, we will never hear that **rhema** word when it is spoken.

Only Caleb and Joshua followed the Lord wholeheartedly (Num 32:12,13); all the others did not follow the Lord wholeheartedly. As a result, 601,730 men died in the desert over a forty year time span (Num 14:30; 26:51). Yet for Joshua, he had a personal **rhema** type of relationship with the Lord.

The first time that it is recorded that the Lord spoke to Joshua was just before the death of Moses:

> *The* L ORD *gave this command to Joshua son of Nun: "Be strong and courageous, for you will bring the Israelites into the land I promised them on oath, and I myself will be with you"* (Deut 31:23).

This was the first recorded word spoken to Joshua. The author of Deuteronomy uses the word Lord, not God, for this introduction of Joshua's new role because of his intimate and personal relationship with the Lord. It was a **rhema** (or personal) word.

After the death of Moses, the Book of Joshua starts with a **rhema** word, where the Lord speaks directly to Joshua:

> *My servant Moses is dead ... I will never leave you nor forsake you. Be strong and courageous, because you will lead these people to inherit the land I swore to their forefathers to give them* (Josh 1:2,5,6).

Notice the similarity to Deuteronomy 31:23 (above).

Without a rhema word, the battle is much more difficult and can sometimes be impossible.

Joshua's Spiritual Warfare

Introduction to the Chiastic Approach

The structure of the Book of Joshua indicates a far deeper meaning than surface descriptions of battles and accounts of the wonders of God. I invite you to join me in analyzing its writing style using what is called the **chiastic (ky'-az-tic) approach**. As we do so, we will see a much deeper meaning than a number of victories through the hand of God. Also, we will see principles for dealing with our daily spiritual battles.

Many people are not familiar with the **chiastic approach**, so this chapter is set aside to help with that understanding. We will start by looking at an example from the Book of Mark that illustrates the chiastic approach. In terms of background, we will then identify when this writing style was first identified. Next, we will look at some chiasms from the Gospels, showing how to identify chiasms and apply them to our overall scriptural usage. Finally, we will look at two other literary styles that are used in Joshua: parallelism and repetition.

In total, this book identifies sixty-seven chiasms which are found in the Book of Joshua. In Parts Two and Three of this book, we will look at the Book of Joshua to reveal these chiasms and the application of the spiritual warfare through the **chiastic approach**.

Illustration of the Chiastic Approach

As we begin to understand the chiastic approach, let us first look at how a familiar set of passages from Mark 11:12-21 are structured:

Verses	Level	Theme
12-14	A	Jesus takes authority over a fig tree by cursing it
15, 16	B	Jesus takes authority over merchandisers at temple
17a	C	My house will be a house of prayer for all nations
17b	C'	You have made my house into a den of robbers
18, 19	B'	Jewish leaders are loosing their authority
20, 21	A'	Disciples recognize Jesus' authority in the withered fig tree

Some theologians refer to the structure of the above verses as an example of a "chiasm" or "chiasmus." A few people refer to it as "inverted parallelism." Others use the term "symmetric parallelism." For the purposes of this book, I will use the term **chiasm** (ky'-az-um). This structured style of writing is called the "chiastic approach."

It is a premise of this book that by analyzing the chiasms of the Book of Joshua, we can uncover key principles of spiritual warfare.

Each chiasm is a repetition of phrases starting at the outside and going in. Look at the similarity of the verses on the previous page: A goes with A', B goes with B', and C goes with C'. The fig tree is the commonality in both vv. 12-14 and in vv. 20,21 (A – A' level), and Jesus shows his authority over the fig tree in these verses. Jesus took authority over the merchandising at the temple in vv. 15,16, and the Jewish leaders realized that Jesus was threatening their authority in vv. 18,19 (B – B' level). The bottom and most important set of verses (v. 17a,b) contrasts how the temple should have been and how the temple had become (C – C' level).

Possibly this chart will help show the structure:

Level	First presentation	Inversion	Theme
A - A'	Jesus takes authority over a fig tree by cursing it (Mark 11:12-14)	Disciples recognize Jesus' authority in the withered fig tree (Mark 11:20,21)	Fig tree is cursed and it is withered, representing Jesus' authority
B - B'	Jesus takes authority over merchandisers at temple (Mark 11:15,16)	Jewish leaders are loosing their authority (Mark 11:18,19)	Authority is taken and authority is given up
C - C'	My house will be a house of prayer for all nations (Mark 11:17a)	You have made my house into a den of robbers (Mark 11:17b)	Contrasting views of the temple

When reading this chiasm, the verses under **First presentation** are to be read from top to bottom, while the verses under **Inversion** are to be read from bottom to top. This is done so that the pairs on each **Level** can be placed together, and then a **Theme** is assigned to each level.

While other experts on the chiastic approach use the style shown on page 23, I prefer to think of chiasms in this chart form. I find that by clearly stating the theme at each level, there is greater clarification of what the Lord is saying to us. This chart format is therefore used throughout the remainder of this book.

Most of the people that have studied the chiastic approach agree that the verses in the center contain the most important part of the chiasm. The chart above shows that bottom row, which is Mark 11:17 (C – C' level), is the center between Mark 11:12 and Mark 11:22. In this book, the bottom row is the center of the chiasm; it is called the **center point**.

Introduction to the Chiastic Approach

Look with me to see why verse 17 is the center point. The phrase *"a house of prayer for all nations"* (Mark 11:17a) is a reference to the same phrase in Isaiah 56:1-8, and the *"den of robbers"* (Mark 11:17b) is a reference to Jeremiah 7:1-11. Some of the verses from Isaiah read:

> *This is what the LORD says: "Maintain justice and do what is right ... love the name of the LORD and worship him"* (Is 56:1,4).

Likewise, the Lord spoke these words through the prophet Jeremiah:

> *"If you really change your ways and your actions and deal with each other justly, if you do not oppress the alien, the fatherless or the widow and do not shed innocent blood in this place, and if you do not follow other gods to your own harm, then I will let you live in this place"* (Jer 7:5-7).

The common theme of these verses from Isaiah and Jeremiah is loving the Lord and treating one another justly. Therefore, when considered together, we see that Jesus took authority over the fig tree and the temple because of the injustices that people committed to the Lord and to one another. In other words, the love for the Lord and the love for one another were far from what was required.

As stated earlier, by looking for chiasms and finding the center point, we can derive a far deeper meaning of the Bible and apply it to spiritual warfare. This chiasm applies to all people, not just the Jews at the temple – having love for the Lord and for one another is a key to obtaining victory in spiritual warfare.

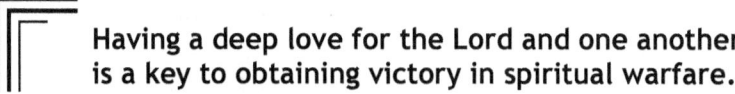

Having a deep love for the Lord and one another is a key to obtaining victory in spiritual warfare.

Background on the Chiasm

Several European publications in the 1700's and 1800's discussed the symmetric arrangement of Scripture, the most notable being John Jebb and Thomas Boys. [9],[10] However, it was not until the 1920's that Nils

---

[9] John Jebb, *Sacred Literature* (London: Cadell & Davies, 1820).
[10] Thomas Boys, *Tactica Sacra* (London: Hamilton, 1824).

Lund published articles about the chiasm in the United States. [11] Since the 1980's, there has been an increasing interest in the chiastic approach.

One of the most comprehensive reviews of this writing style was prepared by Dr. David Dorsey in 1999. [12] In that book, Dorsey studies the structure and meaning of each Old Testament book using this chiastic approach. Dorsey found that the chiastic approach is particularly frequent in Genesis, but he show examples from every book in the Old Testament.

In the New Testament, Bible scholars have also found examples of the chiastic approach in every book, but some books are more known for it than others. I personally find that the chiastic approach appears frequently in the Gospels of Matthew, Mark and John.

The word chiasmus (ky-as-mus) is derived from the Greek word χιασμυσ, where the first letter χ (chi) is indicative of a cross. Chiasmus literally means "placing crosswise, diagonal arrangement." [13] Wade White gives this simple definition: "chiasmus is the reversal of elements in otherwise parallel phrases." [14] Simply put, each chiasm is a structured repetition of themes starting at the outside and moving to the center.

Many attempts have been made to define and redefine chiasms over the years: some see a very simple structure while others provide a wide number of exceptions that becomes very inclusive. In this book, we will see that a chiasm achieves its importance when the central point provides profound insight into the verses; therefore, I generally focus on those with a more simple structure. Where the chiasm has been identified, the center point often gives clarity and understanding of the full intent of these Scriptures either by revealing what is otherwise hidden or by adding particular emphasis.

Within the Book of Joshua, Bible scholars typically focus on the use of the chiasms in chapters 2 and 22. On the World Wide Web, for example, it is very difficult to find sites where chiasms are identified in other parts of the Book of Joshua. Similarly, I have not found any association of chiasms with spiritual warfare on the Internet. Someone

---

[11] Nils W. Lund, "The Presence of Chiasmus in the Old Testament", *American Journal for Semitic Languages 46*, 1929-30.

[12] David A. Dorsey, *The Literary Structure of the Old Testament: A Commentary on Genesis – Malachi*, (Grand Rapids, MI: Baker Publishing Group, 1999).

[13] Nils Lund, *Chiasmus in the New Testament*, (Chapel Hill, NC: University of North Carolina Press, 1942), 31.

[14] Wade Albert White, *Rhetorical Criticism and Zechariah: Analysis of a Methodology for Determining Chiastic Structures in Biblical Hebrew Texts*, (M.A. thesis, Acadia University, 1999), 6.

may have written about it, but as of the writing of this book, it simply does not stand out.

This writing attempts to add to the general understanding of the chiastic approach, namely that the center point of a chiasm can often be applied to the battle known as spiritual warfare. This is particularly true in the Book of Joshua. It is my hope that each of us will come to a new level of understanding with regard to spiritual warfare. We will study how to recognize these chiastic patterns for ourselves so that as we read other books of the Bible, the Lord can speak to us in a new way. Oh the joy of discovering God's word for today!

The Art of Identifying Chiasms

In the example of the chiasm that is on page 24, three levels are identified. Some chiasms have been identified with just two levels, while others have been known to have eight or more levels. Some are very straight forward and therefore obvious; some are surprisingly complex and not easily found.

Chiasms can appear in a linear style (that is, one ends and another one begins), and there can be long gaps between chiasms. There can be one long chiasm with smaller chiasms within the larger one, and there can be overlapping chiasms where one begins before the previous one ends. As an example of the long chiasm with smaller chiasms, Dr. Dorsey points out that the Book of Jeremiah is one long chiasm from chapters 1 - 51 with four levels. The D level (Jeremiah 30 - 33) is the center point, which is a message of hope. Yet Jeremiah 30 - 33 is itself a chiasm with two levels, and Jeremiah 32:1-44 is the center point of that smaller chiasm. [15]

The art of identifying chiasms is still quite new and is somewhat subjective. There is nothing within the Bible that says that the A level starts at a certain point. The A-B-C-C'-B'-A' structure is a nomenclature that was developed by modern day Bible scholars. As such, errors of interpretation can appear. That is why it is important to have discernment regarding the identification and applications of chiasms.

One of my purposes in writing this book is that you will look for chiasms as you read the Bible. As you find them, allow the Lord to speak to you about how to apply each chiasm in regard to spiritual warfare. I only hope that you receive a word from the Lord in confirmation and application of what you believe you are seeing.

---

[15] Dorsey, 236-245.

Examples of the Chiastic Approach

All chiasms start with an outer level and move towards an inner level. At the center point, there can be either one verse or it could be repeated using similar words. Each level has its own theme, although the themes can be related. Let's look at a few chiasms.

- **First example**

I first became aware of chiasms by looking at the footnotes regarding Isaiah 6:10 in my *NIV Study Bible*. In the parallel verses from Matthew 13:15, see if you can identify the levels:

> *For this people's heart has become calloused;*
> *they hardly hear with their ears,*
> *and they have closed their eyes.*
> *Otherwise they might see with their eyes,*
> *hear with their ears,*
> *understand with their hearts ...*

Let us identify the nouns. They are as follows:
- People
- Heart
- Ears
- Eyes
- Eyes
- Ears
- Hearts

Did you see the three levels of the chiasm? With the exception of the word "people," they all have pairs. Did you see the center point? I sense that this verse is speaking about spiritual blindness. What about you?

Here then is the presentation of this first example:

Level	First presentation	Inversion	Theme
A - A'	Hearts are calloused (Matt 13:15a)	Hearts do not understand (Matt 13:15f)	Calloused hearts
B - B'	Ears hardly hear (Matt 13:15b)	Ears do not hear (Matt 13:15e)	Never listening ears
C - C'	Eyes are closed (Matt 13:15c)	Eyes do not see (Matt 13:15d)	Never perceiving eyes

- **Second Example**

    In our next example, we look at Matthew 6:24:

    No one can serve two masters. Either he will hate the one and love the other, or he will be devoted to the one and despise the other. You cannot serve both God and Money.

In this case, it is not just the nouns that identify the levels of the chiasm. I find that frequently I must identify the verbs to see if there is a chiastic pairing:

Level	First presentation	Inversion	Theme
A - A'	Two masters (Matt 6:24a)	God and money (Matt 6:24c)	One master or the other
B - B'	Hate the one (Matt 6:24b)	Despise the other (Matt 6:24b)	Hatred and despising
C - C'	Love the other (Matt 6:24b)	Be devoted to one (Matt 6:24b)	Love and devotion

In this chiasm, we go from identification of the two masters (A – A' level), to hatred (which we should not do) on the B – B' level, to loving (which we should do) on the C – C' level. The center point is about loving the right master: we are to love the Lord our God with all of our heart and with all of our mind and with all of our strength. When we do that, the choice between God and money becomes a moot question.

Therefore, this verse is not as much about the choice between God and money as it is about winning the spiritual battle because we love the Lord that much. When we truly love the Lord, the second master named Money is no longer the focus of our lives.

- **Third Example**

    The story of the transfiguration should be familiar to most Christians. Let's look at how the chiasm appears in Mark 9:2-9.

    In the chiasm shown below, notice the similarity of Mark 9:2a and Mark 9:9. First they're going up the mountain and then going down the mountain. That is the A – A' level, which is the outer most point of the chiasm and presumably the least important.

    The B – B' level is the transfiguration: first Christ is changed from human to a whiter than bleached form (Mark 9:2b-4), and then He is changed back to human form (Mark 9:8). At the same time, Elijah and Moses are changed from invisible to visible, and then are changed back to invisible in the B' portion.

Level	First presentation	Inversion	Theme
A - A'	The four go up a high mountain (Mark 9:2a)	The four go down the mountain (Mark 9:9)	Up and down the mountain
B - B'	Jesus was transfigured, and Elijah and Moses appear (Mark 9:2b-4)	Elijah and Moses disappear, and by inference, Jesus is returned to human form (Mark 9:8)	Transfiguration with the presence of Elijah and Moses
C	Listen to my Son who I love (Mark 9:7)	No inverted verse	Listening to Christ is emphasized

In this chiasm, there is a C level rather than a C – C' level. Most experts in the chiastic approach agree that the center point can be just the one point without an inverse. On the other hand, you could have broken Mark 9:7 into two parts (God's voice comes out of the cloud *and* Listen to Christ's voice), which would create a C and C' level. You would not be wrong either way. Therefore, to identify this as an A-B-C-B'-A' structure is equally correct as stating it is an A-B-C-C'-B'-A' structure.

This C – C' level is where the Lord is trying to draw our attention. He is asking us to be active in listening to what Christ says (Mark 9:7b). This, according to the chiasm, is the most important point and is the emphasis.

What is it about our modern knowledge-centered society? Are you like me in that you were in such awe over the transfiguration that you missed God's emphasis on listening to Christ? Yes I read it, and yes I understood it, but I missed the emphasis on listening to the voice of the Lord until I saw this as a chiasm. The chiasm is so simple yet so profound. On the C level, God is telling us to have an active relationship with Christ; to have spiritual discernment; to be filled with words of wisdom and knowledge; and to have the word of the Lord active in our lives. This, of course, is essential for spiritual warfare.

Identifying Chiasms

Below are some other chiasms to see if you can identify the center points. If you can, not only identify the chiastic structure, but also try to state the principle as it applies to spiritual warfare. The principle should be based on the center point of the chiasm.

John 1:45-49
John 2:3-9
John 2:23 - 3:2

Sometimes the center point is hard to find, while other times it is relatively easy. You might be upset with me over this (is there a spirit of frustration??), but I have chosen not to provide the answers to these chiasms. It is my hope that by attempting this yourself, you will develop this ability on your own.

Here is one technique that I have found helpful in identifying chiasms. When you see a verse repeated or with a very similar thought, you might suspect a chiasm. Count the number of verses between the first and last verse. You can often find the center point by counting half of that number from the first verse. So, if there are 24 verses from the beginning to the end, count 12 verses from the beginning. Although some chiasms can really fool you, that would be a place to start looking for similar themes.

Another technique in identifying chiasms is to identify two verses, one right after the other, that say essentially the same thing. You might suspect that you are looking at the center point of a chiasm. Using this as the center point, look at the thought that was presented in the previous verse or paragraph and in the following verse or paragraph. If they are the same or are similar, you may be reading a chiasm.

Here are two more chiasms to try for yourself:

John 6:35-48
John 17:1-5

Applying Chiasms

I recently wrote a letter to my mom based on John 20:10-16 which is another chiasm. I noticed the chiasm because the words *"Woman, why are you crying?"* are presented in both John 20:13 and John 20:15. From there my eyes went to John 20:10,11 where Mary was crying outside the tomb, and John 20:16 where Mary cried out *"Rabboni!"* (Can you see the entire chiasm?) I did not want to mention the chiastic approach to my mom because it would distract from the message. Instead I pointed out how Mary changed from weeping (John 20:10) to joy (John 20:16) in a matter of seven verses, and then asked her "What changed?" You see, what changed is the center point of this chiasm.

My thought provoking question was followed by this statement: "As we approach Resurrection Sunday, I pray that you will see Jesus for who He truly is." It was that simple. The chiastic approach does not have to be presented in a complicated manner as is done in this book. Instead, it can be bundled in such a way that the center point becomes the focus of our attention. The purpose of understanding the chiasm should be to understand what we are to concentrate on, particularly when spiritual warfare is involved.

As another example, imagine you are a pastor or a home church leader preparing a message, and the Lord has led you to John 6:35-48. The verses start out with *"I am the bread of life,"* and they finish where they started in John 6:48 with the same words. There are fourteen verses so you find that seven verses down from John 6:35 is *"I am the bread that came down from heaven"* (John 6:41), which is similar to the next verse: *"I came down from heaven."* You also see that John 6:41a and John 6:43 discuss how the Jews were grumbling. (Can you see the entire chiasm?)

So as a church leader, you could ask and seek the Lord about which level seems appropriate at this time. (Remember, all of these levels are appropriate for a message because they are all based on the Word of God). Do you believe you should stay at the A – A' level and discuss Jesus as the bread of life and manna? Do you think you should move to the B – B' level in John 6:37-40 and again in John 6:44-47, discussing how to attain everlasting life? Is the Lord prompting you to discuss grumbling from John 6:41a and John 6:43 (C – C' level)? Lastly, you could focus on the center point of this chiasm, where Jesus is the bread of life from heaven (D – D' level).

Some people may choose to mix and match the various levels of this chiasm, or combine it with other Scriptures. But I hope and trust that you will see how to use this rhetorical device. The chiastic approach can add to your toolbox a whole new approach to understanding and presenting the Word of God.

Parallelism

In addition to the frequent use of the chiastic approach in the Book of Joshua, there are two additional writing styles that are noteworthy: parallelism and repetition.

Parallelism is a rhetorical style that is often applied to poetry but can be applied to prose as well. In the Bible, parallelism can be seen where pairs of topics contrast with, are similar to or compliment one another. For example, in Exodus 23:20-28, the angel helps bring in the good while the hornet helps remove the evil, as we will discuss on page 91. The difference between a chiasm and parallelism is that the chiasm is structured towards a central theme, whereas with parallelism, objects seem to stand alone for the sake of comparison by themselves. The comparison or contrast between one parallel object can help to understand the other parallel object:

- **Antithetical parallelism** – derived from the word 'antithesis', these are opposing or contrasting topics. An example would be the comparison of light and darkness: *"God is **light**; in him there is no **darkness** at all"* (1 John 1:5).

- **Synonymous parallelism** – derived from the word 'synonym', these are similar topics. An example is the righteous person in Isaiah: *"You will be a crown of splendor in the **LORD's hand**, a royal diadem in the **hand of your God**"* (Isa 62:3).
- **Synthetic parallelism** – based on the root word 'synthesis', the first set of words are expanded and completed with the second set of words. In these verses: *"I will give you every place where you set your foot, as I promised Moses. Your territory will extend from the desert to Lebanon, and from the great river, the Euphrates – all the Hittite country – to the Great Sea on the west"* (Josh 1:3,4), the second sentence explains and completes the first sentence.

Sometimes chiasms add synthetic parallelism for increased emphasis. Many of the chiasms that are found in the Book of John have this form. In these instances, the first part of the synthetic parallelism is the chiasm, and the second part is prose that complements or emphasizes the point of the chiasm. For example, consider these verses from John 13:31,32:

Level	First presentation	Inversion	Theme
A - A'	"Now is the Son of Man glorified" (John 13:31a)	"God will glorify the Son in himself" (John 13:32b)	The Son of God is glorified
B - B'	"God is glorified in him" (John 13:31b)	"If God is glorified in him" (John 13:32a)	God is glorified in Christ

The chiasm above is the first part of the synthetic parallelism. The second part is the remainder of the sentence: *"and will glorify him at once"* (John 13:32c). In this way, the emphasis is placed on the immediacy of the glory of God to be revealed in Christ – verse 13:32c expands and completes the statements in the chiasm.

Repetition

The last writing style to be mentioned is repetition – it is the most easily understood of the writing styles. For example, there are the seven woes in Matthew 23:13-32. We will see an exceptional amount of repetition in Joshua 6, where the Hebrew words for city, trumpets, ark and encircle appear numerous times.

Repetition is also used for the sake of emphasis. Can you recall times from your childhood where this was used? Repeatedly, my mother told me "Tommy, get that dog out of your bedroom." After a while (a long while I might add), I stopped bringing our brown-haired little dachshund into my bedroom. Why? Repetition taught me that this was very important to my mother.

Structure of the Book of Joshua

I am in total awe at the writing of the Book of Joshua. Just the ability to write a chiasm that maintains the symmetry yet at the same time flows into a story is to me an amazing thing. But what I am about to present leaves me with the highest respect and admiration. This confirms once again that God inspired the writing of the Bible. Let me explain.

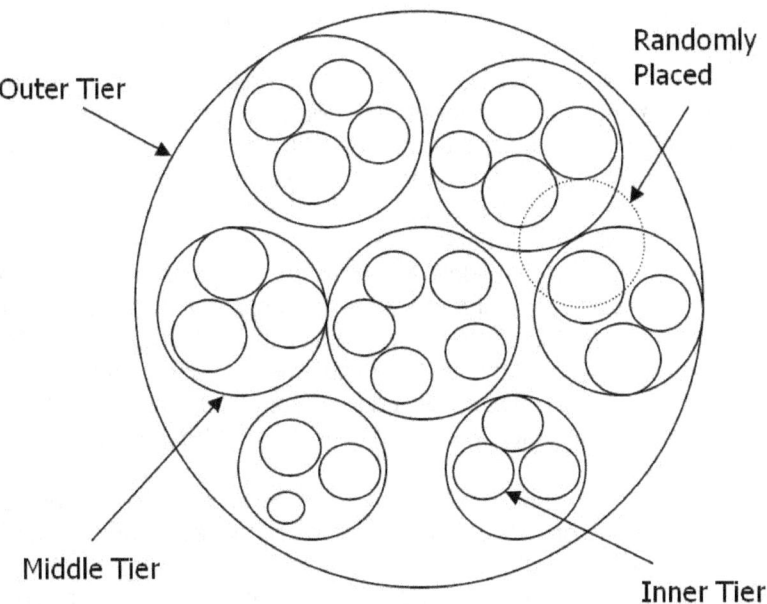

In the Book of Joshua, there are chiasms within chiasms, as illustrated by the circles in the diagram above. Not knowing what to call these chiasms within chiasms, I have given them the names "outer tier", "middle tier" and "inner tier" chiasms.

The outer circle encompasses the seven middle circles, and each middle circle contains three, four or five inner circles. In the same way, there are chiasms that span many chapters, and these have been named outer tier chiasms. The middle tier chiasms typically cover a chapter or two, while the chiasms that represent the inner tier are for a few verses.

To make things more complex, the author of Joshua occasionally adds randomly placed chiasms that seem inappropriate, such as the circle with dashes. These random chiasms overlap into other chiasms.

Outer, Middle and Inner Tiered Chiasms

Chiasms can appear anywhere in the Bible, although they are particularly prevalent in the Book of Joshua. Chiasms can be big in that they cover a number of chapters; and chiasms can be small in that they cover only a few verses. The point is, if a chiasm covers several chapters, what is to prevent the author from putting a five-verse chiasm within that larger chiasm? The answer is "Nothing."

In a person's body, there are many systems: a nervous system, a digestive system, a muscular system, etc. Each system is composed of one or more organs. Each organ contains a number of tissues. Any one cell is located within a tissue which is within an organ that is part of a system belonging in the entire body. All of those parts work together to make the body function properly.

In the same way, the chiasms of the Book of Joshua work together to provide meanings that are not understood by a top-to-bottom reading. By looking at the charts on pages 38 and 39, we can see that there are two outer tiers for the Book of Joshua. Within the first outer tier (chapters 1 - 12), there are nine middle tiers. Each of the middle tiers has two or more inner tiers.

The three tiers (outer, middle and inner) each represent one or more chiasms. For example, the first outer tier is a chiasm that extends from Joshua 1:1 to Joshua 12:24. This chiasm is described on page 41. Of the eleven chiasms that compose the middle tiers, the first middle tier extends from Joshua 1:1 to Joshua 1:18. Within that middle tiered chiasm, there are two inner tier chiasms: Joshua 1:5b-9, and then Joshua 1:9-18.

Confused? I hope not, but rather we can begin to share the sense of awe over God's Word. Studying the charts on pages 38 and 39, and then rereading this section may help clarify any questions.

What is most amazing is the nearly perfect continuity of the three-tiered chiasms, particularly in the first half of the Book of Joshua. Generally speaking, each inner tier chiasm is continuous in that where one chiasm stops, the next one begins. There are hardly any verses missing in each of the three tiers.

Look with me at the third column on page 38, which is labeled **Inner Tier**. The first cell shows "1:5b to 1:9", meaning that this chiasm ends at verse 9 of chapter 1. The second chiasm is shown to extend through 1:18, which is the end of the first chapter. The third chiasm skips two verses and then begins at 2:3. The fourth chiasm skips a verse and then begins at 2:9. And so on. One ends and another begins.

Only a great and awesome Lord could have His hand in such a literary accomplishment. In the New Testament, 2 Tim 3:16 states that *"All Scripture is given by inspiration of God"* (NKJV), and this certainly affirms that statement. Whether Joshua or someone else wrote this book of Joshua, God breathed the words into that author's spirit. That person penned the most complex writing while still having a story line that is easy to follow.

In our modern languages, we use exclamation marks, **bold**, *italics* and underlining to emphasize the points that need to be made. In the ancient Hebrew language, these formatting techniques did not exist. Instead, chiasms were used to show the emphasis, drawing the reader's attention to the center of the chiasm. Something must have stirred in their hearts when, after analyzing the verses, they uncovered that center point: "Oh, now I get it."

In addition to the various tiered chiasms that are presented in this book, there are four randomly placed chiasms. To minimize confusion, we will discuss each randomly placed chiasm as they appear.

First Outer Tier Chiasms

Outer Tier	Middle Tier	Inner Tier
↑ 1:1	↑ 1:1	1:5b to 1:9
	↓ 1:18	1:9 to 1:18
	↑ 2:1	2:3 to 2:7
		2:9 to 2:11
		2:12 to 2:14
	↓ 2:24	2:15 to 2:21
	↑ 3:1	2:22 to 3:2
		3:3 to 3:6a
		3:6b to 3:11
		3:12 to 4:2
		4:3 to 4:9
	↓ 5:1	4:6 to 4:21
		5:2 to 5:8
		5:9 to 5:11a
		5:11b to 5:12
	↑ 5:13	5:13 to 6:2
		6:2 to 6:16
		6:17 to 6:25
	↓ 7:1	6:26 to 7:1
	↑ 7:1	7:3 to 7:5
		7:6 to 7:13
	↓ 7:26	7:15 to 7:25
	↑ 8:1	8:3 to 8:8
		8:10 to 8:17
		8:18 to 8:26
	↓ 8:29	8:28 to 8:29
		8:30 to 8:35
	↑ 9:3	9:4 to 9:13
	↓ 9:27	9:18 to 9:26
	↑ 10:1	10:1 to 10:6
		10:7 to 10:15
	↓ 10:28	10:16 to 10:28
	↑ 10:29	11:1 to 11:11
		11:12 to 11:23
↓ 12:24	↓ 12:24	12:1 to 12:24

Second Outer Tier Chiasms

Outer Tier
↑ 13:1
↓ 24:27

Middle Tier
↑ 22:1
↓ 23:1
↑ 23:2
↓ 24:33

Inner Tier
14:8 to 14:14
15:13 to 15:19
17:13 to 17:18
18:4 to 18:8a
18:8b to 18:10a
22:1 to 22:9
22:10 to 22:16
22:17 to 22:20
22:21 to 22:29a
22:29b to 22:34
23:3 to 23:10
23:12 to 23:16
24:14a to 24:19a
24:14b to 24:23
24:22 to 24:27

Random Chiasms

Ex 12 to Josh 6
Josh 2:1 to Josh 7:1
Josh 2:5 to Josh 6:1
Josh 3:8 to Josh 3:17

Part Two – The Battle

First Outer Tier Chiasm

> *They devoted the city to the* Lord *and destroyed with the sword every living thing in it – men and women, young and old, cattle, sheep and donkeys. Joshua said to the two men who had spied out the land, "Go into the prostitute's house and bring her out and all who belong to her, in accordance with your oath to her"* (Josh 6:21,22).

In these two verses, we see destruction and we see grace. All living creatures in Jericho are destroyed except for a select few. The people and all of their animals are put to the sword, yet a few are allowed to live.

In the "Structure of the Book of Joshua" on page 36, there is a discussion of outer, middle and inner tier chiasms. The chiasm that is shown on the next page represents an outer tier chiasm. That is, it spans a number of chapters which in this case is from Joshua 1 - 12.

Look with me at the similarity of the chapters on page 42. It is easiest to see that the river standing still in chapter 3 is conceptually similar to the sun standing still in chapter 10 (B – B' level). Hopefully we can see how the failure to circumcise the Israelites while in the desert was a sin (chapter 5), which is similar to Achan's sin in chapters 7 and 8. This is the D – D' level. The destruction of Jericho and its king in the first part of chapter 6 is related to how Rahab was spared destruction in the second half of that chapter (E – E' level).

As stated previously, each chiasm is a repetition of themes starting at the outside and going in. Remember to read the column entitled 'First Presentation' from top to bottom, and then read the column entitled 'Inversion' from bottom to top. In this way, the common themes at each level can be easily seen and compared.

As a reminder, if you do not understand chiasms, I invite you to re-read the second chapter. It is my premise that by analyzing these chiasms, we can uncover key principles of spiritual warfare. Most often, these principles are revealed by analyzing the chiasm's inner most level.

Level	First presentation	Inversion	Theme
A - A'	Assurance that the Lord has given the whole land to the Israelites (Josh 1 - 2)	Remainder of the land is given to the Israelites (Josh 10:16 - 12:24)	The Lord has given the whole land to the Israelites
B - B'	Jordan River stands still (Josh 3)	Sun stands still (Josh 10:1-15)	Nature itself stands still
C - C'	Hebrews build piles of stones to show they are transformed to God's community (Josh 4)	Gibeonites fear the Lord God and so are grafted in to God's community (Josh 9)	Israelites and Gentiles can be part of God's community
D - D'	Failure to circumcise is revealed and dealt with (Josh 5)	Achan's sin is revealed and resolved (Josh 7 - 8)	Sin is exposed and is dealt with
E - E'	Jericho's king and its people are destroyed (Josh 6:1-21)	Rahab and her family are saved (Josh 6:22-25)	Judgment of evil and good

At the center of this chiasm, which is the E – E' level, there is the contrast between destruction and salvation; this is the judgment of evil and good. Most of the people in Jericho were killed, but Rahab's family was protected from destruction. In the same way, Jesus stated that many will be lost and a few will be found: *"For wide is the gate and broad is the road that leads to destruction, and many enter through it. But small is the gate and narrow the road that leads to life, and only a few find it"* (Matt 7:13,14). Therefore, in the destruction of Jericho, there is a picture of salvation for those that are willing to pursue it.

Salvation is available to many but few will find it.

Chapter 1 – The Lord Assures Joshua

After the death of Moses the servant of the LORD, the LORD said to Joshua son of Nun, Moses' aide: "Moses my servant is dead. Now then, you and all these people, get ready to cross the Jordan River into the land I am about to give to them — to the Israelites" (Josh 1:1,2).

With these two verses, the transition from Moses to Joshua has been completed and Joshua was now at the helm. Typically, when any new boss takes over, there is a time of adjustment and trials. The people were accustomed to Moses as the leader, so Joshua had the concerns of allegiance of the people. But more importantly, the Lord knew He must first reassure Joshua with what has been previously stated when Moses was alive. Many times, repetition gives reassurance. (I know, I'm repeating myself).

As we begin the study of the Book of Joshua, we continue the series of geography lessons that was started on page 7. The next location to be discussed is the territory east of the Jordan River. With the exception of Mt. Sinai and Shittim, my wife Nancy and I drove to each of the locations that are presented in this book in 1999. That year, we did what we called a 'Joshua tour': within four days, we searched for as many sites as we could find that were mentioned in the Book of Joshua. Little did we realize at the time that I would be writing a book that included this experience!

In this chapter, we will first look at the overall structure of the first chapter of Joshua. In the geography lesson, we will see that the area east of the Jordan is an area of corruption and spiritual darkness. We will conclude with two chiasms: the Lord's command to meditate on His Word of the Law, and entering the Lord's rest.

Structure of Chapter 1

As described on page 36, there are three groupings of chiasms that are presented in the Book of Joshua: outer tier, middle tier and inner tier. For the entire book, there are two outer tier chiasms: chapters 1 - 12 and chapters 13 - 22. Within the first outer tier chiasm, there are nine middle tier chiasms which are described later in this chapter. The first of the middle tier chiasms coincides with chapter 1 of the Book of Joshua:

Level	First presentation	Inversion	Theme
A - A'	Moses, who was the servant of the Lord, is succeeded by Joshua (Josh 1:1,2a)	The people pledge allegiance to Joshua, same as Moses (Josh 1:16-18)	Joshua assumes the position that Moses had with the Lord
B - B'	Repeated three times: the Lord has given the land to the Israelites (Josh 1:2,3,6)	Repeated three times: the Lord has given the land to the Israelites (Josh 1:13-15)	The Lord has given the land to the Israelites
C - C'	Meditate on the word of the Lord (Josh 1:7-9)	Remember the word of the Lord (Josh 1:12)	Importance of the word of the Lord
D - D'	Take possession of the land (Josh 1:10,11a)	You possess the land (Josh 1:11b)	Possession of the land

The D – D' level focuses on possessing the promise. There are times in our lives where doubt can creep in. For example, the Bible can state that the Lord *"forgives all your sins and heals all your diseases ..."* (Ps 103:3). If you have received this promise, cast aside any spirits of doubt and *"take possession of"* (Josh 1:11) that promise.

When we are told that a spiritual promise is ours, then possess that which was promised.

Geography: The Land East of the Jordan (Part I)

Roughly two million Israelites, including wives and children, camped in the valley area east of the Jordan River before their assault upon the Promised Land (Num 26:51,62). If we visited this valley today, we would see a fertile land with ample water, yet extremely dry air. This valley area is known as the Plains of Moab; the city of Shittim was on the eastern edge of the Plains of Moab. Further east of the valley, there is rugged terrain as the elevation climbs two thousand feet to a plateau area. Southwest of the valley is the Dead Sea, only a few miles away. The city of Jericho with its oases is four miles west of the Jordan River, again in the valley area below the mountains.

The prophet Balaam had met Balak while the Israelites camped in the Plains of Moab near Shittim (Num 22:1). Through the influence of Balaam, the Israelite men staying at Shittim began to indulge in sexual immorality with the Moabite women (Num 25:1), which resulted in their worshipping the Baal of Peor.

Geographically, this area is equally as dark. The Dead Sea is the lowest elevation on the face of the earth at 1,310 feet below sea level. The Dead Sea is thirty percent salt, which is eight times saltier than the ocean; no marine life can live in it. Jerusalem, on the other hand, is located only twenty miles west of the Jordan River and is 2,400 feet above sea level. In terms of elevation, Jerusalem is the high point between the Dead Sea and the Mediterranean Sea.

With an elevation difference between the Dead Sea to Jerusalem of 3,710 feet, hopefully we can see how the Lord was taking the Israelites from a deep and dark location to a place of celebration. That is what the Lord was giving to the Israelites. He was giving them the opportunity to re-condition their hearts, from a spiritually low place to joy.

It is equally intriguing to look at the route that the Israelites took into the land of Canaan. Aaron died on Mt. Hor, which is sixty miles south of Jerusalem. Immediately after that, in Numbers 21:1-3, the Canaanite king of Arad was defeated. The Lord could have marched them through Beersheba (only fifteen miles away), Hebron, Jerusalem and then the remainder of the Promised Land. Why did the Lord take them through the vicinity of the Dead Sea? One reason might be to show them the depths from which He would deliver them.

My wife and I were recently involved in establishing a new church in a local city. Each winter evening, large numbers of black cawing and squawking crows would congregate in the downtown area. It was estimated that there were two crows for every person. When women left work, they carried an umbrella for fear of filthy droppings on their heads. Cars parked in this area were constantly peppered with their filth. Plus, the crows made this awful racket, like a family of fifty thousand having one simultaneous argument.

That was two years ago. Today, the crow population is down to normal levels, although every now and then the population starts coming back again. People from the city contend it is by their efforts that this population has decreased. Those of us from this new church understand that the darkness that has been over this city is being broken because the spiritual warfare issues are being addressed. We did not pray for deliverance from the crows; we prayed that the spirits of darkness would be gone in the name of Christ. Even if the city's efforts played a part in the dispersing of the crows, that in itself was an answer from the Lord because of our prayers.

> **What we see in the physical is often a representation of what is happening in the spiritual.**

His Word of the Law

Consider the verses shown below from Joshua 1:5-9.

Level	First presentation	Inversion	Theme
A - A'	*I will never leave you nor forsake you* (Josh 1:5b)	*for the LORD your God will be with you wherever you go* (Josh 1:9c)	The Lord's presence
B - B'	*Be strong and courageous* (Josh 1:6,7a)	*Be strong and courageous. Do not be terrified; do not be discouraged* (Josh 1:9a,9b)	Strength and courage
C - C'	*Be careful to obey all the law... that you may be successful* (Josh 1:7b,7c)	*So that you may be careful to do everything written in it. Then you will be prosperous and successful* (Josh 1:8c)	Obedience ... leading to success
D - D'	*Do not let this Book of the Law depart from your mouth* (Josh 1:8a)	*mediate on it day and night* (Josh 1:8b)	Keep the words of the Lord alive in our spirits

The A – A' level is concerned with the Lord's presence remaining with us. The emphasis on *"Be strong and courageous"* is stated in Joshua 1:6 and Joshua 1:9b. Obedience and success is the theme of the C – C' level.

The inner most level of this chiasm (center point) is the D – D' level in this example, which is Joshua 1:8a,8b. Instead of the NIV's use of the *"Book of the Law"* in Joshua 1:9, a look at the Hebrew shows it is **dabar torah** (word of the Torah). Moses spoke to all of Israel these words at the end of his life:

> *Take to heart all the words I have solemnly declared to you this day, so that you may command your children to obey carefully all the **words of this law**. They are not just idle words for you — they are your life. By them you will live long in the land you are crossing the Jordan to possess* (Deut 32:46,47).

The words of this law were to be their life. They were to eat it, breathe it, think it and consume it, and so it would keep them alive.

The spiritual warfare application of these verses is: by keeping the words of the law alive in our spirits (D – D' level), we will be better prepared to obey the law (C – C' level), thereby keeping us strong and courageous (B – B' level). By keeping the words of the law fresh in our minds, we are more able to obey; by obeying, we can depend on the Lord's strength and courage; and because of all of these (meditating, obeying, depending on the Lord), we will have the Lord with us wherever we go. The progression of meditation, obedience and dependence are essential for fighting the spiritual battle in the Lord's presence. In this way, we overcome in the Lord's strength, not our own.

The *"Book of the Law"* in Joshua 1:8 refers to the requirements on the people and was to be considered as legally binding. The Lord gave these requirements to Moses. So Joshua 1:8 might be paraphrased to read "Do not let these words from the Lord depart from your inner most being, for they are to be your moment by moment life."

After my father passed away, I changed the screen saver on my PC to be a picture of my dad. Although we lived many states away, my dad was very dear to me. In my own way of dealing with the grief over his death, I was able to see his face every time I turned the PC on and off. In essence, I was meditating on his life on a daily basis. Since then, I've removed that screen saver because for the most part, my grief has passed. But during that time, I was keeping the good picture of his face alive in my spirit.

  Keep the words of the Lord alive in our spirit.

Entering the Lord's Rest

The remainder of chapter 1 of Joshua reveals another chiasm (Josh 1:10-18). Most scholars identify these verses with the transition of authority from Moses to Joshua and the people's response to this authority:

Verses	Theme
Josh 1:10,11	Joshua gives directives to all of the people.
Josh 1:12-15	Joshua gives directives to the Reubenites, Gadites and half tribe of Manasseh.
Josh 1:16-18	The people respond with their obedience to the authority that was passed from Moses to Joshua.

The Hebrew word for rest is **nuwach** (noo'-akh) which takes on the sense of quietness. After the long battle, the Lord will give them peace and quietness. The picture of the tribes returning to the eastern side of the Jordan would be one of hope and restoration. The verses from the following chiasm reveal this rest:

Level	First presentation	Inversion	Theme
A - A'	Be strong and courageous (Josh 1:9)	Be strong and courageous (Josh 1:18b)	Be strong and courageous
B - B'	Instructions to the officers, which calls for obedience (Josh 1:10,11)	The officers pledge obedience (Josh 1:18b)	Obedience
C - C'	The 2 ½ tribes are to leave this home and are to fight (Josh 1:12-14)	The 2 ½ tribes may go home after fighting (Josh 1:15b)	2 ½ tribes go to fight and then return home
D	The Lord will give you rest (Josh 1:15a)	No inverted verse	Enter the Lord's rest

The center point of this chiasm is on the D level, which in this case is Joshua 1:15a. There is no corresponding D' verse. Experts in the chiastic approach unanimously agree that the center point can be just the one point without an inverse.

Imagine a time after a long spiritual battle where the evil spirits are no longer tormenting like they once were. The Lord gives this as a promise. To rest in the Lord; to dwell in His presence. The Lord stated: *"I will put my dwelling place among you, and I will not abhor you. I will walk among you and be your God, and you will be my people"* (Lev 26:11,12).

We do not have the authority to make the devil and evil spirits leave this world; but we do have the authority to make them obedient to Christ. Then there is rest.

Like many others, I thoroughly enjoy gardening. At our church, we have a garden that we call the Gethsemane Prayer Garden which I help maintain; it is a meeting place with the Lord. During warm weather, I go there several times a week with a shovel, wheelbarrow, a pair of clippers and any other tools that I may need. Often I am there alone, and there is a deep serenity in this place. The church's indoor sanctuary is a place of praise, worship and teaching. The Gethsemane Prayer Garden, on the other hand, is a sanctuary of intimacy and peace with the Lord. To Moses, *"The LORD replied, 'My Presence will go with you, and I will give you rest'"* (Ex 33:14). That promise of **nuwach** was what the tribes east of the Jordan were to be given.

After an intense spiritual battle, the Lord gives us His rest.

Principalities, Powers, Rulers and Demons

Throughout this book, there are references to the principalities, powers, rulers and evil spirits. The following is explained so that we have a common understanding of terms. The apostle Paul makes two references to this hierarchy in Ephesians 1:21 and Ephesians 6:12. In referring to the armor of God, Paul describes the struggle:

> *For we wrestle not against flesh and blood, but against principalities, against powers, against the rulers of the darkness of this world, against spiritual wickedness in high places* (Eph 6:12 KJV).

As we work through the Book of Joshua in Parts Two and Three of this book, we will see how this hierarchy of principalities, powers, rulers and spiritual darkness were manifested.

The KJV and NIV translate the words principalities, powers and rulers differently from Ephesians 1:21 and 6:12. In this book, I have used the KJV terminology from Ephesians 6:12; for the term *"spiritual wickedness"*, I refer to them as evil spirits or demonic spirits.

Ephesians 1:21		Ephesians 6:12	
KJV	NIV	KJV	NIV
Principality	Rule	Principalities	Rulers
Power	Authority	Powers	Authorities
Might	Power	Rulers of the darkness of this world	Powers of this dark world
Dominion	Dominion	Spiritual wickedness	Spiritual forces of evil

In Tim Mather's book entitled *Prophetic Deliverance*, he explains the difference of each level: [16]

- **Principalities** are "the highest, most powerful class in the hierarchy of the Satanic kingdom"; they rule over church denominations, regions and countries.
- At the next level are the **powers** that are "a major demonic spirit whose primary activity is to envelop a territory with the potency of a particular type of evil." A power can rule over a city, church or area.

---

[16] T. C. Mather, *Prophetic Deliverance - The Missing Ministry of Jesus in the Church*, Tulsa, OK: Insight Publishing Group, 2000, 84-89.

- **Rulers** are at the third level, that are "ranking members of lower ranking demons"; rulers exert their evil upon individuals and small groups.
- The final level is **spiritual wickedness** or **dominion** where an individual "allows a demonic being to exercise some sort of control in their life." Evil spirits are typically seen at this level such as a spirit of anger.

Joshua encountered many kings in the liberation of the Promised Land. When Moses destroyed the kings Sihon and Og along with their cities, he was modeling for Joshua how to conquer the territories. Both of these Amorite territories were *"completely destroyed"* (Deut 2:34 and Deut 3:6); the Lord gave them all to the Israelites.

In the defeat of these cities, there is a focus on the kings Sihon and Og. Sihon was king of Heshbon and Og was king of Bashan, but they had kingdoms that included the cities of the surrounding territories. For example, when Moses gave the territories to the Eastern tribes, they are referred as *"the kingdom of Sihon king of the Amorites and the kingdom of Og king of Bashan – the whole land with its cities and the territory around them"* (Num 32:33). A king ruled over a city while the kingdom had authority over many cities.

In a similar way, Paul in the New Testament refers to powers and ruling spirits (using KJV terminology). There is a direct analogy between the kingdoms and kings of the Old Testament with the powers and ruling spirits of the New Testament. This book, with its focus on spiritual warfare, draws on this analogy for its application to our daily lives. As we progress through this book, other portions of this analogy will be developed.

Kingdom - Has a number of kings under his jurisdiction.	←→	**Powers** - Demonic force that has responsibility over ruling spirits.
King - The person that controls the people of a city.	←→	**Ruling spirit** - One of the devil's angels that controls the other demons.
People of the city - Those that live in the city.	←→	**Demons** - Those angels of the devil that have names like fear, anger and jealousy.

By way of the analogy, Moses came across the **powers** when he met up with the kings Sihon and Og. They had power over broad sections of the land and the people east of the Jordan. The kings of each of the cities that Joshua would come up against, such as the king of Jericho or the king of Ai, are by analogy the **ruling spirits**. Likewise, the people in cities such as Jericho and Ai are analogous to **demons**.

Chapter 2 – The Lord Has Given the Whole Land

> *By **faith** the prostitute Rahab, because she welcomed the spies, was not killed with those who were disobedient* (Heb 11:31).

> *In the same way, was not even Rahab the prostitute considered **righteous** for what she did when she gave lodging to the spies and sent them off in a different direction* (James 2:25)?

The story of the two spies and Rahab is familiar to many Bible readers, yet it leaves some very difficult questions. Hebrews 11:31 (above) states that Rahab's faith led to her meeting with the spies; this action preserved her from being killed. But why did the Lord use a prostitute? Was her faith sufficient to ensure her salvation?

In the same way, James 2:25 (above) refers to Rahab as "*righteous*." But how can an unrepentant prostitute be considered righteous? Why did Rahab's deception to the king's messengers go unpunished?

I may not fully answer these questions because that is not the purpose of this book. The intent of this book is to reveal underlying principles of spiritual warfare using mechanisms such as the chiastic approach. However, if any of these questions are answered, either in part or directly, then praise the Lord.

In analyzing Joshua 2, we will review six chiasms. The theme that flows through this chapter is faith based on a relational covenant with the Lord and His people. Along the way, we will take a look at some examples of parallelism, review another geography lesson on the land east of the Jordan, and investigate the spirits of fear and courage. We will conclude this chapter by comparing the Sinaitic and Deuteronomic covenants. These covenants are the center of a randomly placed chiasm that covers the forty year period represented by Exodus 12 to Joshua 6.

Structure of Chapter 2

Below is the overall chiastic structure of chapter 2. From this middle tier chiasm, we can see that the center point is Rahab's faith, which is what led to establishing the covenant between Rahab and Israel. To the Lord, the covenant relationship between us and Himself is of utmost importance. That is the central theme of chapter 2: faith based covenants. We see the faith of Rahab extended into a promise that was kept. See also Hebrews 11:31 (above).

Level	First presentation	Inversion	Theme
A - A'	The two spies are sent from Shittim to Jericho (Josh 2:1)	The two spies return from Jericho to Shittim (Josh 2:23,24)	Travel across the Jordan River
B - B'	Rahab sends the King's investigators away from Jericho (Josh 2:2-7)	Rahab sends Joshua's spies (investigators) away from Jericho (Josh 2:15-21)	Rahab sends away the investigators
C - C'	Rahab confesses faith based on fear of the Lord (Josh 2:8-11)	Rahab asks for a covenant based on her faith (Josh 2:12-14)	Rahab's faith leads to a covenant relationship

The C – C' level of this chiasm emphasizes the importance of faith in establishing a relationship with the Lord. Rahab's faith became the basis for entering the covenant relationship and ultimately her protection.

What if the two spies went back to Shittim and forgot about Rahab? That type of scenario happens all the time within the church: "I'll keep you in my prayers." That person desperately wants to be free, but somehow we either forget or think it unimportant. The enemy will attempt to use these broken oaths to create bitterness in that person. Our failure to keep our commitments, whether it is a sports game with our children, a phone call that we never make or a prayer we don't pray, can do harm which the devil attempts to take advantage of. I like the way Stasi Eldredge puts it:

> "Demons smell human brokenness like sharks smell blood in the water, and they move in to take advantage of the weakened soul."[17]

All of this because someone says they will do something and they never do.

> **We are to honor our commitments so we don't inadvertently increase the spiritual warfare in ourselves or others.**

---

[17] John and Stasi Eldredge, *"Captivating"*, (Nashville, TN: Thomas Nelson, Inc., 2005), 192.

Antithetical Parallelism

As described on page 32, parallelism is the study of similar or contrasting topics. The topics described in this section are antithetical because they contrast with one another:

Jericho - This city is at the base of the hills, three miles west of the Jordan River and is exactly opposite Shittim. It was a strong fortress with a walled city. To the two spies, Jericho was a place of high risk.

←→

Shittim - This city is at the base of the foothills, three to four miles east of the Jordan River. At the time of these two spies, the Tent of Meeting would have been set up in Shittim. Shittim would be a place of safety to the two spies.

King of Jericho - The word "king" connotes authority and power. Therefore, he would have ruled the city.

←→

Joshua - In chapter 1, Joshua received his direction from the Lord. Joshua 2:1 is the first directive that Joshua gave: "*Go, look over the land ... especially Jericho.*" He has now replaced Moses as the Lord's leader of the Israelites.

Investigators from the king - The king sent out some men to investigate this intrusion into the stronghold of Jericho. Because they were accustomed to being around the lies of the devil, they had no discernment about Rahab's statements.

←→

Two spies - These two men were sent by Joshua to determine the lay of the land, especially Jericho. They went to the home of Rahab, were sent away, hid in the hills for three days and then returned to Shittim. They discerned that Rahab's statement about their discouragement was of greater importance than the lay of the land, so they stopped their investigation.

Rahab the prostitute - She was a prostitute, a deceiver and a manipulator. She sold her body to men, and she deceived and manipulated the king's messengers so that she could get from the spies the kindness of protection.

←→

Rahab the woman of faith - Hebrews 11:31 and James 2:25 lift her up as a great woman of faith and righteousness. She also had a son named Boaz (from the story of Ruth); David and Christ's lineage come from Rahab's son Boaz (Matt 1:5).

In each of these examples of antithetical parallelism, there is a common thread:
- Jericho and Shittim were opposites both geographically and spiritually. Because of the way that the walls fell, hopefully we

can see that Jericho had a significant spiritual stronghold. In contrast, Shittim is where His presence was dwelling between the two cherubim over the ark (Num 7:89 and 1 Chron 13:6).
- The king of Jericho represents a ruler of the people in darkness, as compared to Joshua, the leader of the enlightened people.
- The investigators from the king do not have discernment, whereas the two spies had discernment.
- Rahab the prostitute shows her nature before coming to faith, and Rahab the woman of faith shows her nature afterwards.

As most readers of chapter 2 of Joshua should agree, Rahab is the center of attention in these verses. We will see on page 59 that her concern is to rescue herself and her family from the doom that is expected. Clearly she was a woman undergoing intense spiritual warfare.

Geography: The Land East of the Jordan (Part II)

Back in Genesis, we read that Lot had two illegitimate sons because of incest with his two daughters. His older daughter had a son named Moab and he is the father of the Moabites (Gen 19:37). His younger daughter had a son named Ben-Ammi, and he is the father of the Ammonites (Gen 19:38). The Moabites settled in the land east of the Dead Sea, as well as the valley area between the Jordan River and Shittim (the Plains of Moab). The Ammonites settled in the plateau area east of the Jordan and north of the Moabite territory (which would be east and northeast of Shittim).

Assuming you have installed Google Earth on your computer (see page 7 for instructions), type the following longitude and latitude which will take you to the approximate location of Shittim:

31 49.9'N, 35 39.7'E

Shittim is located at the edge of a valley and at the base of a significant incline. The fertile valley that is to the west of Shittim is the Plains of Moab. Possibly you can see the stream whereby water would have been provided. At the top of the hillside is a large plateau area where modern day Amman, Jordan is located. Shittim's location between the valley and the hillside may indicate that a transition was about to take place.

Sihon and Og

In Joshua 2:10, Rahab expresses the basis of the fear that is in Jericho: the parting of the Red Sea and the destruction of Sihon and Og. The kings Sihon and Og were Amorites. [It is easy to get the Ammonites and the Amorites confused: the Ammonites were descendents of Lot

(Gen 19:38), while the Amorites were descendents of Noah and Canaan (Gen 10:15,16)]. The Amorites had originally settled in areas west of the Jordan River: Jerusalem, Hebron and cities to the south and west. Prior to the arrival of the Israelites, the Amorites had invaded the territory east of the Jordan where the Ammonites and Moabites lived. Many of the Ammonites and Moabites were relocated to adjoining territories (Num 21:26).

The Amorites were one of the seven nations that the Lord promised would be driven out (Canaanites, Hittites, Hivites, Perizzites, Girgashites, Amorites and Jebusites), and they were the first to experience defeat. The expanded territory of the Amorites extended from the Arnon River near the Dead Sea to the Golan Heights towards Damascus.

The false god of the Moabites was Chemosh, and the false god of the Ammonites was Molech (1 Ki 11:33). While the Bible does not directly state this, we can infer that the Amorites, by invading and defeating the Moabites and the Ammonites, had been able to overcome Chemosh and Molech. As Christians, we know that these two gods had no power unto themselves.

Because the Moabites and Ammonites were defeated, the people of Jericho would have perceived the gods of kings Sihon and Og (Amorites) as having more power than the gods Chemosh and Molech. Further, in a figurative sense, these two kings would have been considered the rulers of their strongholds: Heshbon and Bashan.

Therefore, when the story went out that the kings Sihon and Og were defeated by the Israelites, it was not just the Israelites that the people in Jericho feared. Rather, the Canaanites realized that the spiritual powers of the great Sihon and Og were nothing, and the Lord of Moses and Joshua was the one **to be feared**. The Lord had used the sword (Num 21:24) to drive out the Amorite kings. This is why Rahab stated that the people of Jericho were "... *melting in fear because of you*" (Josh 2:9).

Spirits of Fear and Courage

Two types of fear are described in Joshua 2: Rahab looked at the fear as an opportunity to escape, while the king of Jericho feared loosing his position and his life. Rahab's fear might be called 'respect', but it was probably more than that – Rahab knew the depravity of the people in Jericho, and she was in the middle of it. More than fearing death and destruction, she was choosing a new life. Her fear gave her knowledge of what to do; it gave her hope.

This type of fear was described by Moses forty years earlier. The Israelites saw the thunder and lightning, heard the trumpet and saw the mountain in smoke. Moses then spoke to the people in Exodus 20:20:

"Do not be afraid. God has come to test you, so that the fear of God will be with you to keep you from sinning." This type of fear recognizes our own weaknesses and helps us see sin and demonic oppression as repulsive.

Another example is provided by Flavius Josephus, a Hebrew historian in the first century AD, who wrote a parallel account of the Book of Joshua in *Antiquities of the Jews*. He states: *"Now while Joshua, the commander, was in fear about their passing over Jordan, for the river ran with a strong current ..."* [18] Apparently Joshua's fear may have been something like: "How can we get the people, their belongings and most importantly the ark of the Lord from getting wet? I have no clue about how to do this." We see that very shortly, his fear changed to courage because the Lord gave him direction.

The second type of fear was exemplified in the king of Jericho as he "took on" fear when he realized that some spies had entered his territory. Joshua 2:11 states *"everyone's courage failed."* The word courage is the Hebrew word **ruwach**, which we discussed on page 13, meaning spirit or wind. A more literal way of translating these words is "the spirit of every man did not remain." What was that spirit? Courage.

There is an alternating play on the concepts of "strong and courageous" versus "fear and discouragement" in the books of Deuteronomy and Joshua. In Deuteronomy 31, Moses instructed the people generally and Joshua specifically to be *"strong and courageous."* In Joshua 1, the Lord gave this same instruction four times to Joshua. Rahab confessed, in essence, that her people had lost their strength and courage. As we go through the remainder of Joshua, notice the incidents where the fear came and the courage left. Courage and discouragement are "antithetical."

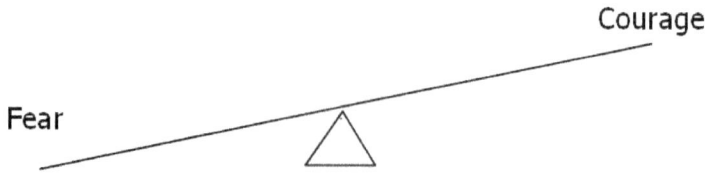

I like to think of this imbalance in the same way as how two people sit on a teeter totter. When one person is high, the other person is low. When the second person then goes up, the first person goes down.

---

[18] Flavius Josephus, *Antiquities of the Jews*, trans. William Whiston, bk. V, chap. 1, sec. 3

In the same way, we can have strength and courage, or we can have fear and discouragement. When the Lord is our strength, we go up and we feel courageous. When the devil has stolen our strength, we feel fearful and discouraged. This boils down to a choice: we either allow a spirit of strength and courage to control us, or we allow a spirit of fear and discouragement to have power over us.

This is how it is with "strong and courageous" versus "fear and discouragement." The more we take on the spirits of strength and courage, the more the enemy is fearful and discouraged. This can be a daily battle, but there is victory in the name of Jesus.

> **The more we allow the Lord to be our strength,
> the more fear we put in the devil and his demons.**

Rahab's Spirit of Deception

Rahab was a prostitute in a city that was destined to die, but she also believed by faith in the Lord of the Israelites (Josh 2:11). This is the classical scenario of a person coming out of bondage – as a person coming to a new faith, her fear of the king and her fear of the Lord of the Israelites led her to plead ignorance. She knew that if she told the investigators what she knew, there would be adverse consequences for both her and the two spies. She had faith, but she still had a spirit of deception.

This chiasm emphasizes her statements to the king's investigators on the C – C' level:

Level	First presentation	Inversion	Theme
A - A'	King of Jericho sends investigators within city (Josh 2:3)	Investigators pursue spies outside the city (Josh 2:7)	Investigators are in the city and the vicinity
B - B'	Rahab hides the two spies (Josh 2:4a)	Rahab had hidden the two spies under stalks of flax (Josh 2:6)	Rahab hides the two spies
C - C'	Rahab says she does not know where they came from (Josh 2:4b)	Rahab says she does not know where they have gone (Josh 2:5)	Rahab pleads ignorance

Rahab reminds me of how many new believers behave with regard to their previous lifestyle; she had not yet gotten rid of that **spirit of**

deception. This, of course, was only the beginning of her walk with the Lord. She needed a deliverance from the spirit of deception.

Everything Bows Down to the Lord

Those Biblical scholars who are familiar with the chiastic approach often point to the chiasm that is in Joshua 2:9-11. What is unique to this book is the application of chiasms to spiritual warfare:

Level	First presentation	Inversion	Theme
A - A'	I know that the Lord has given this land to you (Josh 2:9a)	For the Lord your God is God in heaven above and the earth below (Josh 2:11b)	Profession of faith
B - B'	We are all melting in fear of you (Josh 2:9b)	Our hearts melted and everyone's courage failed because of you (Josh 2:11a)	Effect: Courage is replaced with fear
C - C'	The Lord dried up the water of the Red Sea when you came out of Egypt (Josh 2:10a)	The territories of Sihon and Og, the two kings of the Amorites east of the Jordan, were completely destroyed (Josh 2:10b)	Cause: Both the physical earth and the spiritual powers bow down to the Lord God

Notice how perfectly this chiasm is constructed. In modern Western World logic, we would expect the structure to be something like this:

Cause: "We have seen the great things of the Lord."

Effect: "Fear of the Lord has overcome us."

Profession of faith: "The Lord is God."

But in the chiastic approach, the sentence structure is completely different:

- On the A – A' level of Rahab's testimony, she briefly professes her faith by acknowledging the Lord's dominion over heaven and earth.
- The effect on the B – B' level is the report that the spies are looking for: everyone has lost their courage.
- On the C – C' level, Rahab recognized how the Lord has control over all nature by opening up the Red Sea on demand, and how He has the ability to defeat the demonic spiritual forces that the Amorites called gods.

Chapter 2 – The Lord Has Given The Whole Land

The chiasm shows that the parting of the Red Sea and the defeat of Sihon and Og are given equal importance. The opening of this large body of water is repeated in the Bible many times to emphasize its importance. The defeat of Sihon and Og, which really was the defeat of the ruling spirits and gods of the Amorites, emphasizes the importance of spiritual warfare.

I am reminded of a modern day prostitute who gave up that lifestyle when she committed her life to Christ. She was brought to our church two years ago by the pastor of a small downtown church for her baptism. In her testimony before the congregation, this woman stated that she had been hooked on crack cocaine for many years. Her lifestyle was supporting the devil's wishes: to keep her eye on her own addiction and off of Christ. The spiritual oppression that had been on this woman was reportedly immense.

This pastor and others from that church provided her with food from their Food Pantry, genuinely showed the love of Christ, and prayed in the name of Jesus that the binding spirits would be loosed. I have heard that she is now eagerly serving the Lord in any way that she can, holds down a regular job, and confesses the love of Christ to other women who are caught in the same struggle.

Similarly, Rahab became the mother of Boaz. She became the wife of an Israelite, becoming an ancestor of King David. Her faith helped in the defeat at Jericho and her family was spared judgment.

> **Effective spiritual warfare can not only defeat the enemy's stronghold; it can lead people to Christ.**

Covenant With Rahab

After Rahab's testimony, she immediately asks for a sign that her family would be spared:

Level	First presentation	Inversion	Theme
A - A'	Rahab: "Please show kindness to my family" (Josh 2:12)	Spies: "We will treat you and your family with kindness" (Josh 2:14b)	Kindness requested and granted
B - B'	Promise that you will spare me and my family (Josh 2:13)	Spies commit to the promise (Josh 2:14a)	Covenant of protection is requested and established

At the beginning of this chapter (page 51), we saw that these verses are the center point of the overall chiasm for this chapter. This brief chiasm brings out Rahab's hope that she and her family would be saved from the spiritual oppression of Jericho and would not have to face the impending death and destruction.

What motivated Rahab? Joshua 2:9 and Joshua 2:11a state very clearly that it was the fear of the Lord. No doubt she was desperate. In the same way today, many people seem complacent about the apparent heaviness that holds them down, while others crave to be free. Desperation from oppression should be desperation for the Lord.

> **Be desperate for freedom from demonic oppression for ourselves and for others.**

Another Passover

Let's look at the last chiasm in this chapter. I have relied on the teachings of Peter J. Leithart in the *Biblical Horizons Newsletter* for the analysis in this section: [19]

Level	First presentation	Inversion	Theme
A - A'	Spies escape through window (Josh 2:15)	Scarlet cord is tied in the window (Josh 2:21b)	Window is path to escape
B - B'	Rahab tells them: "Go to the hills" (Josh 2:16)	Rahab sends them into the hills (Josh 2:21a)	Sent to hills of safety
C - C'	Scarlet cord must be in the window (Josh 2:18a)	Blood will be on your head if conditions are not met (Josh 2:19b)	Scarlet cord equated with blood (red)
D - D'	Bring all your family (Josh 2:18b)	Everyone must stay in your house (Josh 2:19a)	Entire household will be passed over

There are two opposites that are noteworthy here. On the C – C' level, the scarlet cord is identified with the blood. Some people say that the scarlet cord is a fore-telling of the blood of Christ. For example, Numbers 19:6 uses scarlet wool for cleansing along with the blood of a red heifer. Leithart suspects, however, that the red is a reminder of the

---

[19] Peter J. Leithart, "Passover and the Structure of Joshua 2", *Biblical Horizons Newsletter*, 99, Nov 1997, 2,3.

Passover in Egypt because blood was placed over the doorway so that the destroyer would not harm the first born. In this way, hanging the scarlet cord out the window would be equated with the blood placed over the doorway during the plague of the first born in Egypt.

The center point of this chiasm is that the whole family must stay inside the house. This should further bring to mind the Passover from forty years earlier: *"Not one of you shall go out the door of his house until morning"* (Ex 12:22). Similarly, the oath would not be binding if Rahab or her family did not do their part. Therefore, Joshua 6 represents a **second Passover**. Most of the people of Jericho were killed in that chapter, but Rahab and her family were passed over.

A Forty Year Chiasm

As covered in the previous section, the protection of Rahab, her family and her house was a second Passover. Let us compare the second Passover to the first Passover and then look at the resulting chiasm. I have labeled this type of chiasm as a "randomly placed chiasm" because it does not follow the pattern of one chiasm leading to another, as in the tiered chiasms. This chiasm extends from Exodus 12 to Joshua 6 and spans forty years:

Level	First presentation	Inversion	Theme
A - A'	Passover and deliverance out of Egypt (Exodus 12)	Deliverance and Passover in Jericho (Joshua 6)	Destruction and grace
B - B'	Consecration of the first born out of Egypt (Exodus 13)	Circumcision of the first generation into Promised Land (Joshua 5)	Preparation of the first people before the Lord
C - C'	Red Sea parted (Exodus 14)	Jordan River parted (Joshua 3 - 4)	The power of God in parting the waters
D - D'	Song and first 2 months in the desert (Exodus 15 - 18)	Song and last 2 months in the desert (Deuteronomy 31 - Joshua 2)	Song and 2 months in desert
E - E'	Covenant at Mt. Sinai (Exodus 19 - 34)	Covenant at Plains of Moab (Deuteronomy 1 - 30)	Two covenants
F - F'	Next 10 months in the desert (Exodus 35 - Numbers 19)	Last 10 months in the desert (Numbers 20 - 36)	First and last years in the desert

Considering the A – A' level, the Passover from Egypt resulted in the Israelites being spared which was followed by their deliverance from Egypt. Forty years later, Jericho was delivered into the hands of the Israelites (Josh 6:2), and Rahab's household was passed over. The B – B' level matches the consecration of the first born before they left Egypt with the circumcision of the first generation shortly after they entered the Promised Land.

At the C – C' level, there is the comparison of the parting of the Red Sea with the Jordan River. In both events, the Lord had the people walk on dry land even though it had previously been mud. Joshua reminded the Israelites of this comparison in Joshua 4:23,24: *"The LORD your God did to the Jordan just what he had done to the Red Sea when he dried it up before us until we had crossed over. He did this so that all the peoples of the earth might know that the hand of the LORD is **powerful** and so that you might always fear the LORD your God."*

The first and last two months in the desert are identified in the D – D' level. Exodus 19:1 states that two months had passed since they entered the desert. A comparison of Deuteronomy 1:3 (first day of eleventh month) with Joshua 4:19 (tenth day of first month) reveals that there were roughly two months between Moses speech at the plains of Moab and their crossing the Jordan River. Further, Moses and Miriam sing a song of celebration in Exodus 15; at the end of his life, Moses recites a song of celebration even though he is no longer able to sing.

On the E – E' level, there is reference to two covenants: one at the plains of Moab and the other at Horeb (Mt. Sinai):

> *These are the terms of the covenant the LORD commanded Moses to make with the Israelites in **Moab**, in addition to the covenant he had made with them at **Horeb**.* (Deut 29:1)

We will discuss these two covenants in the next section.

On the F – F' level, the remainder of the first year in the desert is compared with the last year in the desert. The F level begins in Exodus 35 where the tabernacle and all of its elements were created. That timeframe extends all of the way to Numbers 19 and includes one form of rebellion after another. For some reason, the Bible does not record the events of the next thirty-eight years. Then the Bible picks up the events of the last year, describing them in Numbers 20 – 36.

The severely legalistic commandments from Leviticus and Numbers were not given at either Mt. Sinai or in the Plains of Moab. Instead, they were given to Moses in the desert while he was in the Tent of Meeting. These commandments were given in their first year in the desert, and to a much smaller extent, in the last year in the desert.

Sinaitic and Deuteronomic Covenants

Many theologians consider the covenant at Horeb (Mt. Sinai) and the covenant at Moab to be different aspects of the same covenant. They contend that the promises and requirements at Horeb and Moab are part of the same package from the Lord. For example, Keil and Delitzsch state that the words spoken at Moab *"consisted literally in a renewed declaration of the covenant which the Lord had concluded with the nation at Horeb."* [20]

More recently, some theologians have distinguished between the two covenants, calling them the Sinaitic covenant and the Deuteronomic covenant. According to that theology, the Sinaitic covenant was given at the beginning of the forty years in the desert, and it represents all of the commands given in Exodus 19 - 34. The Deuteronomic covenant was issued before entering the Promised Land; it begins with a review of the Sinaitic covenant in Deuteronomy 4 – 5, but the heart of the Deuteronomic covenant extends from Deuteronomy 6 - 30.

The theology supporting two covenants is not as well formed as the classical theology of one covenant from Exodus through Deuteronomy. The basic premise of Deuteronomy is that the Lord promised success in possessing the land and promised prosperity provided that His commands are met. Conversely, failure to keep these commands was intended to create a proper fear of the Lord.

The covenant at Sinai has its cornerstone in the Ten Commandments which are clearly delineated. The Deuteronomic covenant, on the other hand, does not have a single list of commands; in my research, no theologian has presented such a list. Therefore, I humbly present the list of seven commands below for consideration to the theological community. The verses that support these distinctions are listed after each command:

- Fear the Lord your God (Deut 10:12, 20)
- Love the Lord your God (Deut 10:12; 30:6, 16, 20).
- Obey the Lord your God (Deut 10:13; 30:2 8, 10, 14).
- Walk in the ways of the Lord (Deut 10:12; 30:16).
- Listen to the Lord's voice (**rhema**) (Deut 30:20).
- Hold fast to the Lord (Deut 10:20; 30:20).
- Serve the Lord your God (Deut 10:12, 20).

---

[20] Keil & Delitzsh, *Commentary on the Old Testament, Vol 2: Joshua, Judges, Ruth, Samuel* (Peabody, MA: Hendrickson Publishers Inc., 1866-1891), Electronic database from PC Study Bible 2007

In addition, Deuteronomy 30 states each of these seven commands, and they are repeated many other times throughout the Book of Deuteronomy, such as chapters 4, 6, 11 and 19. The fear of the Lord is the basis for the list of curses in chapters 27 and 28. Note also that the seven commands of the Deuteronomic covenant, emphasizing the relational aspects, are consistent with the words taught by Jesus.

Back to the last chiasm – hopefully we can see how the Passover and deliverance in Exodus 12 and Joshua 6 (A – A' level) points towards the two covenants (E – E' level). Once we see that, hopefully we can see that this gives equal importance to the second covenant when compared to the first.

> **With effective spiritual warfare, we are to fear the Lord, love the Lord, obey the Lord, walk in His ways, listen to His voice, hold fast to the Lord and serve the Lord.**

Chapters 3 and 4 – Transformed at the Jordan

He did this so that all the peoples of the earth might know that the hand of the LORD is powerful and so that you might always fear the LORD your God (Josh 4:24).

The story of the parting of the Jordan River is just as amazing as the parting of the Red Sea. By faith, twelve men step into the Jordan River and it immediately stops flowing. The water backs up to Adam (modern Damiya) which is a community approximately twenty miles away.

The battle of Jericho had not started, but with the crossing of the Jordan there already was a spiritual victory. Just as the hearts of the people in Jericho had melted because of the parting of the Red Sea and defeat of kings Sihon and Og, now they had even more to fear. After all, as Joshua 4:1 states, the entire nation of Israel had crossed over the Jordan. Of the roughly two million people that crossed the Jordan, there were forty thousand men in their armed forces (Josh 4:13). Courage was certainly on the side of the Israelites.

After reviewing the structure of chapters 3 and 4, we will again look at the geography of this area, this time focusing on the vicinity of the Jordan River. Then we will consider eight chiasms that appear in Joshua 3 and 4, where we will see the effect that the crossing the Jordan had on the Israelites. We will also look back at the forty years that the Israelites were in the desert in a comparative sense, for they were transformed at the Jordan.

Structure of Chapters 3 and 4

In one sense, Joshua 3 and 4 should be treated as separate chapters because Joshua 3 is more about the river crossing, whereas Joshua 4 more emphasizes the stones to remember the river crossing. Modern Bibles of course separate this story into two chapters.

On the other hand, the two chapters belong together because they weave the story of transformation that the people experienced while crossing the Jordan River. We will see how the Israelites were transformed into a faithful people that are ready for battle. In addition, there is a middle-tiered chiasm that covers both chapters 3 and 4.

At the E – E' level in the chiasm shown below, the priests carried the ark of the covenant, and the Israelites crossed the river in the presence of the Lord. As we will see, not only was the flow of the river changed but the people were changed: they had a life changing experience.

Level	First presentation	Inversion	Theme
A - A'	Prophecy that the Lord will help them cross the river (Josh 3:1-6)	Today, the Lord dried up the Jordan before you (Josh 4:15 - 5:1)	Future and backward views of the Lord's favor
B - B'	Lord says He will exalt Joshua just as He did to Moses (Josh 3:7)	Lord exalted Joshua, and the Israelites revered Joshua, just like Moses (Josh 4:14)	Joshua earns respect of the Israelites, just like Moses
C - C'	You will know that the living God is amongst you (Josh 3:9,10)	Memorial stones are set up to show they understood that God was amongst them (Josh 4:4-9)	Recognition that the living God will help them conquer the land
D - D'	Choose twelve men to carry the ark of the Lord (Josh 3:11-13)	Choose twelve men to take up the stones (Josh 4:1-3)	Twelve men representing the twelve tribes
E - E'	Priests carrying the ark of the covenant step into the riverbed, so that the people crossed over (Josh 3:14-16)	Priests carrying the ark of the covenant stand in the riverbed, allowing people to pass by the Lord (Josh 3:17)	Priests take the presence of the Lord into the riverbed and the people pass by

Geography: The Jordan River

The Jordan River extends some sixty miles between the Sea of Galilee and the Dead Sea. Bible maps often do not show how the river meanders in the vicinity of Jericho. To my knowledge, no credible individual knows or even speculates on the exact location where the Israelites crossed the Jordan. By typing the following longitude and latitude into Google Earth, you will be taken to an area of the Jordan River that is between Shittim and Jericho:

31 50.1'N, 35 32.85'E

If we were to visit the Jordan River today near where Joshua presumably crossed the river, we might wonder what the big deal is all about: there is very little water in the river. When the water comes out of the Sea of Galilee, the river is thirty or forty feet wide and possibly eight to ten feet deep because there is a dam a short distance downstream. At the dam, water is drawn out and sent to other areas of Israel for irrigation and other purposes. [Note: many Christian tourists are baptized at that location. However, the likely location of the baptism site for Jesus was probably much closer to Jericho, near where Joshua led the people across].

As a result of the irrigation, today we see that much of the water in the Jordan does not reach the place where the Israelites crossed the river. That is not what Joshua saw in the spring of that year:

> Now the Jordan is at **flood stage** all during harvest (Josh 3:15).
>
> No sooner had they set their feet on the dry ground than the waters of the Jordan returned to their place and ran at **flood stage** as before (Josh 4:18).

Clearly the river was a much bigger problem than it is today.

A second point of interest is what caused the river to back up. Amos Nur of Stanford University has observed that there may be a natural solution. He reports that in 1927, an earthquake measuring 6.5 on the Richter scale caused a mudslide which stopped the Jordan River from flowing for 21 hours. The epicenter of that earthquake was near Adam, where the Jabbok River empties into the Jordan River. [21]

In response, let me say that the Lord does not need a mudslide to stop a river from flowing, but if this is how He caused the water to back up, praise the Lord!! The real miracle is that when the need came for Israel to pass through the water, the men stepped into the river and the water stopped flowing. The Lord knows our needs and He satisfies them in His way and in His time.

Land Has Been Delivered

The previous inner tier chiasm ended with Joshua 2:21 (page 60). The next chiasm extends from Joshua 2:22 to Joshua 3:2 and focuses on deliverance of the land:

Level	First presentation	Inversion	Theme
A - A'	Two spies wait on mountain for three days (Josh 2:22)	Officers wait for three days (Josh 3:2)	A three day wait
B - B'	Two spies cross the Jordan and return to Shittim (Josh 2:23)	Joshua leads people from Shittim to the Jordan (Josh 3:1)	Movement between Shittim and Jordan River
C - C'	Wisdom: *"the LORD has surely given the whole land into our hands"* (Josh 2:24a)	Wisdom: *"all of the people are melting in fear because of us"* (Josh 2:24b)	Israelites are assuming land; Canaanites are giving up the land

---

[21] Amos Nur, "And the walls came tumbling down", *New Scientist*, 6 (July, 1991), 39-42

In the C – C' level of this chiasm, the NIV translates the Hebrew word **nātan** as "has surely given." In comparison, both the KJV and the NKJV translated this word as "delivered." In the same way, we will see in the fall of Jericho, the Lord delivered that city:

> Then the LORD said to Joshua, "See, I have delivered Jericho into your hands ..." (Josh 6:2).

The two spies received a revelation from the Lord that the land would become theirs. This wisdom was based on the fear that Rahab had described to them. Strength and courage were being given to the Israelites, and fear was taking courage away from the Canaanites.

> **In seeking freedom from demonic attacks, remember that our enemy the devil can be filled with fear, and demons can tremble and shutter.**

The Living God is Amongst Us

The chiasm for Joshua 3:3-6 reveals a new or possibly deeper understanding regarding the officer's instructions to stay a long distance from the ark. Joshua knew that the people needed greater proximity with the Lord, yet the instructions from the officers were to stay a significant distance away:

Level	First presentation	Inversion	Theme
A - A'	People instructed by officers to follow the ark when see priests carrying it (Josh 3:3)	Priests instructed by Joshua to carry the ark past the people (Josh 3:6a)	People are instructed to follow the priests carrying the ark
B - B'	People instructed by officers to be separated from the ark (Josh 3:4)	People instructed by Joshua to be consecrated so they can go past the ark (Josh 3:5)	Conflicting instructions: be separated versus prepare yourself to pass by

On the A – A' level, the Lord is to be followed. The people are told to follow after the ark of the covenant (Josh 3:3), and the priests are told to lead the way by going ahead of the people (Josh 3:6a).

The B – B' level focuses on the two conflicting set of directions: be separated from the ark versus be consecrated so that they can draw near the ark. The Lord did not want separation; He wanted proximity. That is why the B – B' level of the chiasm reveals the conflict. After all,

if the Lord's desire was for the sinful Israelites to stay away from the ark, then why would the Lord have them march around Jericho with the ark in the middle of the people (Joshua 6)?

The officers instruct the people to *"keep a distance of about a thousand yards between you and the ark; do not go near it"* (Josh 3:4). The officers thought it best to separate the people from the Lord because of their sinful state. They also knew that no one was to touch the ark. In that way, they would not contaminate the purity of the Lord.

The events of Joshua 3:1-6 are similar to the first time that Moses went up Mt. Sinai (Ex 19:1-24):

Exodus 19	Joshua 3
Israelites are camped in front of the Holy Mountain (Ex 19:1)	Israelites are camped in front of the Holy Land (Josh 3:1)
"on the third day" (Ex 19:11)	*"After three days"* (Josh 3:2)
Consecrate the people (Ex 19:10)	Consecrate yourselves (Josh 3:5)
Lord said that the people cannot go near the Lord (Ex 19:24)	Officers said people cannot go near the Lord (Josh 3:4)

The officers, in remembering the events at Mt. Sinai from Exodus 19, thought they knew what the Lord wanted. They called for separation from the ark by more that one-half of a mile.

This was spiritual warfare because the officers were not hearing from the Lord. Our Lord does not take sinful people and call Himself to be separate from them. He takes us, as sinful people, and says:

> *Draw near to God and He will draw near to you. Cleanse your hands, you sinners; and purify your hearts, you double minded* (James 4:8 NKJV).

Joshua understood that the Lord does not want separation, He wants proximity.

The directions of the officers appear as a challenge to Joshua's authority. Joshua was, of course, the new leader of the people. Imagine a situation at work where a new boss takes over a department or business. At some point early in the new boss's tenure, he or she is challenged by other workers with more experience. That is what the officers were doing by giving their own directions.

Note that immediately following these instructions, the Lord clarified Joshua's position of authority:

> *Today I will begin to exalt you in the eyes of all Israel, so they may know that I am with you as I was with Moses* (Josh 3:7).

By exalting Joshua, he will no longer be challenged by the people.

Joshua gave the directive to *"consecrate yourselves"* (Josh 3:5) as a way of preparing to be near to the Lord. By consecrating themselves, they would be able to go near to the ark rather than being separated from it. The KJV and NKJV translate this as the words *"sanctify yourselves"* (Josh 3:5) which may help with your understanding.

Consecrate had two aspects: physical cleanliness and separation. Regarding cleanliness, Moses instructed the people first to wash their clothes and then to be separated from one another:

> ... *he consecrated them, and they washed their clothes. Then he said to the people, "Prepare yourselves for the third day. Abstain from sexual relations"* (Ex 19:14,15).

In Leviticus, Moses had taught that consecration was associated with removing physical concerns like unclean food (Lev 11:1-47), infectious skin diseases (Lev 13:1-46), mildew (Lev 13:47-59), and improper sexual relations (Lev 18:6-23). At first blush, the directive to *"consecrate yourselves"* in Joshua 3:5 may recall these physical directives from Leviticus.

But when looked at from the viewpoint of the chiasm, it becomes clear that consecration is more than physical purification; the consecration was to help overcome the separation with the Lord. The purification did not change their hearts, but it helped restore the separation that caused them to be one thousand yards away.

> **As we come to understand our own sinfulness, do not be separate from the Lord, but draw near to Him in cleansing and purification.**

Repetition in Chapters 3 and 4

Two of the most frequently used words in Joshua 3 and 4 are the Hebrew words **'abar** (aw-bar') which means to pass on or cross over, and **nasa'** (naw-saw') which means to carry or to take:

Hebrew	English	Repetitions
'abar	pass on or cross over	22
nasa'	take up or carry	15

For example, in the center point in the middle tier chiasm (page 66), the priests carried **(nasa')** the ark of the covenant, and the Israelites went past **('abar)**. In Joshua 3:5,6, which was just covered, Joshua instructed the people to be consecrated so they can go past **('abar)** the ark.

The Israelites passed by the ark two times on their way to Gilgal. First, in Joshua 3:6-14, the priests carry **(nasa')** the ark of the covenant past **('abar)** the people on the way to the Jordan River. The Israelites had been camped next to the Jordan, and the ark had been at the furthest point away from the Jordan. Joshua said to the priests:

> Take up the ark of the covenant and pass on ahead of the people (Josh 3:6).

Once the ark was in the riverbed, the Israelites passed by **('abar)** the ark a second time (Josh 3:16 - 4:13). The people, referring to the tribes that would settle to the west of the Jordan, along with the two and one half tribes that would settle east of the Jordan, and the armed guard, all passed by the ark of the Lord that was in the riverbed.

If that were not enough, the stones were carried past the people in Joshua 4:1-8. The stones, which were to memorialize this effort, were carried **(nasa')** from the riverbed to Gilgal where they would be camping for the night, which passed **('abar)** by the people.

Why all of this emphasis on **nasa'** and **'abar**? Again, it is for the purpose of proximity with the Lord. The people needed to see first-hand that the miracle that was being performed was being done by the Lord. If they had been separated from the Lord, the miracles of the Jordan River parting would not have transformed their lives.

The Water Stood In a Heap

Another repetition appears in Joshua 3, although this time it is embedded into a chiasm. The repeated word is `**amad** (aw-mad), which means to stand, remain or endure (Josh 3:8, 13, 16, 17):

Level	First presentation	Inversion	Theme
A - A'	Priests are told to stand (`amad) in the river (Josh 3:8)	The priests stood (`amad) on dry ground in the riverbed (Josh 3:17)	Priests stand firm
B - B'	The water will stand (`amad) in a heap (Josh 3:13)	The water stood (`amad) in a heap (Josh 3:16)	The water stood firm
C - C'	The ark goes ahead of the people (Josh 3:14)	The ark reaches the water's edge (Josh 3:15)	The presence of the Lord reaches the water's edge

In the above randomly placed chiasm, notice the transition from priests standing (A – A' level) to water standing (B – B' level) to the movement of the ark (C – C' level). The verbs carry the secret for unlocking this chiasm. On the A – A' level in Joshua 3:8, the Lord told Joshua to tell the priests to go and `**amad** (stand) in the river. Likewise, at the end of the event in verse 17, it is stated that the priests `**amad** firmly on dry ground.

Notice what happened at the B – B' level: the water will `**amad** (stand) in a heap (Josh 3:13). Again in Joshua 3:16, the water `**amad** in a heap, only here the NIV uses the word "piled" instead of "stood." In other words, the water stood just like the priests stood. Let me repeat in a different way: **the water stood because the priests stood first**.

At the C – C' level, the ark of the covenant carrying the presence of the Lord reached the Jordan River. Immediately the water honored the presence of the Lord by standing, just as the priests honored the presence of the Lord. The water imitated the priest's action (A – A' level) because of the presence of the Lord (C – C' level).

The priests stood, and they stood, and they stood. There were roughly five hundred thousand men that crossed the Jordan plus their women, children, carts and animals. [22] That was probably around two million people. Potentially that took a long time.

The New Testament is rich in statements about standing firm. Here are some examples:

> ... **stand firm**. Let nothing move you ... (1 Cor 15:58).
>
> Be on your guard; **stand firm** in the faith; be men of courage; be strong (1 Cor 16:13).
>
> ... it is by faith you **stand firm** (2 Cor 1:24).
>
> It is for freedom that Christ has set us free. **Stand firm** ... (Gal 5:1).
>
> For now we really live, since you are **standing firm** in the Lord (1 Thes 3:8).
>
> ... **stand firm** and hold to the teachings we passed on to you, whether by word of mouth or by letter (2 Thes 2:15).

---

[22] The second census identifies that there were 601,730 men from the twelve tribes plus some number of Levites (Numbers 26). The tribes of Reuben, Gad and half tribe of Manasseh comprised 110,580 men, yet only their armed guard went across the Jordan (Deut 3:19). The Bible does not state how many men from those Eastern tribes went to fight and how many stayed to protect their homeland. We can only estimate that the number was around 500,000 men.

Just think: where would the body of Christ be if we all stood firm against abortion, drugs, mediocrity, false gods, family dysfunction, etc.? When the priests stood, the water stood. They kept on standing until the mission was complete.

> Stand firm against the devil's schemes (Eph 6:11).

Priests Carry the Ark Past the People

The next inner tier chiasm begins at Joshua 3:6b:

Level	First presentation	Inversion	Theme
A - A'	Priests carry the ark of the covenant past the people (Josh 3:6b)	Ark of the covenant crosses past the people into the Jordan (Josh 3:11)	Ark is carried past the people on the way to the Jordan
B - B'	The Lord was with Moses, and He will be with Joshua (Josh 3:7)	The people will know that the Lord is with them (Josh 3:10)	The Lord is with Joshua and the people
C - C'	Priests are instructed to stand in the river (Josh 3:8)	Israelites are told to see the priests stand in river and hear the Lord (Josh 3:9)	Come and see the miracle and hear its meaning

The Lord was about to do something that had to be seen for the Israelites to believe. First, the Lord passed by the people on the way to the Jordan (A – A'). Then the Lord reminded them that He was among them (B – B'). Then, Joshua beckoned them to go to the waters edge to see the miracle (C – C').

The Bible is full of exhortations to see and hear so that the people understand, such as:

> *"Hear this, you foolish and senseless people, who have eyes but do not see, who have ears but do not hear: Should you not fear me?" declares the LORD* (Jer 5:21,22).

Jesus asks the same question to the disciples after the feeding of the four thousand, attributing their condition to hardened hearts (Mk 8:17,18). Jesus concluded with these words: *"Do you still not understand?"* (Mk 8:21).

At the Jordan, the hearts of the Israelites were prepared, so they would understand what they saw and heard. The difference between this experience at the Jordan and the experiences that the Israelites had in later years is that at this time, their hearts were ready to receive.

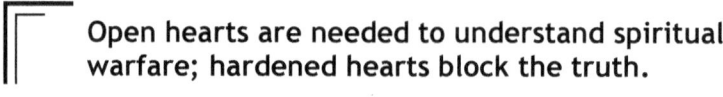

Open hearts are needed to understand spiritual warfare; hardened hearts block the truth.

Priests Carry the Ark Into the Riverbed

The next inner tier chiasm defies science: the ark did not get wet.

Level	First presentation	Inversion	Theme
A - A'	Take twelve men, one from each tribe is chosen (Josh 3:12)	Take twelve men, one from each tribe is chosen (Josh 4:2)	Choose twelve good men
B - B'	Soles of the feet of the priests go to the Jordan, the water is cut off, the water stands in a heap, people set out to cross over, and the priests carry the ark (Josh 3:13,14)	The feet of the priests touch the edge of the water, the water rises in a heap, the waters are cut off, the priests stand on firm ground in the Jordan, and the people crossed over (Josh 3:15 - 4:1)	Feet touch the water's edge, the water is cut off and stands in a heap, priests stand where the water was, and people cross over

The A – A' level of this chiasm is very straight forward: it is a call for twelve men. The B – B' level is a bit more difficult to see because there are five parts which appear in roughly the same order. Moses had instructed the people:

> *For if you carefully keep all these commandments which I command you to do – to love the LORD your God, to walk in all His ways, and to hold fast to Him – then ... every place on which the **sole of your foot** treads shall be yours ...* (Deut 11:22-24 NKJV).

The Lord spoke similar words about the sole of their feet to Joshua:

> *Every place that the **sole of your foot** will tread upon I have given you, as I said to Moses* (Josh 1:3 NKJV).

By these verses, we can see that the Lord kept His promise: the priests touched the waters edge and everyone saw the Lord's miracle.

Take Twelve Stones

The next inner tier chiasm looks at the twelve stones which are to be a memorial for all generations:

Level	First presentation	Inversion	Theme
A - A'	Take twelve stones from where the priests stood firm (Josh 4:3a)	The twelve stones were set up where the priests stood (Josh 4:9)	Twelve stones from where the priests stood
B - B'	Carry the stones to where you will spend the night (Josh 4:3b)	Twelve stones are carried to the place they spent the night (Josh 4:8)	Stones moved to Gilgal where they spent the night
C - C'	Twelve men are called by Joshua (Josh 4:4)	Twelve men are instructed to cross before the ark (Josh 4:5)	Twelve men pass before the ark

There is a discrepancy between the NKJV and NIV Bibles with respect to Joshua 4:8,9. The NKJV (and KJV) reveals two piles whereas the NIV shows only one pile (although the footnote in the NIV for Joshua 4:9 indicates the possibility of a second pile). Here are the verses in question from the NKJV:

> *8And the children of Israel did so, just as Joshua commanded, and took up twelve stones from the midst of the Jordan, as the LORD had spoken to Joshua, according to the number of the tribes of the children of Israel, and carried them over with them to the place where they lodged, and laid them down there. 9Then Joshua set up twelve stones in the midst of the Jordan, in the place where the feet of the priests who bore the ark of the covenant stood; and they are there to this day* (Josh 4:8,9 NKJV).

In Joshua 4:8, the twelve stones are moved to Gilgal where they were camped. In Joshua 4:9, Joshua sets up another twelve stones in the middle of the Jordan where the priests stood.

By looking at the A – A' level of this chiasm, it becomes readily apparent that there were two piles. The A' verse is needed to satisfy the A verse. But even more so, the two piles have a different meaning. The stones from Joshua 4:3a, which is the A verse, are to be a memorial for the Israelites. The stones in Joshua 4:9, which is the A' verse, are hardly a memorial for these people; these stones are an example of antithetical parallelism, meaning that they contrast to the first set of stones. If the first stones represent a new life for the Israelites, the second stones represent a new death for the enemies of Israel.

This contrast between the first and second set of stones is similar to the contrast in Joshua 4:24: *"He did this so that all the peoples of the earth might know that the hand of the LORD is powerful and so that you might always fear the LORD your God."* In other words, do not underestimate God's strength when you need help, but He is also a Lord to be feared.

The effect of this power is seen by the statement made about the Amorite kings who lived west of the Jordan River. Joshua 5:1 states that *"... their hearts melted and they no longer had the courage to face the Israelites."* The courage of these Amorites had changed into fear. The implication is that the Israelites had even more courage.

 The power of the Lord sets the captives free and causes the enemies of the Lord to fear Him.

Disobedience During the Forty Years

As preparation for the next inner tier chiasm, let us look back over the previous forty years in the desert. During those forty years, they stumbled and fell many, many times:

- The whole Israelite community **grumbled** about the lack of food, so the Lord provided manna (Ex 16:1-4). In time, the manna became very distasteful because of repetition.
- Some of the Israelites **disobeyed** Moses by keeping the manna for the following morning, but the manna bred worms and stank (Ex 16:20).
- The people **quarreled** with Moses about the lack of water at Massah, so the Lord had Moses strike his staff on the rock (which was Christ) causing water to come out (Ex 17:1-7).
- Aaron and the Israelites **rebelled** against Moses and the Lord by casting a golden idol, causing the Lord to bring a plague against the rebels (Ex 32:1-6, 25-35; Deut 9:15-17).
- Aaron's sons Nadab and Abihu, upon seeing the glory of the Lord in the form of a fire, **boldly** offered unauthorized fire before the Lord, so they died before the Lord (Lev 9:23 - 10:2).
- The son of an Israelite woman **blasphemed** the Lord's name and cursed, so the Lord had him stoned to death (Lev 24:10-14).

- Some Israelites **complained** about their hardships, which aroused the Lord's anger and caused Him to burn and consume some of them (Num 11:1-3).
- The people **coveted** meat and **complained** about the manna, so the Lord provided quail which turned into a plague (Num 11:4-33).
- Miriam and Aaron, the sister and brother of Moses, **questioned the authority** of Moses, so the Lord gave Miriam leprosy for seven days (Num 12:1-10).
- The ten spies **lacked the faith** that the Lord would be with them in conquering the land. The Lord struck them down and they died of a plague (Num 13:26-33, 14:36,37).
- When the Israelites **disbelieved** the two spies and then **treated the Lord with contempt** by **grumbling** against Moses and Aaron, the Lord condemned all men twenty years old or older to death (that is 601,730 men) over a forty year period so they would not enter the Promise Land (Num 14:1-29).
- Against the advice of Moses, some people attempted to conquer a part of the Promised Land using just their own strength **(self reliant)**. The Lord was not with their effort and they were defeated by the Amalekites and Canaanites (Num 14:39-45).
- A man **disobeyed** one of God's laws by gathering wood on the Sabbath day, so the Lord had him stoned to death (Num 15:32-35).
- Korah, Dathan and Abiram **rebelled** and **disrespected** Moses and the Lord, so the Lord judged the rebellious people by opening the earth and swallowing them (Num 16:1-33).
- Two-hundred and fifty people **followed Korah's example**, so they were consumed with fire from the Lord (Num 16:2,35).
- In the same disobedience, 14,700 people died by a plague from the Lord because they too had picked up this same **rebellious** attitude (Num 16:41-49).
- Moses and Aaron, after being instructed by the Lord to speak to the rock, instead struck the rock. Even though water came out, this disobedience **failed to honor the Lord as holy**, so the Lord prevented them from entering the new land (Num 20:1-12).
- The Israelites became **impatient** about having to go around Edom and **spoke against** the Lord and Moses, so the Lord sent snakes that bit and killed many of the people (Num 21:4-6).

- Israelite men **indulged in sexual immorality** with the Moabite women, so the Lord brought a plague which killed twenty-four thousand people (Num 25:1-9).
- When the Israelites passed through the land of the Amorites, the Lord gave king Sihon a **stubborn** spirit and an **obstinate** heart, so the Lord delivered the Amorites into their hands, killing them all (Deut 2:24-34).

It may be easy, when reviewing a list as long and challenging as this, to dwell in our minds on the judgments from the Lord. But look again at this list: could some of these examples be from an evil force pulling these people away from the Lord? Today we see or experience rebellion, deception, criticism, individualism, lust, selfishness, etc., and the list goes on and on. It was the same way during the time of Moses – the disobedience was often prompted by demonic forces, pulling a person down and pulling them away from God. That was the devil's purpose then, and it is his purpose today.

Two of the above examples questioned the authority of Moses:

- Korah challenged the authority of Moses, and he (and his followers) was put to death by the earth opening up and swallowing him (Num 16:1-33).
- Miriam and Aaron questioned their brother's authority, and she was sent out of the camp for seven days with leprosy (Num 12:1-10).

While both questioned the authority of Moses, Korah was put to death but Miriam and Aaron were disciplined. Why? May I suggest that the difference is spiritual motivation? Korah had a spirit of rebellion, while the poor choice of Miriam and Aaron was followed by a heart of confession and repentance.

The story of Korah in chapter 16 of Numbers is particularly instructive of how a spirit of **rebellion** can attempt to defeat us. Korah, as leader of the rebellion, first got Dathan and Abiram to go against Moses. Pretty soon they were joined by another 250, and ultimately another 14,700 were caught in this spirit of rebellion. This exponential increase shows how quickly the problem can spread, just like a virus can spread in our places of work. If the problem had not been addressed with the 14,700, the entire camp would have been infected.

The Israelites had lived four-hundred years in Egypt. Even though they had lived separately from the Egyptians, they had been in bondage to them. But the most serious problem was the rebellious spirits that they had picked up while in Egypt. These spirits caused them to sin and to move further away from purity. For forty years, the Lord had to deal with the rebellion and disobedience of the people because they were not ready to enter into the Promised Land. Their wickedness, caused by bad personal choices and by demonic spirits, needed to be purged. The battle for their minds was clearly illustrated by their frequently stated desire to return to Egypt.

Years later, Samuel the prophet reminded the people of Israel what the Lord said: *"I brought Israel up out of Egypt, and I delivered you from the power of Egypt and all the kingdoms that oppressed you"* (1 Sam 10:18). Egypt had a power of oppression. Truly, that forty year period was a time of intense spiritual warfare.

Notice how quickly the Lord dealt with the many issues above. Spirits of rebellion, complaining, deceit, coveting, etc. must have been at work attempting to defeat the Israelites. But the Lord had to quickly take action because He knew how quickly the damaging fire can spread. Let this be our motto, whether the problems are in our homes, our workplaces or our churches: do not let the problems fester!

> **Issues of spiritual warfare should be dealt with quickly.**

Transformed

As we did in chapter 2, let's look at the parallelism that is found in chapters 3 and 4. In this case, the objects are called synonymous because of their similarity:

Jordan River - The river changed form, from a river flowing with spring runoff from Mt. Hermon to a river with no water.	←→	**Riverbed** - When the water stood in a heap, the mud of the river turned into dry ground.
Twelve Stones - The stones were relocated from the stream to their camp.	←→	**Twelve Priests** - These twelve men stood in awe as these events unfolded.

Notice the transformations: the river was transformed from flood stage to no water; the riverbed was changed from mud to dry ground; the stones were relocated from the river to a pile; and the minds of the men were transformed from disbelief to belief. Therefore, the Jordan represents the place of transformation from the bondage of Egypt to the holiness of the Promised Land. Like the river, the riverbed and the stones, the tribes were transformed.

Prior to their entry into the Promised Land, the Lord stated this about the new generation:

> *Moreover your little ones and your children ... who today have **no knowledge of good and evil**, they shall go in there; to them I will give it, and they shall possess it* (Deut 1:39 NKJV).

The children did not know the difference between good and evil because their rebellious parents had not taught them.

God's problem prior to the crossing of the Jordan was that rebellious parents do not normally raise faithful children. Rebellious parents often raise children who have a worse problem than they do. In a spiritual sense, the curses on the parents are normally passed down to subsequent generations. How does He reach the two million people who have not understood His love and desire for them to know Him? His answer: an experience that everyone would understand.

The many forms of rebellion and sin that plagued the first generation coming out of Egypt were listed on page 76. If our faith is not strong, we will not believe it until we have experienced it. The priests stood in the middle of the river with the ark, the Jordan River stood still, and they all passed through on dry ground: they now understood and were transformed.

A natural question to ask at this point is "Why didn't the previous generation understand when the plagues hit Egypt?" In Egypt and in the desert after the Exodus, their rebellion got in the way of understanding what God had truly done. At Gilgal, however, their deliverance from this rebellion was now complete as they were transformed through the experience of the Jordan River. They understood what the Lord had done, and they were changed people.

Ephesians 4 describes the effect of this change process:

> *... put off your old self, which is being corrupted by its deceitful desires; to be made new in the attitude of your minds; and to put on the new self, created to be like God in true righteousness and holiness* (Eph 4:22-24).

The miracle of the Jordan River demonstrates the power of the Lord that transforms people. A changed life should no longer dwell on evil things but instead focus on what is good.

> **Transformed lives should understand the Lord's might, power and love, and His requirements for righteousness and holiness.**

Armed for Battle

In Ephesians 6, there are two nearly identical statements that emphasize putting on the full armor of God so that we can stand:

> Put on the full **armor** of God so that so that you can take your **stand** against the devil's schemes. (Eph 6:11)

> Therefore put on the **full armor** of God, so that when the day of evil comes, you may be able to **stand** your ground, and after you have done everything, to **stand**. (Eph 6:13)

In a similar way, the center point (E – E' level) from the next inner tier chiasm from Joshua 4:6-21 shows they were armed for battle. Also, the C – C' level of this chiasm shows how the priests were able to stand:

Level	First presentation	Inversion	Theme
A - A'	When children ask "What do these stones mean?," tell them that the flow of the water was cut off (Josh 4:6b,7)	When descendents ask "What do these stones mean?," tell them that Israel crossed on dry ground (Josh 4:21)	Explanation why the stone piles were built
B - B'	They took twelve stones from middle of the river (Josh 4:8,9)	Joshua set up the twelve stones (Josh 4:20)	Stones are selected and piles are built
C - C'	Priests carrying the ark stood in the water until everything was completed (Josh 4:10)	Priests carrying the ark got out of the water, which causes the water to flow again (Josh 4:18)	The power of standing is again emphasized
D - D'	The ark of the Lord and the priests go to the far side of the river (Josh 4:11)	The ark and the priests come out of the river (Josh 4:15-17)	The presence of the Lord shifts
E - E'	The men of 2 ½ tribes were armed for battle (Josh 4:12)	There were 40,000 men that were armed for battle (Josh 4:13)	Be armed for the battle

Ephesians 6:10-18 tells us how to be strong in the Lord by putting on the full armor of God: the belt of truth, the breastplate of righteousness, feet of readiness, shield of faith, helmet of salvation, and sword of the spirit. Joshua's army was prepared for war. In the same way, we must be prepared for spiritual battle.

By the way, did you see the chiasm in Ephesians 6:10-18? The center point of that chiasm is found in Ephesians 6:12. It is interesting that Ephesians 6:10 says to be strong in the Lord and His power, whereas Ephesians 6:14-18 describes how to be strong in the Lord and how to use His power.

I greatly admire the pastor of the church in that city where all the crows used to flock. Even though he is a employed full time along with full time ministry, he is constantly ready for the battle. He is a man of integrity, he preaches righteousness, he is constantly ready for attacks from the enemy, he is deeply concerned about the salvation of the people, and he is always searching for the deeper word of God which he regularly uses. He wears the full armor of God and he stands.

> **Put on the full armor of God (Eph 6:11,13).**

The Courageous Crows

The crows are back! (If you don't understand this reference, I explained on page 45 that crows have been known to infect the downtown area of a nearby city each evening in the winter). As I was sitting at a stoplight this evening around 5:30pm, I watched hundreds and hundreds of these flying rebels descend over the State Prison and into the downtown area. I probably saw over a thousand in just the minute that I sat at that traffic light, and there was no sign that their number was decreasing. They turned the leafless trees into black statues, where they were squawking and cawing loudly.

Perhaps we have let up on our prayers too much. Perhaps there are new spiritual forces that have made their way into this city. I don't know; but I do know that just last week they had been down to reasonable numbers. It is no wonder that the Lord instructed the Israelites to completely destroy the Hittites, Amorites, Canaanites, Perizzites, Hivites and Jebusites.

The City personnel use newly acquired technology to bring fear upon these crows, thereby scattering them to other areas. This technology, which was obtained from the USDA, allows them to shine laser beams at the congregation of crows and to play recordings of wounded crows. The City personnel will assuredly be out again to deal with them, possibly tonight. To the people of this city, they receive courage in the form of encouragement when the crows are dispersed. To the crows, their courage to re-enter the city will again be displaced by fear. Then the city will once again be transformed.

Chapter 5 – Sins of the Fathers

Now when all the Amorite kings west of the Jordan and all the Canaanite kings along the coast heard how the LORD had dried up the Jordan before the Israelites until we had crossed over, their hearts melted and they no longer had the courage to face the Israelites (Josh 5:1).

Hold on to your hat!! There is a fresh wind blowing.

The layout of chapter 5 is fairly straight forward: more geography is discussed, the men get circumcised, the Israelites celebrate the Passover, the manna stops, and the commander of the army of the Lord visits Joshua. In this chapter, four more chiasms are identified and analyzed.

At the beginning of chapter 5 (shown above) is an account of how the spirit of fear filled the Amorite and Canaanite kings. Do you remember the teeter totter example regarding fear and courage (page 56)? In this one verse, we see that the Amorite and Canaanite kings had lost their courage. The KJV reads *"neither was there spirit in them,"* where the Hebrew word **ruwach** (page 13) is translated *spirit* or *wind*. If the kings lost their courage, the implication is that the Israelites had gained it.

But there is more, much more. Remember the **rhema** word? Please allow the rhema word of God to minister to you as you read through the next two chapters. Stay tuned for the fresh wind (**ruwach**) that is blowing.

Geography: In Search of Ancient Gilgal

There are conflicting definitions for the name Gilgal. Josephus, in the *Antiquities of the Jews*, states in the quote shown below that Gilgal means *'liberty'* – he states the reason for this name is that they now had liberty from their miseries:

> *Now the place where Joshua pitched his camp was called Gilgal, which denotes **liberty**; for since now they had passed over Jordan, they looked on themselves as freed from the miseries which they had undergone from the Egyptians, and in the wilderness.* [23]

---

[23] Josephus, 5.1.11

According to the footnotes in the NIV for Joshua 5:9, the name Gilgal sounds like the Hebrew word for 'roll'. Other Bible theologians identify the name Gilgal with 'wheel'. The common thread of all of these definitions is that they had received liberty (came around full circle) as a result of the transformation described in chapter 4 of Joshua.

Josephus also identified that Gilgal was fifty furlongs (approximately six miles) from the Jordan River, and ten furlongs (a little over one mile) from Jericho. [24] Others have placed Gilgal somewhat closer to the Jordan River; some have identified a possible hill (or tell) which may qualify as "the hill of foreskins" (Gibeath Haaraloth). The precise location of Gilgal may be lost, although we know it was somewhere east of Jericho (Josh 4:19).

When my wife and I drove through this area in 1999, we looked for Gilgal but did not find it. We spent roughly one hour in this area, which reveals that we are not archaeologists; but none the less, there were no obvious signs of an ancient civilization that we came across. The land around this area has a few occasional trees and it is very sandy. The sand storms for the last 3,500 years could easily have hidden Gilgal.

Circumcision

Once the Israelites had crossed the Jordan and had set up the memorial stones, they took a "time out" for circumcision (Josh 5:2-9). What if the history books were rewritten: after the Allied troops crossed the English Channel to land at Normandy, the general got out his knife and barked "Attention! All who have not been circumcised step forward." Those men were under severe attack; it would be no time to care for these needs. It should have been addressed before they crossed the English Channel if not many years earlier.

Does it seem odd that the Lord calls for a circumcision at this time? As odd as that timing may appear, it was at the Lord's instruction: *"At that time the LORD said to Joshua, 'Make flint knives and circumcise the Israelites again'"* (Josh 5:2).

The Israelites would have been familiar with the story of Dinah (Genesis 34), where the men of Shechem were tricked into being circumcised in exchange for their daughters. Three days later, while they were still very weak, Simeon and Levi killed every one of them with their swords (Gen 34:25).

In Joshua 5:2-8, both Joshua and the Israelites obeyed. The people of Jericho could have attacked at any moment. Just a few days after their circumcision at Gilgal, these men would be pursuing Jericho.

---

[24] Josephus, 5.1.4

Was Moses negligent in not circumcising the Israelites according to Genesis 17:10-14? Possibly this inner tier chiasm will explain the situation:

Level	First presentation	Inversion	Theme
A - A'	Lord instructs Joshua to circumcise the Israelites (Josh 5:2,3)	The whole nation was circumcised (Josh 5:7,8)	Circumcision is ordered and fulfilled
B - B'	Every man twenty years old or older died in the desert because they grumbled (Josh 5:4)	The Lord had sworn that they would not see the Promised Land because they grumbled (Josh 5:6b)	Num 14:1-29: Consequences of disobedience are remembered
C - C'	Those born in Egypt had been circumcised, but the people born in the desert were not circumcised (Josh 5:5)	Those who did not obey the voice of the Lord were consumed (Josh 5:6a)	Rebellion is revealed

On the C – C' level, we see that in Joshua 5:5, the fathers were circumcised but their sons were not:

> For all the people who came out had been circumcised, but all the people born in the wilderness, on the way as they came out of Egypt, had not been circumcised (Josh 5:5 NKJV).

Then in Joshua 5:6a, we see that these disobedient fathers, who did not obey the voice of the Lord, were consumed:

> For the children of Israel walked forty years in the wilderness, till all the people who were men of war, who came out of Egypt, were consumed, because they did not obey **the voice of the LORD** (Josh 5:6 NKJV).

The "voice of the Lord" is in bold because some translations, including the NIV, do not mention this. The disobedient fathers of Israel had neglected their responsibility: they had not circumcised their sons and they had ignored the voice of the Lord. The fathers, not Moses, were responsible. This points to the extent of their rebellion, and why the Lord had to deal so harshly with their spirit of rebellion.

Rebellion could be defined as "knowing the right thing to do, but doing your own thing." Rebellion is a matter of following the wrong voice: a false voice that deceives us rather than the voice of truth.

In the discussion of the synthetic parallelism (page 33), we saw that the verse following the chiasm sometimes adds clarity. In Joshua 5:9, we see that summary verse: *"Today I have rolled away the **reproach of Egypt** from you."* Reproach means disgrace and that disgrace was rebellion. They had been rebellious in Egypt and they had been rebellious in the desert. But now they had changed hearts.

   When we come across a spirit of rebellion, deal firmly and directly with that spirit.

Circumcised Hearts

Not only was the sword (**chereb** was described on page 17) used for the destruction of unholy people, but it was used in the circumcision process. In this chapter, Joshua had the Israelites circumcised by flint knives after crossing the Jordan River. Both the KJV and the NIV translated the word **chereb** as flint knives in that verse:

> *At that time the LORD said to Joshua, "Make flint knives and circumcise the Israelites again." So Joshua made flint knives and circumcised the Israelites at Gibeath Haaraloth* (Josh 5:2,3).

Circumcision was part of a covenant that God made with his people. A circumcised Jew is one who has been set apart, hence consecrated.

A little anatomy might be appropriate at this point. There is very little of the human body that God created as unnecessary: we can cut some of our hair off and it is not missed; we can cut back our finger nails and our fingers seem to work better; we can even undergo liposuction to get rid of unwanted fat.

Many believe that circumcision is important from a health standpoint because filth and bacteria will collect in this area, which can lead to infection and contamination of the surrounding area. Remember: some translations of the Bible translate "sin" as "flesh." Therefore, the circumcision process removes flesh (which represents sin) because the body is better off without it. Holiness has no part in sin. The flint knives (**chereb**) were used in removing the cause of the contamination (sin) from the body.

Now that the transformation of chapters 3 and 4 has taken place, the removal of the sin through circumcision is most appropriate. The Lord was seeking people that would obey Him without the infusion of sin.

Four days after their circumcision, they would be celebrating the Passover. If there was any pride in these men, the recovery from the circumcision would have been humbling. Yes women, I understand that the experience of childbirth is often very painful; but doesn't adult circumcision without anesthesia sound painful?? It seems somehow appropriate that they are celebrating Passover in their time of weakness. *"For when I am weak, then I am strong"* (2 Cor 12:10). Adult circumcision was being used to teach dependence on the Lord.

And another thing ... I don't know how other men react to adult circumcision, but what gets me is that they never complained. Their fathers had grumbled over their need for water, for meat, even over their indecision to follow Caleb and Joshua. But this new generation doesn't complain!! Good for them.

Therefore, their commitment to be circumcised represented their circumcised hearts:

> *The LORD your God will circumcise your hearts and the hearts of your descendants, so that you may love him with all your heart and with all your soul, and live* (Deut 30:6).

The Lord was and is looking for circumcised hearts. While the Bible does not say this directly in Joshua 5, their willingness to go through circumcision without grumbling or complaining immediately before the battle indicates their faith and their circumcised hearts.

Passover

Immediately following the rite of circumcision was the celebration of the Passover (Josh 5:10). The Lord gave Moses these regulations regarding who could celebrate the Passover:

> *An alien living among you who wants to celebrate the LORD's Passover must have all the males in his household circumcised; then he may take part like one born in the land.* **No uncircumcised male may eat of it.** *The same law applies to the native-born and to the alien living among you* (Ex 12:48,49).

Note the regulation that the Lord spoke to Moses: *"No uncircumcised male may eat of* [the Passover].*"* The Lord could not have been clearer: no circumcision, no Passover.

If the new generation of Israelites wasn't circumcised, had they even celebrated the Passover while in the desert? The last recorded celebration of the Passover was thirty-nine years earlier in Numbers 9:1-5, which was the first anniversary of their Exodus from Egypt. For that generation, the Passover was not a celebration; they wanted to return to

Egypt. Based on the extent of their rebellion, possibly they had not celebrated Passover for thirty-nine years.

If they celebrated the Passover without circumcising their sons, it would have been a violation of their law (Ex 12:48,49). If they did not celebrate the Passover, that too was defiance of their law (Lev 23:4-8). Either way, they violated their law, but possibly they never celebrated for thirty-nine years. We may never know the answer to that question.

It seems fitting, however, that Joshua 5:10 records that the Passover was celebrated by a faithful generation immediately after the crossing of the Jordan, their transformation and their circumcision:

Level	First presentation	Inversion	Theme
A - A'	The Lord removes the disgrace of Egypt (Josh 5:9)	The Lord removes the manna punishment by allowing to eat from the land (Josh 5:11a)	Disgrace and punishment for rebellion is removed
B - B'	On the fourteenth day of the first month, as per Lev 23:5 (Josh 5:10a)	Passover was celebrated (Josh 5:10b)	Passover celebration

At the center of this simple chiasm, we see the emphasis on the Passover. The similarity of the two water crossings is interesting: immediately before the Exodus, on the tenth day of the first month, the Jews took a lamb in preparation for the Passover (Ex 12:3). Before the invasion of Jericho, they set up stones of remembrance on the tenth day of the first month (Josh 4:19). The Passover in Egypt happened on the fourteenth day of the first month, and the celebration in the land of Canaan occurred on the same day forty years later.

The Passover was celebrated by eating three things: roasted lamb, bitter herbs and bread made without yeast (Ex 12:8). The blood of the lamb was placed on the doorposts so that the death angel would pass by their house (Ex 12:23); the bitter herbs represent their lives of slavery to the Egyptians (Ex 1:14); and the bread was without yeast because they did not have time to prepare regular bread while in the desert (Ex 12:39).

Therefore, to this new family of Jews, the Passover celebration was more than a reminder of the Passover from forty years earlier. As they received their transformation through their Jordan River experience, this celebration reminded them of both the Red Sea and Jordan River crossings. As a side note, John the Baptist stood in approximately the same area near the Jordan declaring that Jesus is the sacrificial *"Lamb of God"* (John 1:29,36).

Manna

Once they ate from the produce of the land in Joshua 5:11, the manna stopped. Exodus 16:1-4 describes how manna first came to the people: they grumbled and the Lord provided manna. *"In this way, I will test them and see whether they will follow my instructions"* (Ex 16:4). The people called this substance *"manna"* meaning "What is it?" (Ex 16:31). What if we said to our mother-in-law at the dinner table: "Please pass some of that 'whatever it is'." They didn't know what it was or what to call it. Would the mother-in-law be offended?

Possibly we can come to some understanding of this manna through the lens of a chiasm. In the previous chiasm, Joshua 5:11,12 were the A' level. But those two verses are a chiasm in itself:

Level	First presentation	Inversion	Theme
A - A'	The Israelites ate unleavened bread and roasted grain (Josh 5:11)	The Israelites ate the produce of the land (Josh 5:12c)	The Lord's new provision: bread that was made from the land
B - B'	The manna stopped when the Israelites ate the unleavened bread (Josh 5:12a)	The Israelites no longer had manna available to them (Josh 5:12b)	The Lord's old provision (manna) stopped

This chiasm shows that these verses are addressing more than the manna going away. Notice the contrast between the A – A' level and the B – B' level. On the A – A' level, we see the new provision of bread which is contrasted with manna (a type of unleavened bread) on the B – B' level. This is significant because Christ was described as the unleavened bread (1 Cor 5:6-8). Therefore, we will investigate to see whether Christ was the giver of the manna or His flesh was the manna.

First, in the Book of Revelation, Jesus says to the church in Pergamum: *"To him who overcomes, I **will give** some of the hidden manna"* (Rev 2:17). The manna is hidden in that Christ makes visible or apparent what was not previously visible or apparent. From this, we see that Christ is the giver of the manna.

Secondly, in John 6, Jesus supernaturally feeds bread made with yeast to the five thousand, and then some Jews follow Jesus to the other side of the lake. Remembering the manna, they want to know how the bread that fed the five thousand compares with the manna. Jesus replies *"... it is my Father who **gives** you the true bread from heaven"* (John 6:32). God, of course, gave His son who is the bread of life. Jesus is the new manna, greater than the manna in the desert. With this bread, they will hunger no more.

Thirdly, Jesus continues the dialog with the Jews by clarifying in a figurative sense, the manna in the desert:

> *I am the bread of life. Your fathers ate the **manna** in the wilderness, and are dead. This is the bread which comes down from heaven, that one may eat of it and not die. **I am the living bread which came down from heaven.** If anyone eats of this bread, he will live forever; and the bread that I shall give is **my flesh**, which I shall give for the life of the world. ... This is the bread which came down from heaven – not as your fathers ate the **manna**, and are dead. He who eats this bread will live forever* (John 6:48-51, 58 NKJV).

Jesus confirmed in John 6:48-58 that this bread of life is His flesh in the form of living bread. He is the bread of life which is offered to give eternal life to this world. He is the new manna, being better than the first manna. The first manna brought life in the desert; this manna offers eternal life. It is possible that Jesus was stating that He was the manna in the desert, but it could be argued that this was only in a figurative sense.

Fourthly, the manna also taught them: they were fed *"with manna ... to teach you that man does not live on bread alone but on every word that comes from the mouth of the LORD"* (Deut 8:3). Therefore, the manna was to teach them to hear and live by the **rhema** word from God. From the beginning, Jesus was the word: *"In the beginning was the Word ... and the Word became flesh"* (John 1:1,14). This manna was intended to point them to Christ.

From these passages, we see that Christ is either the hidden dispenser of the manna (Rev 2:17), or His flesh was dispensed in the form of manna. Either way, Christ was with them for the forty years.

Spirit of Complaining

Besides the question of what is the manna, there is a question as to why it went away in Joshua 5:11,12. If there had been a thirty-nine year interruption in celebrating the Passover, then punishment with manna for thirty-nine years fits with Exodus 16:4 where they were tested for obedience. They were showing obedience by celebrating the Passover in Joshua 5:10. This new generation did not complain that they would get their clothes and supplies wet on the Jordan River, complain about the people they would fight in the Promised Land, or complain about getting circumcised. Because of their circumcised heart, the Lord blessed them by removing the manna.

The manna was supernaturally provided while in the desert for nearly forty years. The fathers, mothers and children, that is everyone, ate the manna. The first generation grumbled against the manna and they died. This second generation also ate this manna, yet they were allowed to enter into the Promised Land.

Of the first generation, everyone except Caleb and Joshua had grumbled and complained against the Lord. These rebels ate but did not worship this manna as their path to life. If they had fed on the manna as their very own source of life, they would have lived. John 6:58 might be paraphrased this way: "if they had the faith to daily eat and worship this bread, they would have lived." Their complaining led to death and they missed Christ.

> **If we want success in our spiritual warfare, stop complaining.**

Angels and the Hornet

After the manna is stopped, the topic suddenly changes and the Commander of the Army of the Lord is introduced. At first, Joshua does not know who he is talking to (Josh 5:13). To help us understand his confusion, let us first look back to Exodus 23 to see the angel and the hornet.

As described in Exodus, Joshua learned about the angel and the hornet in these words spoken to Moses:

> *See, I am sending an **angel** ahead of you to guard you along the way and to bring you to the place I have prepared. Pay attention to him and listen to what he says. Do not rebel against him; he will not forgive your rebellion, since my Name is in him. If you listen carefully to what he says and do all that I say, I will be an enemy to your enemies and will oppose those who oppose you. My **angel** will go ahead of you and bring you into the land of the Amorites, Hittites, Perizzites, Canaanites, Hivites and Jebusites, and I will wipe them out. Do not bow down before their gods or worship them or follow their practices. You must demolish them and break their sacred stones to pieces. Worship the LORD your God, and his blessing will be on your food and water. I will take away sickness from among you,*

> *and none will miscarry or be barren in your land. I will give you a full life span.*
>
> *I will send my terror ahead of you and throw into confusion every nation you encounter. I will make all your enemies turn their backs and run. I will send the **hornet** ahead of you to drive the Hivites, Canaanites and Hittites out of your way* (Ex 23:20-28).

These verses were spoken by the Lord to Moses as part of their promise about entering into the Promised Land. The people would be tempted by the evil one to adapt the ways of the Amorites, Hittites, Perizzites, Canaanites, Hivites and Jebusites. No doubt these nations, like the Egyptians, had all sorts of spiritual baggage. But the Lord did not want spiritual contamination, so the Israelites were instructed to do their part in avoiding and destroying that which would cause this contamination.

- **Angel**

These verses begin with a reference to an angel, which is the Hebrew word **mal`ak** (mal-awk'). In verse 20, the Lord stated that this angel will protect and lead: *"I am sending an angel ahead of you to **guard** you along the way and to **bring you** to the place I have prepared"* (Ex 23:20). The Lord told them to *"listen carefully to what he **says** and do all that I say"* (Ex 23:22). This angel **(mal`ak)** will lead the Lord's people into the Promised Land.

During the invasion of the land, the only reference to a heavenly being is in Joshua 5:13-15. That heavenly being is identified as the Commander of the Army of the Lord. Thinking he was an angel, Joshua asked this being *"What message does my Lord have"* (Josh 5:14). As we work through the Book of Joshua, particularly chapters 5 and 6, we will see how this Commander was more than a messenger or angel.

- **Hornet**

The second spiritual being that is presented in the above verses is the hornet, which in Hebrew is **tsir`ah** (tsir-aw'). The Septuagint (the first Greek translation of the Old Testament) translated this word as "wasp." Unlike the angel that was to help bring in the good, the purpose of the hornet was to *"drive ... out"* the evil by sending *"terror"* and *"confusion"* (Ex 23:27,28). The hornet is described in Deuteronomy with these words:

> *Moreover, the LORD your God will send the **hornet** among them until even the survivors who hide from you have perished. Do not be **terrified** by them, for the LORD your God, who is among you, is a great and*

awesome God. The LORD *your God will **drive out** those nations before you, little by little. ... But the* LORD *your God will deliver them over to you, throwing them into great **confusion** until they are destroyed.* (Deut 7:20-23)

Most modern Bible authorities seem to agree that the hornet is not a literal wasp with a black body, six legs and an impressive stinger. However, there is no consensus on what it really was: one commentator thought it was an illustration of the harm that the hornet does, while another thought it might represent invading armies from Egypt, and a third thought it was a form of divine terror like the plagues of Egypt.

I tend to agree with what *The Bible Knowledge Commentary* states regarding Exodus 23:27,28:

*"God also promised to give the Israelites the land gradually. Their enemies, terrorized by God, would be confused and would retreat. Like running to escape the sting of a **hornet**, they would flee in **fear** and **panic** (cf. Ex 15:15; Num 22:3; Josh 2:9-11,24; 5:1; 9:24)."* [25]

This fear would come because of what the enemy would hear, see or experience. We discussed the spirits of fear and courage on page 55. Suffice it to say at this point that fear played a significant role in the conquest of the land of Canaan as well as in spiritual warfare.

Let us look at some modern military uses of the hornet:

- Boeing Corporation designed the F/A-18C Hornet in the 1970s as a strike fighter jet that was designed to attack both air and ground targets. In its time, it was both highly versatile and reliable. The "Blue Angels," which are often seen in aircraft shows, are F/A-18C Hornets.
- Boeing Corporation has recently produced for the U.S. Navy a strike fighter aircraft named the F/A-18E Super Hornet. This plane is fully capable of being a fighter, a bomber and a tanker, and conducts both air-to-air and air-to-ground combat missions.
- On November 17, 2006, Israel announced it is developing a 'bionic hornet' weapon. This wasp sized robot would be capable of flying into otherwise unreachable areas, photographing its targets or potentially killing them. It would be capable of flying

---

[25] John F. Walvoord and Roy B. Zuck, *The Bible Knowledge Commentary: Old Testament*, (Dallas: Victor Books, 1988), 145.

through narrow alleys in crowded cities without drawing attention.

Modern military personnel have correctly identified the hornet as a weapon that would be capable of doing the very unusual. But the military technology that man produces will never be able to match what God so easily produces. Fighter planes, bionic hornets and nuclear weapons can do a great deal of harm thereby creating a spirit of fear, but far greater is the fear that comes from the Lord.

The sword, angel and hornet, when looked at from a spiritual standpoint as in Leviticus 26:3-8 and Exodus 23:20-28, gives the Lord's assurance a special meaning. When the sword (whose purpose is to cut out the sin that does not belong) is put with the angel (whose purpose was to protect, lead and instruct what is good) and the hornet (whose purpose was to drive out evil by sending terror and confusion), the combination was truly effective. In this way, Joshua learned from Moses to be "strong and courageous." You, too, can have this same confidence.

> **As with the angel and the hornet, Jesus Christ and the Holy Spirit have the authority and power to protect us, lead us and destroy demonic spirits that are tormenting us.**

The Commander of the Army of the Lord

Joshua 5:13 starts a new theme: a man with a drawn sword introduces himself as the Commander of the Army of the Lord. Who is this Commander of the Army of the Lord? There are two Hebrew words that are translated into "Commander of the Army": **sar** (chief, general, keeper or ruler) and **tsaba'** (a mass of persons especially regarding an army for war or for a campaign). These two Hebrew words, **sar tsaba'**, appear a number of times in the Old Testament but almost always in regard to an army of humans led by a human commander. Only in Joshua 5 do the words **sar** and **tsaba'** combine with a third word, **YHWH**, which is Lord. This combination of three words takes on a different meaning: this commander was the **sar tsaba' YHWH**.

Because this combination of three words is not used elsewhere in the Bible, we have to look elsewhere for the meaning. Possibly the actions of this commander will help:

- Joshua 5:13 states that He is carrying a drawn sword. Jesus stated:

> Do not suppose that I have come to bring peace to the earth. I did not come to bring peace, but a **sword** (Matt 10:34).

- The Book of Revelation identifies that the Son of Man had a sharp double-edged sword in His mouth (Rev 1:16). The Son of Man, of course, is Christ.
- In addition to the sword, the reference to sandals in Joshua 5:15 is very reminiscent of the experience of Moses:

Exodus 3:5	Joshua 5:15
Take off your sandals, for the place where you are standing is holy ground.	Take off your sandals, for the place where you are standing is holy.

God spoke to Moses in Exodus 3 from within a bush. Could it be God speaking?

- Joshua 6:2 starts, *"Then the LORD said to Joshua..."* The original Hebrew never had chapters and verses; these were added years later. The flow of the sentences from Joshua 5:15 - 6:2 indicate that the Commander is speaking as the Lord.

Some people may instantly agree that the Commander of the Army of the Lord is Jesus Christ, while others may remain skeptical. The discussion in the remainder of this chapter and the next chapter should help with that understanding.

A Christophany can be loosely defined as either the pre-incarnate appearance of Jesus Christ (that is, before His birth) or His appearance after ascending to heaven. For example, Paul had a Christophany on the road to Damascus (Acts 9).

If we agree that the appearance of the Commander of the Army of the Lord was a pre-incarnate appearance of Jesus Christ, then we agree that this was a Christophany. Other examples of Christophanies include: *"I am God Almighty; walk before me and be blameless"* (Gen 17:1), *"I looked up and there before me was a man dressed in linen ..."* (Dan 10:5), *"With them was a man clothed in linen who had a writing kit at his side"* (Ezek 9:2) and *"My grace is sufficient for you, for my power is made perfect in weakness."* (2 Cor 12:9).

Metamorphosis

The next chiasm, which is another of the randomly placed chiasm, has the center point on the transformation that is presented in Joshua 5:12.

Level	First presentation	Inversion	Theme
A - A'	Rahab, due to her faith, becomes an Israelite; is promised deliverance from destruction (Josh 2:1-24)	Achan, due to his lack of faith, is treated as a Canaanite and is destroyed (Josh 7:1)	Contrast between faithfulness and lack of faith, and the consequences there in
B - B'	Three days of preparation before crossing the Jordan plus four days for the healing from circumcision (Josh 3:1 - 5:9)	Seven days of encircling the city of Jericho (Josh 6:6-27)	Seven days before and after the appearance of the Passover celebration
C - C'	Remembrance of the Passover, where the Lord struck down the firstborn (Josh 5:10-11)	Lord states He has delivered the first city to the Israelites (Josh 5:13 - 6:5)	Firstborn Egyptians are compared with the first city
D - D'	The manna stopped (Josh 5:12a)	Manna was no longer received (Josh 5:12b)	A transition: the manna stopped

The A – A' level is described in David Howard's his excellent book entitled *"The New American Commentary: Joshua"*, where he contrasts the faithfulness of Rahab with Achan's lack of faith. He points out that Rahab, a Canaanite, became in effect an Israelite; conversely, Achan was an Israelite but became like the other Canaanites because of his lust and rebellion. Rahab was to be saved from destruction, while Achan was stoned to death. [26]

The B – B' level is also identified in Howard's commentary as two seven-day periods that were "climaxed by a mighty work of God: the stopping of the Jordan's river in the first instance and the destruction of Jericho in the second." [27] This is simple mathematics – three days plus four days equals seven days.

The C – C' level presents a comparison between what the Lord did at the Passover in Egypt with what the Lord did at the second Passover. (See page 61 for the description of the second Passover.) In this way, *"the LORD struck down all the firstborn in Egypt"* (Ex 12:29) is similar to the Lord stating to Joshua *"I have delivered Jericho into your hands"* (Josh 6:2).

Please pay attention to the D– D' level which focuses on the transition that is represented by the manna. Prior to Joshua 5:12, Christ was either the invisible dispenser of the manna, or He was the manna

---

[26] David M. Howard, Jr., *The New American Commentary: Volume 5 – Joshua* (Broadman & Holman Publishers, Nashville), 187.
[27] Ibid, 144.

itself (see Manna on page 89). In Joshua 5:12, however, the manna was no longer provided. What did Christ do in Joshua 5:13? He immediately made an appearance to Joshua. Christ was **transformed** from the manna to the form of a man with a drawn sword!

What is it about the thought process of our western world? We seem to have a hard time seeing and accepting the supernatural. We accept as a scientific wonder the metamorphosis of a cocoon into a beautiful butterfly. But the Bible is full of supernatural events. At the time of the conversion of Moses, God was transformed into a burning bush (Ex 3:2-6). A man in linen appeared to Ezekiel by coming out of four cheribum with interlocking wheels (Ezekiel 10:2). Jesus was transformed into a human being when He was conceived in Mary's womb by the Holy Spirit (Matt 1:18).

More than that, Christ did not just appear at the time of His birth in Bethlehem. John 1:1,12 states that in the beginning was the Word, and that Word was Christ. Christ was present at the time of Creation (Gen 1:3) and He was in the rock when Moses struck it (1 Cor 10:4). Today, if we are born again Christians, the living Christ is within us. Christ can manifest His presence whenever or wherever He chooses.

Therefore, if we agree that Christ was the manna (or dispenser of the manna if you prefer) and that He was the Commander of the Army of the Lord, then Josh 5:12 is indicating that a metamorphosis took place. Christ, the manna, was transformed into the Commander of the Army of the Lord. The disappearance of the manna represents a change in the spiritual realms.

Joshua Asks For A Word From the Lord

The next natural question might be "Why did Christ appear to Joshua prior to the invasion of Jericho?"

Level	First presentation	Inversion	Theme
A - A'	Commander appears with a drawn sword **(chereb)** (Josh 5:13, 14a)	Commander states He has already delivered Jericho into the hands of Israel (Josh 6:2)	Reference to Lev 26:3-8 - "*your enemies will fall by the sword*"
B - B'	Joshua falls to the ground in worship, with his face to the ground (Josh 5:14b)	Commander confirms that the ground is holy (Josh 5:15b)	Standing on Holy ground
C - C'	Joshua asks for a rhema word from the Commander (Josh 5:14c)	The Commander gives a rhema word (Josh 5:15a)	Ask and you shall receive

The A – A' level reiterates what has been discussed in the section entitled "Joshua and the Sword" on page 16: the Lord had reassured Moses that the sword would be used to deliver the Lord's enemies into the hands of the Israelites (Lev 26:3-8).

The B – B' level emphasizes the holiness that was associated with the Commander of the Army of the Lord. Joshua 5:13 stated that He was standing. When Joshua assumes the facedown posture, he is not only worshipping the Commander, but also giving reverence to the ground that He was standing on. Then the Commander confirms that yes, even the ground is holy.

We see at the C – C' level, which is the center of the chiasm, this request: *"What message does my Lord have for his servant?"* (Josh 5:14). Joshua, the Lord's servant, is eager to listen to the **rhema** word of God. Joshua is at a point of complete dependence on the Lord. If he had a battle plan for Jericho, he knows that the Lord has a better one. The servant's job is to obey. Joshua wants to do the will of God; he is all ears. He wants to hear, understand and obey. Then the Commander responds in Joshua 6:2.

Ask the Lord for a Word and be ready to receive.

The Presence Disappears

Are you still with me? I hope so. We were investigating the appearance of Jesus as the Commander of the Army of the Lord.

Level	First presentation	Inversion	Theme
A - A'	The gates of Jericho were shut up (Josh 2:5-7)	Jericho was tightly shut up (Josh 6:1)	The gates of Jericho were shut tight
B - B'	Two spies receive a rhema word via Rahab (Josh 2:8-24)	Joshua receives rhema word via Commander (Josh 5:13-15)	Rhema word is given
C - C'	Israelites come to a new faith in crossing the Jordan (Josh 3:1 - 4:13)	Lord's blessings for faithfulness: Amorites fear; manna is removed (Josh 4:15 - 5:12)	Faithfulness results in blessings
D - D'	The Lord exalted Joshua in the sight of all Israel (Josh 4:14a)	People exalted Joshua just as with Moses (Josh 4:14b)	Joshua is put on the same level as Moses

Chapter 5 – Sins of the Fathers

Most theologians, regardless of who they believe the Commander of the Army of the Lord is, view His appearance as starting at Joshua 5:13 and ending at Joshua 5:15. They state that chapter 6 starts another thought process: *"Jericho was tightly shut up ..."* (Josh 6:1), and then in Joshua 6:2, the Lord spoke to Joshua as was done in previous chapters.

The above randomly placed chiasm presents an alternative perspective on when the Commander of the Army of the Lord departed. The A – A' level indicates how the gates in the city of Jericho were shut tight. The rhema word of the Lord is provided in the B – B' level. The reward for faithfulness is revealed on the C – C' level as the Amorites are filled with fear (Josh 5:1) and the manna is withdrawn (Josh 5:11,12).

The center point of this chiasm (D – D' level) and a major theme of the Book of Joshua, although not emphasized in this book, is that Joshua was a "second Moses." It can be shown that Joshua assumed the power and position that Moses had. You may wish to research that on your own, although you may see that Joshua was given a different form of authority.

The point in bringing out this chiasm is what appears on the A – A' level. Here we see that Joshua 6:1 is the end of a chiasm that began in Joshua 2:5. Therefore, Joshua 6:1 was inserted between Joshua 5:13-15 and Joshua 6:2 to fill the needs of this chiasm. Consequently, contrary to what most theologians believe, Joshua 6:2 is a continuation of Joshua 5:13-15.

If Joshua 5:13 - 6:5 is one continuous dialog with Joshua and the Lord speaking to each other, then when does the presence of Christ get removed? The Bible does not state when the presence of the Lord left, but no doubt it is when defiant sin enters!

Assuming you are familiar with the Book of Joshua, you know that the sin of Achan led to their defeat at Ai in Joshua 7. At the end of the seven days, after the fall of Jericho, *"... the LORD's anger burned against Israel"* (Josh 7:1). Achan had taken for himself what was to be devoted to the Lord.

In the next chapter, we will see that His presence remained for seven days, which is represented as Joshua 6 in the Bible. At the end of Joshua 6, the Lord became angry over the disrespect of things that were to be devoted to the Lord. Therefore, after the fall of Jericho and the presence of Achan's sin on the seventh day, His presence disappeared.

> **Sin can cause the presence of the Lord to disappear.**

Chapter 6 – The Deliverance of Jericho

Then the LORD said to Joshua, "See, I have delivered Jericho into your hands, along with its king and its fighting men" (Josh 6:2).

Many scholars over the years have written about the Book of Joshua. Oftentimes the emphasis is on the conquest of the land of Canaan through the power of the Lord. For example, the dramatic book entitled *A Table in the Presence* describes many miracles that a Chaplin witnessed in the US led invasion of Iraq in 2003. [28] In that book, the encounters with the enemy and the protection from harm by the Lord are likened in some ways to the events of the Book of Joshua.

As we have seen, the Book of Joshua is about both the miraculous takeover of the Promised Land and the application of spiritual deliverance in individual lives. When the Bible states that Jericho was destroyed, I completely agree that the physical city was conquered by the Israelites. If the Bible states it, I believe it happened or prophetically will happen. But, as explained on page 45, what is seen in the physical is often a representation of what is happening in the spiritual. In this way, the destruction of Jericho is analogous to the freeing of a person from the stronghold of demonic spirits:

- As the city of Jericho was released of the worshippers of foreign gods, so can a person be released from the torments of many demonic spirits.
- A physical wall was constructed around Jericho to prevent intrusion into their city. Figuratively, some people may not appear reachable because a spiritual wall protects demonic spirits that hide in a persons mind.
- Jericho had a man with the title of king; he can be likened to a ruling spirit that controls the demons which can haunt a person.
- Rahab desired that she and her family would be saved from destruction. In the same way, spiritual freedom means the release from bondage and oppression that comes from demonic spirits.

---

[28] Lt. Carey H. Cash, *A Table in the Presence*, (Nashville, TN: W Publishing Group, 2004)

Therefore, these analogies illustrate more than just the physical demise of Jericho – they have personal application to our daily struggles.

Review of Previous Chapters

As identified in the section entitled "First Outer Tier Chiasm" on page 41, the events at Jericho are the central chapter of a twelve chapter chiasm. The first five chapters took the Israelites across the Jordan. Chapter 6 is the destruction of Jericho along with the escape of Rahab's family. The next six chapters (chapters 7 - 12) take the Israelites into the heart of the Promised Land. Chapter 6 is the central chapter because the miraculous fall of Jericho emphasizes the presence of the Lord as judge for the destruction of many and liberator of a few.

In preparation of understanding what happened at Jericho and the application to our lives, it may be important to review some of the key points that we have discussed up to this point:

- The Israelites who came out of Egypt were a very rebellious and sin-infected generation.
- Rebellious parents do not normally raise faithful children.
- The second generation, when they crossed the Jordan River on dry ground, was converted to a true faith.
- The second generation willingly underwent physical circumcision, which represents their circumcised hearts.
- The prior rebellious generation probably did not celebrate Passover for thirty-nine years because to them, it was no celebration.
- The second generation celebrated Passover.
- The manna, which was Christ, disappeared.
- The presence of the Lord Jesus Christ immediately appeared to Joshua as Commander of the Army of the Lord (metamorphosis).
- Joshua fell down in reverence at the presence of his Lord.
- Rahab, a Gentile, was grafted in to the Jewish faith.
- After the fall of Jericho, in the presence of Achan's sin, the presence of the Lord disappears.

Therefore, in a spiritual sense, the major theme of the previous five chapters of the Book of Joshua is the transformation of the Israelites from ungodliness to faith in the Lord. In chapter six, we see the deliverance of Jericho, as shown in the chiasm in the next section. The remainder of Joshua shows the transformation of the people from faithfulness to holiness.

Structure of Chapter 6

Here is the overall structure of Joshua 6, which actually begins in Joshua 5:13 and ends at Joshua 7:1.

Level	First presentation	Inversion	Theme
A - A'	The presence of His Holiness appears to Joshua (Josh 5:13-15)	The presence of His Holiness leaves (Josh 7:1)	The Lord Jesus Christ appears and disappears
B - B'	Instructions regarding deliverance (Josh 6:2-5)	Deliverance is completed and Rahab escapes (Josh 6:16-27)	Deliverance of Jericho
C - C'	March around city for six days (Josh 6:6-14)	March around city seven times on the seventh day (Josh 6:15)	Encircling the city

My guess is that most people would not have thought that the encirclement around Jericho was the center point of Joshua 6. I certainly did not. More likely, I suspect that most people would have thought the central point concerned the deliverance of the city. As important as the deliverance might be, it is only the B – B' level. We will discuss the C – C' level, "Encircling the City," on page 108.

In this chapter, we begin with another geography lesson. Then we will look how a number of words are repeated an unusually large number of times, apparently for the purpose of emphasis. In addition to the repetitions, there are three inner tier chiasms within this chapter: Josh 6:2-16; 6:17-25; and 6:26-7:1. We will also discuss a number of other topics that make this chapter very rich. At the end of this chapter, there is a summary of the amazing events that are described.

Geography: In Search of Ancient Jericho

Today, the City of Jericho is recognized as perhaps the oldest community on earth that has been continuously lived in. Jericho is part of the West Bank, which refers to the west bank of the Jordan River. Of the nineteen thousand people that live there today, most are Muslim. There are high mountains to the west towards Jerusalem. A number of oases provide water throughout the year, yet it is surrounded by dry parched land. In Deuteronomy 34:3, Jericho is identified by a second name: City of the Palms.

There are two ancient communities in Jericho that we could see today if we were there: Tell es-Sultan and Wadi Qilt. The first, Tell es-Sultan, is the Jericho from Joshua 2 and 6. The second, Wadi Qilt, is the community where Jesus met Zacchaeus before his final entry into Jerusalem (Luke 19:1-10).

Tell es-Sultan is an oblong mound that is fifty to ninety feet high, eleven hundred feet long and four hundred feet wide. The perimeter is 3,200 feet; this means that if we marched around the ancient city of Jericho, it would be a little over a one-half mile walk.

If you have installed Google Earth on your computer (see page 7 for directions on installing Google Earth), type the following longitude and latitude in the address located at the top left corner of the screen:
31 52.25'N, 35 26.65'E
Once you have entered this, you can see the extensive archaeological digging over the entire Tell. In the diggings, the archaeologists have found walls, buildings, wells, pottery and a brand new Mercedes Benz (just kidding, seeing if you were paying attention).

Remembering there were forty thousand men in the armed guard (Josh 4:13), here is a math question for your twelve-year old:

> If there is a parade of 40,000 people, the parade is 3,200 feet long, and each person is spaced every four feet on the front, back and sides, how many rows of people are there and how many people are in each row?

The answer is there would be 800 rows with 50 people in a row.

An archaeologist named Bryant Wood found that the wall of Jericho, that is Tell es-Sultan, was actually two walls, one on top of the other. [29] The lower wall goes from the bottom of the hill to the top of the hill; the upper wall was the outside of the homes that were built around the perimeter. Rahab's house, for example, was built on top of the lower wall, and the exterior wall of her house was the upper wall.

Repetition in Chapter 6

In Joshua 6, some of the words repeated most often are:

Hebrew	English	Repetitions
YHWH	Lord	16
'iyr	City	16
sheba' and shebiy'iy	Seven and Seventh	14
shophar	Trumpets	14
'arown	Ark	10
ruwa' and teruw'ah	Shout and Shouted	8
taqa'	To blow	8
cabab	Encircle	7

---

[29] Bryant Wood, "The Walls of Jericho", *Creation Magazine* (Creation 21(2):36-40, March 1999) Online: http://www.answersingenesis.org/creation/v21/i2/jericho.asp, [7 April 2007]

In one way or another, we will be discussing each of the above words in the remainder of this chapter. By the use of repetition, the author of Joshua is emphasizing certain concepts.

For example, the Hebrew words for "seven" and "seventh" appear fourteen times in chapter six. The number seven is believed by many to be the number for perfection. In Joshua 6:4, seven priests with seven trumpets were to circle Jericho seven times on the seventh day. Also, in Joshua 6:15,16a, after circling the city for the seventh time on the seventh day, there were seven priests blowing seven trumpets. The perfection, of course, is the presence of Christ at Jericho.

Each of these words, in one way or another, helps weave the story of deliverance. The repetitions emphasize the **synergy** or **interrelationship** in accomplishing the defeat at Jericho. A trumpet sound, but itself, did not perform the work. A great shout, by itself, did not deliver the people. Encircling the city, by itself, did not accomplish the relief. Carrying the ark, by itself, was not sufficient. When all of these worked together, great things were done through the power of the Lord.

The Ark of the Covenant of the Lord

'**Arown** (aw-rone'), which is the Hebrew word for "ark," appears ten times in chapter 6. For example, "ark" appears twice in Joshua 6:6 – Joshua instructed the priests to *"Take up the ark of the covenant, and let seven priests bear seven trumpets of rams' horns before the ark of the LORD"* (Josh 6:6 NKJV). The ark is clearly important because the Lord was to be found between the two cheribum that were on top of the ark:

> When Moses entered the Tent of Meeting to speak with the LORD, he heard the voice speaking to him from between the two cherubim above the atonement cover on the ark of the Testimony. And he spoke with him (Num 7:89).

The presence of the Lord would be essential in the deliverance of Jericho.

Feast of Unleavened Bread

In chapter 5, we saw the Israelites celebrate the Passover perhaps for the first time in thirty-nine years. Josephus, in his historical documentation of the Jews, stated that

> ... *on the first day of the feast [of the Passover], the priests carried the ark round about, with some part of the armed men to be a guard to it.* [30]

Immediately after the Passover, the Israelites were to celebrate the Feast of Unleavened Bread (also known as the Feast of Passover) starting on the fifteenth day of the month. They celebrated the Passover starting at sunset on the fourteenth day of the month, eating the meat of the lambs that night and burning the remaining portions before morning (see below). Therefore, Josephus was stating that they marched around Jericho on that first day of that Feast of Unleavened Bread, and it continued for seven days.

Look with me at these regulations:

> *The LORD's Passover begins at twilight on the fourteenth day of the first month. On the fifteenth day of that month the LORD's Feast of Unleavened Bread begins; for seven days you must eat bread made without yeast. On the first day hold a sacred assembly and* **do no regular work**. *For seven days present an offering made to the LORD by fire. And on the seventh day hold a sacred assembly and* **do no regular work** (Lev 23:5-8).

The Lord instructed Moses in these verses to do no regular work on the first day (Passover) and seventh day (last day of the Feast). Yet on the last day of the Feast of Unleavened Bread, look how far they walked: a little over a mile to Jericho, seven times around the city at half a mile each time around, and the return trip. That's a total of roughly six miles.

Some people suggest that we should not conduct spiritual warfare, such as casting out demons, on the Sabbath, because we are to do *"no regular work."* But the Lord gave these instructions to Joshua for the entire period of the Feast, including the last day. If the devil is holding you, a friend or an acquaintance in spiritual bondage of some form, deal with it right then and there. Don't allow the devil to have a foothold by waiting until a future time. The Lord set the example in Jericho, and Jesus followed that example by healing people on the Sabbath.

> **Be willing and available to conduct spiritual warfare on all seven days of the week, including the Sabbath.**

---

[30] Josephus, 5.1.5

Purpose of the Feast

Because the Feast of Unleavened Bread immediately follows Passover for seven days, it was a celebration of the time when they were brought out of Egypt. In Egypt, they had been in bondage as slaves. Hence, the purpose of the Feast was to celebrate their new life without bondage.

The leaven, or yeast as it is commonly called today, is fermented dough that is left from the bread made on the previous day, and has turned acidic. Yeast is compared to sin several times in the Bible, such as:

> *Your boasting is not good. Don't you know that a little **yeast** works through the whole batch of dough? Get rid of the old **yeast** that you may be a new batch without yeast — as you really are. For Christ, our Passover lamb, has been sacrificed. Therefore let us keep the Festival, not with the old yeast, the yeast of malice and wickedness, but with bread without **yeast**, the bread of sincerity and truth* (1 Cor 5:6-8).

These verses compare bread made with yeast with bread made without yeast. The bread with yeast represents malice and wickedness; the bread made without yeast is likened to sincerity and truth. Therefore, the Feast of Unleavened Bread uses bread that is made without sin (acidic yeast).

There is only one "bread" that is without sin: Jesus Christ (John 6:51). The beauty of this revelation is that the Lord Jesus Christ was with the Israelites for the Feast of Unleavened Bread. It was a seven-day celebration of the presence of Jesus Christ.

The Process of Delivering Jericho

Levels A – A' thru E – E' of the following chiasm are shown in more detail on the following pages. In this first inner tier chiasm within Joshua 6, please use either the KJV or the NKJV translation because the NIV translation removes certain key words from the Hebrew that are essential for this chiasm. When taken together, these verses describe a miracle that only the Lord could have provided.

The Hebrew word **nātan** (given or delivered) is used in the A – A' level to accentuate what the Lord has provided – see page 131 for a description of nātan. The B – B' level looks at encircling the city of Jericho, and this is analyzed on page 108. The C – C' and E – E' levels of this chiasm reveal a strong use of the numbers seven or seventh, and this is discussed on page 109. The shout is the focus of the D – D' level, and this is described on page 110.

Level	First presentation	Inversion	Theme
A - A'	Lord says He has given Jericho to Joshua (Josh 6:2)	Joshua says the Lord has given Jericho to the people (Josh 6:16)	Lord has delivered Jericho
B - B'	March around the city for six days (Josh 6:3)	They marched around the city for six days (Josh 6:14)	Encircle the city for six days
C - C'	Send seven priests with seven trumpets of rams' horns to march around the city ... and the priests are to blow trumpets (Josh 6:4)	Seven priests with seven trumpets of rams' horns went on ... and the priests blew the trumpets (Josh 6:13)	Seven priests with seven trumpets of rams' horns; priests are blowing trumpets
D - D'	People shall shout with a great shout ... and the priests shall take up the ark of the Lord (Josh 6:5,6a)	When Joshua says to shout, then shout ... and the priests took up the ark of the Lord (Josh 6:10-12)	Shout, shout, then take up the ark of the Lord
E - E'	Seven priests carry seven trumpets before the Lord; Joshua says march around with armed guards ahead of the ark of the Lord (Josh 6:6b,7)	Seven priests with seven trumpets are ahead of the ark of the Lord; they advanced with armed guards before and after the ark (Josh 6:8,9)	Seven priests with seven trumpets of rams' horns, and armed guard before and after the ark

Before we move on to look individually at each level, please take a moment to compare the left column with the right column. In the left column, which is the first presentation, the directions are given through the Lord's rhema word. In the right column, which is the inversion, the directions were followed precisely. That should be a model for us.

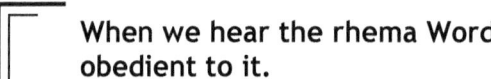

When we hear the rhema Word, we are to be obedient to it.

Encircling the City

On the B – B' level of the above chiasm, the Lord gave instructions to *"march around the city"* (Josh 6:3) while the Israelites were still healing from the wounds of circumcision. The Hebrew word for "march around" is **cabab** (saw-bab'), which means to encircle, surround or encompass. They were instructed to **cabab** for six days, and then on the seventh day, they were to **cabab** the city seven times. The Lord knew they were healing from their circumcision. He knew the Feast of Unleavened Bread had just started. He knew they were too weak to fight a battle; He was teaching dependency.

We saw on page 94 that His manifest presence was in Gilgal immediately before the deliverance of Jericho. We also saw on page 99 that His presence likely disappeared when Achan's sin occurred.

Consider this: by performing the **cabab** (march around), His presence was potentially moved from Gilgal to Jericho. *"For where two or three come together in my name, there am I with them"* (Matt 18:20). It took forty thousand armed men to surround Jericho because the city was so tightly locked up. I imagine it may have been similar to Joshua 5:13 where the Commander of the Army of the Lord stood with his sword drawn: Christ as the Commander was over the city of Jericho. The illustration on cover of this book, from the year 1372, depicts the Commander of the Army of the Lord to be in the clouds.

Certainly the people of Jericho never saw the manifestation of Christ because of their sinful ways and their worship of false gods. Possibly the army of forty thousand never saw His presence, or any of the two million or so Israelites; possibly only Joshua. Nevertheless, if this image is correct, then Christ was in Jericho in all of His glory.

> **As we deliver a person from demonic spirits, surround the individual with people and prayer so that Christ is in our midst.**

The Sevens

Both the C – C' and E – E' levels of the previous chiasm (page 108) have the use of paired sevens. The Hebrew words for "seven" and "seventh" appear fourteen times in chapter six. Each of the sevens appears as a pair, as shown on these seven verses:

Verse	Text
Josh 6:4a	Seven priests with seven trumpets of rams' horns
Josh 6:4b	On the seventh day, encircle seven times
Josh 6:6b	Seven priests with seven trumpets of rams' horns
Josh 6:8b	Seven priests with seven trumpets of rams' horns
Josh 6:13	Seven priests with seven trumpets of rams' horns
Josh 6:15a	On the seventh day, encircle seven times
Josh 6:15b,16	Encircle seven times; on the seventh time, "Shout"

(Note: to see the above pattern of sevens from the Hebrew, use either the KJV or NKJV because the NIV says it in a different way.) There are seven instances where the pairing of seven or seventh appear. While Genesis, Revelation and other books make frequent use of the number seven, nowhere else in either the Old or New Testament is there such a clustering of the words "seven" or "seventh." Clearly, the author was attempting to point out that the Perfection was with them as they encircled Jericho.

The Shout

The two Hebrew words **ruwa'** (roo-ah') and **teruw'ah** (ter-oo-aw'), which are translated as "shout" and "shouted," are used eight times in chapter 6. The shout was the D – D' level of the first chiasm of this chapter (page 108). For example, in both Joshua 6:5 and Joshua 6:20, they *"shouted with a great shout."* The shouting was the last step before the wall collapsed.

Verse	Text
Josh 6:5	Shout with a great shout
Josh 6:10	You shall not shout until I say shout
Josh 6:16,20a	People told to shout; then the people shouted
Josh 6:20b	Shouted with a great shout

The symmetry between the first and last occurrences is used to emphasize the enormous shout and the power that is in our voices.

The Trumpet of Rams Horns

The Hebrew word for trumpet in Joshua 6:4, 5, 6, 8 and 13 is **shophar yobel** (sho-far' yob-ale'). The Lord had instructed Moses to use silver trumpets in battle (Num 10:1, 9). These, however, were **shophar yobel** which are literally "trumpets of rams' horns." Possibly when the trumpet of rams' horns was used in Jericho, it reminded them of the Passover event that was celebrated a few days earlier; each family had to slaughter a lamb in preparation of the Passover meal.

I am not an advocate of loud noises. I think it would be a mistake to believe that the Lord would honor going up to a severely oppressed person, blowing a trumpet in one ear and shouting in the other. "I know the devil must be in there somewhere, and we'll just blast him out." No, no, no, a hundred times no. The trumpet served other purposes.

First of all, remember that it was the Lord that delivered Jericho. The priests and the army were only obedient to the instructions. Man did not deliver Jericho; the Lord did it all. There is no power, per se, in the trumpet or the shout. The power belongs to the Lord.

Second, the deliverance happened during the Feast of Unleavened Bread. Deliverance is an event to celebrate. The release of a person from spiritual bondage should be a joyous occasion. Look at the results.

Third, the trumpet blast usually precedes a change in the spiritual realm (1 Cor 15:52). In this case, the change is the judgment of the demonic spirits in Jericho along with the release of the spirit within Rahab and her family.

Fourth, remember that deliverance is not a formula. What worked in Jericho was unique to that situation: seven priests with seven trumpets on the seventh day after the seventh **cabab** (encircling). This method was not repeated elsewhere in the Bible.

> All deliverances are unique; what worked previously may not work again.

The Walls Fall Down

In the last section, four purposes were identified for the trumpet. There is one more purpose and that is related to the seventh trumpet that is found in the Book of Revelation:

> *The seventh angel sounded his **trumpet**, and there were loud voices in heaven, which said: "The kingdom of the world has become the kingdom of our Lord and of his Christ, and he will reign for ever and ever." And the twenty-four elders, who were seated on their thrones before God, **fell on their faces and worshipped God** ...* (Rev 11:15,16).

When the last angel sounded the trumpet, the twenty-four elders fell on their faces and worshiped God. Likewise, the sound of the trumpet and the loud shout in Joshua 6:20 heralded the presence of the Lord and the start of the judgment at Jericho. In Revelation 11:18, the elders state that *"The time has come for judging the dead, and for rewarding your servants the prophets and the saints."* Not only did the elders fall on their faces in worship, but they also recognized that this was a time of judgment: the spiritually dead and the saints. So it is that the sounds of the trumpet and the shout signaled the start of the judgment.

Look at this next sequence of events in Joshua 6:20 with me:

> *And it happened when the people heard the sound of the trumpet, and the people shouted with a great shout, that the wall fell down flat* (Josh 6:20 NKJV).

Notice the similarity of events:

Revelation 11:16	Joshua 6:20
The twenty-four elders in the presence of God heard the sound of the seventh trumpet, and they fell to the ground in worship.	The walls of Jericho, in the presence of Christ, heard the sound of the seventh trumpet and fell to the ground.

The Hebrew word for 'fell down flat' in Joshua 6:20 is **naphal** (naw-fal'), which means to fall, cast down, cause to lie down, overwhelm or perish.

Please consider this progression of logic:

- Joshua, when the Commander of the Army of the Lord met him, *"... fell facedown to the ground in reverence ..."* (Josh 5:14). That word is **naphal**.
- The twenty-four elders fell to the ground in worship (Rev 11:16).
- The walls of Jericho fell (**naphal**) to the ground because the presence of the Lord had come upon the city when the forty thousand armed guard, the seven priests and the ark of the Lord encircled the city on the seventh time.

It is normal to think of walls collapsing because of some power such as the force of a great wind or the shaking of an earthquake. However, what makes this story so phenomenal is that there was no wind, earthquake or the like. The Lord may have pushed them over, but based on the evidence, the walls appear to have fallen down in reverence to the presence of the Lord. Please allow me explain why.

As the disciples joyfully praised God on his entering Jerusalem, Jesus spoke these words to the Pharisees: *"I tell you,"* he replied, *"if they keep quiet, the stones will cry out"* (Luke 19:40). Someone might ask "How can a wall, which has no ability to think, make a decision to fall?" I can't fully answer that except to refer to what the Scriptures state.

Now please turn to Hebrews 11. The author of Hebrews discusses great men of faith: Abel offered a better sacrifice by faith; Noah built an ark by faith; Abraham offered Isaac by faith; Isaac blessed Jacob and Esau by faith; Jacob blessed his sons by faith; Joseph gave instructions about his bones by faith; and Moses led the people out of Egypt by faith.

These were examples of people who had great amounts of faith; they are not inanimate objects who have no flesh and bones. That is, with one exception – look what that author says about Jericho:

> *By faith the walls of Jericho fell, after the people had marched around them for seven days* (Heb 11:30).

All of the other references to faith in Hebrews 11 are about what people did. But here, an inanimate object had faith, which caused the wall to physically collapse. What were the walls doing? The walls fell down in worship in the presence of Jesus Christ, just as the twenty-four elders fell down in worship in Revelation 11:16.

> **When looking for a release from demonic attacks, develop a strong and sincere practice of worship.**

An Application to Spiritual Warfare

Some people have put up a wall of protection around themselves. These people can be very hard to reach because their wall does not allow penetration of the Word of God. In the case of Jericho, the wall was very high and formidable. Yet the walls of Jericho were broken. Likewise, people can be broken and we should not hinder that process because it's God's process. Broken people, with their walls shattered, are the ones that the Lord can now reach.

Let us consider a hypothetical man whose heart is hard and unreachable. He might be a braggart, an alcoholic, an insensitive father, or any number of other problems. For the sake of the analogy, let us call him Jerry (short for Jericho – please counsel his wife not to purchase a trumpet, as tempted as she might be). Let us now consider that Jerry loses his job, which brings a great deal of economic and emotional hardship onto the family. What is his wife to do? The tension seems unbearable at times and she does not know if she can handle another day. It seems that the devil is taking advantage of every opportunity to steal, kill and destroy.

Please tell his wife that the attacks are often for the purpose of collapsing that wall. Discernment is needed here because at the right time, when Jerry is completely surrounded and there is no way out, the Lord will appear. But have confidence that the Lord's plans are perfect. Patient endurance is essential, along with a prayerful analysis of how his wife might have some changes that must be made first. When the walls collapse out of reverence for the Lord, rather than being pushed over by another person, then true change can begin.

> *A patient man has great understanding,*
> *but a quick-tempered man displays folly* (Prov 14:29).

> **Patiently seek discernment from the Lord to distinguish between demonic attacks and the hand of the Lord.**

Guarding the Presence of the Lord

On the E – E' level of the first inner tier chiasm of this chapter (page 108), we saw the emphasis on sevens followed by the emphasis on the positions of the armed guard. That is the center point of this inner tier chiasm: seven priests with seven trumpets of rams' horns are with the ark, and the armed guard is both before and after the ark.

Those who have been armed were to surround the ark; some marched ahead and some behind:

Verse	Text
Josh 6:9	Armed guard marched ahead and the rear guard marched behind the ark
Josh 6:13	Armed guard marched ahead and the rear guard marched behind the ark

Not only was the city encircled, but the ark of the Lord was encircled as well. Who is the armed guard?

> *... let him who is armed advance before the ark of the LORD* (Josh 6:7 NKJV).

According to Joshua 4:13, there were forty thousand armed men that were prepared for battle. Now look at that same question with a New Testament lens: who is the armed guard? If Christ is in our hearts and we daily go into battle, isn't it our responsibility to protect the ark?

> *Above all else, guard your heart, for it is the wellspring of life ... Do not swerve to the right or the left; keep your foot from evil* (Prov 4:23,27)

The best way for protecting our hearts and the presence of the Lord is to avoid temptations of every kind of evil. *"Be very careful, then, how you live – not as unwise but as wise"* (Eph 5:15). Use the wisdom that the Lord gives us, which will guard against the intrusion of evil.

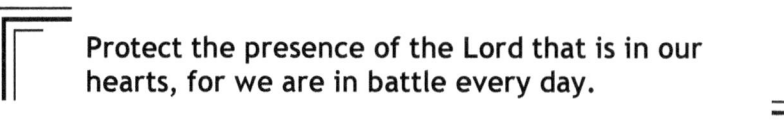

Protect the presence of the Lord that is in our hearts, for we are in battle every day.

The Authority of Christ

We have already established that Jesus Christ was the Commander of the Army of the Lord (Josh 5:14), and that He stayed with the Israelites until Achan sinned (Josh 7:1). We have also seen how the Israelites, by surrounding Jericho, caused the presence of Christ to be within that city. Finally we have seen that the walls of the city collapsed in worship out of reverence for the presence of Christ.

Jesus not only showed His authority over Jericho, but He passed on that authority to us. He gave authority to the twelve apostles to *"drive out demons"* (Mark 3:15) and He *"... sent them out two by two and gave them authority over evil spirits"* (Mark 6:7). This authority has been given to all born again believers:

> *I have given you authority to trample on snakes and scorpions and to overcome all the power of the enemy; nothing will harm you* (Luke 10:19).

> **Speak with the authority of Jesus Christ when engaging in spiritual warfare.**

Judgment of Jericho

Another chiasm begins at Joshua 6:17 – we see the contrast of the people destroyed within Jericho with the salvation of a faithful family.

Level	First presentation	Inversion	Theme
A - A'	Joshua instructs men that only Rahab and family are to be spared (Josh 6:17)	Joshua spared Rahab and her family (Josh 6:25)	Grace is given to the family of a Gentile
B - B'	Joshua instructs men to keep away from silver, gold, bronze and iron articles because they are sacred to the Lord (Josh 6:18,19)	Men put silver, gold, bronze and iron articles in the treasury of the Lord's house (Josh 6:24)	Devote the firstfruits to the Lord
C - C'	Unfaithful men and women of Jericho were destroyed by the sword (Josh 6:20,21)	Rahab and family were saved (Josh 6:22,23)	Christ judges the wicked but frees the faithful

The A – A' level shows how Rahab, a Gentile, was spared because of the grace that was based on her faith. The B – B' level gives the directions about the firstfruits: put aside certain articles because they belonged to the Lord. In the defeat of other cities, the Israelites were allowed to keep the plunder; at Jericho, it belonged to the Lord.

In the C – C' level of this chiasm, the contrast between the unfaithful and the faithful becomes very apparent. The unfaithful were destroyed while the faithful were saved. As Christians, we know that only Christ has the authority to judge between the unfaithful and the faithful, between the living and the dead. In a spiritual sense, Christ was exercising His authority over both the demonic forces in Jericho and the faithful captives.

> *For we must all appear before the judgment seat of Christ, that each one may receive what is due him for the things done while in the body, whether good or bad* (2 Cor 5:10).

In Joshua 6:2-5, the instruction from the Lord was to encircle Jericho for six successive days. This would have allowed the people of Jericho to fear both the Israelites and the Lord of the Israelites. Therefore, the **cabab** (march around) gave the people of Jericho the opportunity to come to the same fearful respect that Rahab had understood. On the seventh day, they were given seven opportunities during the march around: make a decision before it's too late. But in the end, Joshua 6:21 states that all were destroyed except Rahab and her family.

Joshua 6:21 also states that the Israelite army destroyed everything that was living in Jericho with the **sword**. Remember the image of Christ holding a drawn sword in Joshua 5:13?

At the end of the Book of Joshua, Joshua reminded the Israelites what the Lord said regarding the many accomplishments. He stated that Jericho was conquered with a sword that was not their own: *"You did not do it with your own sword and bow"* (Josh 24:12).

> **Spiritual warfare ultimately ends at the judgment seat of Christ; the Lord watches how the short term battles are handled for their long term consequence.**

The Curse

The curse in Joshua 6:26 has been a stumbling block for many:

> *At that time Joshua pronounced this solemn oath: "Cursed before the LORD is the man who undertakes to rebuild this city, Jericho:*
> > *At the cost of his firstborn son will he lay its foundations; at the cost of his youngest will he set up its gates"* (Josh 6:26).

Chapter 6 – The Deliverance of Jericho

After the destruction of Jericho, Joshua put a curse on that community stating that if anyone rebuilds Jericho, it will cost the life of his firstborn son and his youngest child.

Many people believe that this curse was fulfilled in 1 Kings 16:34 when Hiel rebuild Jericho. This happened during the time of Ahab in 874BC when Hiel of Bethel rebuilt the city. Both his firstborn son Abiram, and his youngest son Segub, died as a result of this effort (1 Kings 16:34).

Today, the city of Jericho has nineteen thousand inhabitants and tourism is a significant source of income for the people of this city. Yet it is predominantly a Muslim city. Is Islam the curse that is being referred to in Joshua 6:26?

Let us look at the chiasm of Joshua 6:26 - 7:1 to see if this holds up:

Level	First presentation	Inversion	Theme
A - A'	Joshua places a curse on Jericho (Josh 6:26a)	Achan brings a curse on Israel (Josh 7:1)	Curses prophesied and happened
B - B'	Firstborn son will lay its foundation (Josh 6:26b)	Youngest son will set up its gates (Josh 6:26b)	Firstborn and youngest son

The first thing we note is that on the A – A' level, a curse is prophesied by Joshua, which is paired with the curse that Achan brought upon the Israelite community by stealing the Lord's firstfruits. Achan was not attempting to rebuild the city; but the emphasis on a curse is provided in both sides of this chiasm. If someone else rebuilds the city, such as Hiel, we see from 1 Kings 16:34 that physical death is the result. So in this sense, Islam could well be a curse from rebuilding Jericho.

The second thing we note is that the curse is not an everlasting curse. From the Book of Revelation we know that Jericho does not remain under a curse forever; every city, including Jericho, is freed when the rider on a white horse, with a sharp sword in His mouth, captures the beast and the false prophet (Rev 19:11-21). If the curse lasted forever, Jericho would be in more of a hopeless situation.

Thirdly, we know that Christ spoke to both a blind man and Zacchaeus in Jericho (Luke 18:35 - 19:27). **Jesus was spiritually rebuilding Jericho.**

Surprisingly, the unexpected answer to the question: "Who rebuilt the Jericho, what was the curse and what was the cost?" belongs to Jesus Christ. The "*curse*" that was placed upon Jericho was how Christ became a curse for us – no one else can properly rebuild Jericho; no one else could overcome that curse. The "*cost*" (Josh 6:26b,c) was the death of God's first born and only son (who is therefore His youngest son). Let me explain.

We have previously concluded that Jesus Christ was present in Jericho from Joshua 5:13 - 7:1. This prophecy is referring to Christ rebuilding Jericho through His death and resurrection.

The curse is identified on the A – A' level in Joshua 6:26a. We know that Christ became a curse for us: *"Christ redeemed us from the curse of the law by becoming a curse for us"* (Gal 3:13).

The cost is identified on the B – B' level. Notice how this prophecy was fulfilled:

Joshua 6:26	Fulfillment
*At the cost of his **firstborn** son will he lay its foundations* (Josh 6:26b)	*For no one can lay any foundation other than the one already laid, which is Jesus Christ.* (1 Cor 3:11)
*At the cost of his **youngest** will he set up its gates* (Josh 6:26c)	*"I am the gate; whoever enters through me will be saved"* (John 10:9)

Christ is the firstborn and the youngest, the foundation and the gate.

Joshua 6:26a states that everyone that attempts to rebuild this city is to be cursed. Jericho had just been set free by the power of Jesus Christ as Commander of the Army of the Lord. If anyone in the future attempts to build Jericho in some other way, that person is attempting to take Jericho away from their faith in Christ. The devil, of course, is cursed. If Jericho is rebuilt in some way besides Christ, that born-again believer has lost their relationship with Christ.

All is not lost, however; the rider on the white horse reminds us that the only one that can withstand the curse that is on Jericho is Jesus Christ. A sincerely repentant individual would be able to have a new foundation and to walk through that gate once again. The spiritual warfare application of this verse is that, whatever curse is on that person, that curse can be broken through Jesus Christ.

> **Christ, through His death and resurrection, wants to remove any curses that have been placed on us.**

Summary of Chapter 6

At the start of this chapter, it was stated that chapter 6 is the center point of a twelve chapter chiasm. Because it has this central position, let us summarize what we have seen:

Chapter 6 – The Deliverance of Jericho

- The presence of the Lord Jesus Christ appeared to Joshua at the end of chapter 5.
- Joshua fell down in reverence at the presence of his Lord.
- The seven days of encircling Jericho coincided with the seven days of the Feast of Unleavened Bread.
- The ark of the covenant, which had been identified as a dwelling place for the Lord, encircled the city.
- The Feast of Unleavened Bread was a seven-day celebration of the presence of Jesus Christ.
- While the army encircled the city, the presence of the Lord was over Jericho.
- The frequent use of the number seven indicates that Christ, the Perfection, was with them.
- The sound of the trumpet and the loud shout heralded the start of the judgment at Jericho, but the power belonged to the Lord.
- The walls of Jericho fell down in worship of the presence of the Lord.
- The people of Jericho were given the opportunity to accept the Lord on each of the seven days.
- The Lord judged between the faithful and the unfaithful when determining who would live and who would die.
- The curse that was placed upon Jericho is broken by Jesus Christ.
- The Lord's presence disappeared when Achan took items that were to be devoted to the Lord.

Chapter 7 – Achan's Sin

But the Israelites acted unfaithfully in regard to the devoted things; Achan son of Carmi, the son of Zimri, the son of Zerah, of the tribe of Judah, took some of them. So the LORD's anger burned against Israel (Josh 7:1).

In the previous chapter, the firstfruits were devoted to the Lord (see page 115). The Lord had given a gift of firstfruits to the Israelites: the first defeat in the Promised Land, Jericho, and the first converts, Rahab and family. There would be many other victories; after the death of Joshua, there would also be an astounding number of defeats.

In return for the victory at Jericho, the Lord was looking for the firstfruits of the plunder to be devoted back to Him. In future raids, the Lord would allow the plunder to be kept by the Israelites. But in this first victory, the Lord was looking for faithfulness to be represented by giving back to the Lord what He has already provided. He was expecting one-hundred percent participation; and He was most disappointed by the rebellion of just one person. One man's sin caused the whole nation to fail.

In this chapter, we will review the overall structure of chapter 7, study another geography lesson including the deforestation of the vicinity of Ai, and then review three chiasms: The Defeat at Ai, Conversation with the Lord, and A Spirit of Lust. We will conclude this chapter with a brief discussion about why Achan's entire family was stoned to death.

Structure of Chapter 7

Our church offers an intensive summer camp for teenagers on our church property for a two-week period. The new teens come to Boot Camp, as we call it, not really knowing what to expect. The experienced teens know that hearts and lives are often changed through the events that happen at Boot Camp.

One year, I remember that the Lord did not appear to be moving as had happened in previous years. There was a blockage of some sort. The adults entered a time of intense prayer for the release of whatever was holding back the Spirit of the Lord. The blockages continued to come and adversity was followed by more adversity. People were getting sick or injured and some teens abandoned the camp.

Then the message came: the sins of Achan. Specific sins were revealed as teens confessed their offenses to God, yielding a heart of repentance. Once the blockages were understood, the issues were addressed with boldness. In the remainder of the Boot Camp, the Lord moved mightily in the lives of these young people, and they went out to minister to others.

In this chapter, we see the middle tiered chiasm as:

Level	First presentation	Inversion	Theme
A - A'	The Lord's anger burns against the Israelites (Josh 7:1)	The Lord turns from his fierce anger (Josh 7:26)	The Lord's anger
B - B'	Joshua is overwhelmed with grief (Josh 7:6-9)	Joshua's grief is resolved (Josh 7:19-25)	Joshua's grief
C - C'	The Lord's explanation of the sin (Josh 7:10-12)	The Lord's direction to resolve the sin (Josh 7:13-16)	The Lord reveals the sin and shows the resolution

It should probably come as no surprise that the center point of Joshua 7 is the explanation and direction regarding the seriousness of this sin. On the A – A' level, we see how angry the Lord was with sin. Then on the B – B' level, Joshua took a similar stand towards sin. Praise the Lord for the revelation that He gave Joshua on the C – C' level.

Geography: In Search of Ancient Ai (Part I)

My wife and I had the pleasure of visiting Ai in 1999, or at least we thought we did. Traveling in the West Bank by ourselves was difficult: we had a Bible Atlas, two road maps of Israel written in English, and street signs that were written in Aramaic and occasionally Hebrew. One other thing we had: the Lord was with us and guided us. He provided me with a sense of direction, without which we would not have seen any of the sites that we did.

It is clear from the Bible that Ai is east of Bethel near a community called Beth Aven (Josh 7:2). A map in the *Atlas of the Bible* showed Ai near Bethel [31], so off we went in our rental car. Because we were driving in the West Bank, Avis had us sign some special papers that we were liable for anything and everything that might happen on our excursion including demolition of the vehicle. They strongly discouraged us from going into Palestinian territory because they would not be responsible if anything happened.

---

[31] John Rogerson, *Atlas of the Bible*, (New York: Facts on File Publications, 1986), 148.

Modern day Bethel is fifteen miles north of Jerusalem. East and slightly south of Bethel are two long and narrow hills with steep sides. Both hills run in an east-west direction. The road is in a valley that is on the north side of the northern hill. The location we found for Ai seemed to fit the description (more in the next chapter), but we really didn't know. There were no tour guides to tell us if we were in the right area or not, so we were clearly at a disadvantage. On the other hand, archaeologists struggle to this day with where ancient Ai was located, and we were just interested tourists. Therefore, while I will present the site that we found in this chapter and the next chapter, we really don't know for sure if this was Ai.

Cities in the Promised Land from this era were usually built on a hill. If an enemy army were to attack, then the army on the uphill side had the clear advantage.

If the people of Ai had lived on either of the two hills that we found, it would have been a very good choice for a city. The slopes on the south, east and north sides are very steep; only the western side offers some easier access. On both hills, the northern slope is barren and severely eroded, and the north-east corner of both hills could be quarried for stone (Josh 7:5).

Deforestation near Ai

Today, we could travel for miles around Ai and see very few trees. The land is dry and there is hardly any good soil to grow vegetation on. There are many areas where rock outcroppings appear and a few small bushes appear amongst the scattered brush. The likely reason: erosion.

It was not always like this. Let us look at two Bible references:

- Gibeah is just a few miles south of Ai. In 1 Samuel 14:25,26, woods were located there: *"The entire army entered the **woods**, and there was honey on the ground. When they went into the **woods**, they saw the honey oozing out ..."*
- Bethel is two miles west of Ai. In 2 Kings 2:24, there were two bears that mauled some youth because they called Elisha baldhead: *"He turned around, looked at them and called down a curse on them in the name of the LORD. Then **two bears** came out of the **woods** and mauled forty-two of the youths."*

We certainly did not see any bears on our visit to this area; nor did we see any woods where bears might have lived.

This was not a problem isolated to this area. We found one area near Beth Shemesh, which is thirty miles to the southwest, that had some trees, and there was a reforestation project south of Hebron which would have been forty or so miles away. Other than that, it was essentially barren.

John Rogerson, archaeologist and Professor of Biblical Studies at the University of Sheffield, England, suggests that the erosion was caused by deforestation to support the large amounts of animal sacrifice. [32] Much wood was needed to fuel the fires, such as when:

Solomon	*Offered a sacrifice of twenty-two thousand head of cattle and a hundred and twenty thousand sheep and goats* (2 Chron 7:5).
Asa	*Sacrificed to the LORD seven hundred head of cattle and seven thousand sheep and goats ...* (2 Chron 15:11).
Hezekiah	*Provided a thousand bulls and seven thousand sheep and goats for the assembly, and the officials provided them with a thousand bulls and ten thousand sheep and goats* (2 Chron 30:24).
Josiah	*Provided ... a total of thirty thousand sheep and goats for the Passover offerings, and also three thousand cattle ....* (2 Chron 35:7).

There are other instances in the Old Testament where large numbers of animals were sacrificed. Rogerson's theory suggests that it is not the animal sacrifice, per se, that caused the deforestation; it was the amount of trees that had to be cut to support this much fire. Once an area is stripped of its trees, the soil erodes and the forests are gone.

How is this related to spiritual warfare? Because the indulgence of large numbers of animals would not have been necessary if the people had been consistent in their faith. Periodically, the people turned away from the Lord, so when repentance or a special dedication came, they had a huge celebration.

> *For I desire mercy, not sacrifice, and acknowledgment of God rather than burnt offerings* (Hos 6:6).

The Lord's plan was for a morning and evening sacrifice every day. Man's plan called for celebration and over indulgence. That opened the door to spiritual warfare, and the effect is even seen today.

> **Overindulgence, even when done in the name of the Lord, can leave a curse that lasts for generations.**

---

[32] Ibid, 164.

Chapter 7 – Achan's Sin

The Defeat at Ai

When the presence of the Lord left Jericho and Gilgal in Joshua 7:1, Joshua was on unfamiliar ground: the Lord became angry with Israel. Previously, the Lord provided instructions about what to do next, but now He was silent. In Joshua 1 - 6, Joshua had not asked the Lord what to do at each step, but instead relied on the Lord to tell him. The Lord had given him instructions on being strong and courageous, how to cross the Jordan River, how to prepare memorial stones for future generations, when to circumcise the second generation of men, and how to defeat the stronghold of Jericho. Only in his encounter with the Commander of the Army of the Lord did Joshua ask *"Are you for us or for our enemies?"* (Josh 5:13) and then *"What message does my Lord have for his servant?"* (Josh 5:14).

After Jericho was defeated, there is no record that Joshua asked the Lord what to do next; if he had, there was no response. He did not realize that the Lord was angry with Israel. So in Joshua 7:2, Joshua gives instructions to his army without the Lord providing directions on what to do next.

Level	First presentation	Inversion	Theme
A - A'	In boldness, Joshua sends a small portion of his army to Ai (Josh 7:3)	In fear, the hearts of the people melted (Josh 7:5c)	Contrast between being courageous and fearful
B - B'	Three thousand men go up from Gilgal (Josh 7:4a)	Men are chased down the hill towards Gilgal (Josh 7:5b)	Contrast between up and down
C - C'	The army was routed past stone quarries (Josh 7:4b)	Thirty-six of army were killed (Josh 7:5a)	Defeat at Ai

In the A - A' level, we see how quickly a spirit of courage turned into a spirit of fear. Like a slap from the Lord, the defeat at the hands of the enemy on the C - C' level was the consequence of sin.

Likely there are times in each of our lives where the Lord does not speak. We have to ask ourselves "Why is the Lord being quiet?" We press in, still no answer, "What are You wanting to say, Lord?" we ask, and still no answer. So we set out on our own.

> **If the Lord is quiet about whatever direction we are to take, setting out on our own can give opportunities for the devil to advance.**

Conversation with the Lord

In Joshua 7:6-13, Joshua had another dialogue with the Lord. This conversation is similar to Joshua's dialogue with the Lord in Joshua 5:13-15 because again Joshua falls facedown before the Lord, demonstrating his reverence to the Lord. Because of his personal encounter with Christ at Gilgal, he begins speaking out of reverence: *"Ah, Sovereign LORD ..."* (Josh 7:7). Joshua's relationship had now reached a new level of intimacy – he is now conversing. This is the personal relationship that the Lord wants with each of us. Joshua spoke to his Lord as if He was standing in front of Him, letting Him know what is on his heart.

Paraphrasing the Bible, Joshua asked "Lord, why were we defeated?", "What are You doing Lord?", and "Lord, what are we to do now?" And finally and most importantly, Joshua asked "Lord, what about Your great name?" Joshua was more concerned about the Lord's name than about the fate of the Israelites. Praise the Lord.

Joshua needed that deeper, more intimate relationship with the Lord from chapters 5 and 6 because he was about to deal with a new level in spiritual warfare. As Pastor Joy Clarke (no relation) of Hamilton, Ontario states: "New level, new devil." Joshua's previous leadership skills had navigated the people into the Promised Land. But now, having just led the people through the success at Jericho, Joshua received his first defeat. Thank God that Joshua was provided with the presence of the Lord just in time for him to have a frank conversation with the Lord.

Level	First presentation	Inversion	Theme
A - A'	Joshua asks the Lord if He is intending to destroy them (Josh 7:6-9)	Lord replies that an Israelite is leading them to destruction (Josh 7:13c)	Joshua asks "why?"; Lord reveals "why"
B - B'	Lord recognizes that Joshua is sanctified (Josh 7:10)	Lord instructs Joshua to have Israelites be sanctified (Josh 7:13b)	Emphasis on importance of sanctification
C - C'	The Lord states that sin has broken the covenant between Himself and the people (Josh 7:11)	With the covenant broken, the Lord withdraws His promise of protection (Josh 7:12)	Broken covenant by sin; not binding on either party

The covenant in Joshua 7:11 refers to the agreements made between the Lord and the Israelites, such as Deuteronomy 29 and 30. Under this covenant, the people were to obey the Lord in everything, which in this case was the requirement to set aside the firstfruits for the

Lord from Joshua 6:18. In return, the Lord promised success in possessing the land and promised prosperity.

This covenant was clearly defined as a conditional covenant. In other words, if the people maintained the conditions that the Lord laid out, then the Lord would honor His promises. However, if the people did not maintain those conditions, then the Lord's promises would no longer be binding. If the people didn't do their part, then the Lord was not obligated to do His part either. That is the curse that Achan put on them.

Christians often refer to this sin as "Achan's Sin" or "The Sin of Achan." The focus is often one of obedience versus disobedience, or of sin versus purity. To put it in contemporary terms, there are consequences of our sins. All this is correct.

On the C – C' level of this chiasm, we see that the Lord is reminding His people that in a covenant, both parties are expected to do their portion. But if one bails out, the other is not obligated to fulfill that party's portion. For example, see also Deuteronomy 30:17,18.

The same is true with the New Testament covenant of salvation; both parties are expected to do their portion. The Lord freely grants us salvation based on our faith: we confess that our sins have separated us from our Lord, we seek forgiveness for these sins, we repent and we believe in the salvation that is offered by Jesus Christ. The promise from the Lord is everlasting life with Him.

Theologians have battled over the years with what happens to the backslidden individual. There are those that contend that a saved man has an eternal destiny with the Lord. They go on to say that if someone's moral fiber has severely deteriorated, that person could not have been saved in the first place. Others say that the severely backslidden person has no hope for salvation without sincere repentance. May I suggest that we are not the judge? Only God knows whether a person was saved or not, and He alone knows a person's eternal destination. We can all have our own thoughts, but they are only opinions; God knows.

One thing I believe we can all agree on is that sin harms our relationship with the Lord. If events turn sour when they were going well, we need to ask ourselves if the Lord has seen something that is not right. The Lord will allow us to continue up to a point, and from there, He needs to get us back on the right path.

> **Sin, both overt and hidden, eventually breaks the covenant promise of protection.**

Spirit of Lust

The central point of the next inner tier chiasm deals with exposure of sins:

Level	First presentation	Inversion	Theme
A - A'	The man who is guilty will be destroyed along with all belongings (Josh 7:15a)	Achan, who was guilty, is stoned and belongings are burned (Josh 7:25c)	Destruction of the guilty sinner
B - B'	Achan confesses to taking the plunder (Josh 7:20,21)	Achan's plunder is taken to the valley of trouble (Josh 7:24,25b)	Plunder is confessed and taken away
C - C'	Plunder is found by men (Josh 7:22)	Plunder is exposed to the Lord (Josh 7:23)	Sin is exposed

When Achan finally confessed his sin in Joshua 7:21, he was admitting that he saw, coveted, took and hid the items. Notice the progression. That is the problem with sin without restraint:
- we see it so we want it
- we want it so we take it
- we take it and we hide it in shame

When the thought first enters our mind, we must deal with it right there so it never gets to the 'took' and 'hid' stages. Many preachers have made this topic the central point of their Sunday message.

Remember that the Lord knew what happened to the devoted things way back in Joshua 7:1, which is well before the first Israelite climbed through the valley to Ai. Josephus the historian from the first century AD stated that Achan supposed he was concealing the plunder not only from his fellow soldiers but also from God himself. [33] That is because his deception was patterned after the great deceiver himself.

The point is when we hide something, "What do others see?" In Exodus 2:11-14, we remember the Moses thought no one had seen him kill the Egyptian. The problem is that Moses was seen and the sin was exposed by a fellow Hebrew. If Moses tried to lead the people out of Egypt at that point, he probably would not have succeeded.

Even if a person's sin is never found out, there is a spirit of deception that is carried around that can be discerned by others. Our poor choice of sin invites other negative spirits to come in and eventually take over. That demonic spirit does not have to be in the same 'family' as our sin. If we have a sin of coveting, as Achan did, it may invite a

---

[33] Josephus, 5.1.10.

spirit of lust into our presence, or it might invite a spirit of anger which could be a cousin of lust.

The Achan within us must be dealt with. Intentional and willful sin makes the person weak. Remember how quickly in Joshua 7:4,5 the army's spirit of boldness changed to a spirit of fear?

> *He who conceals his sins does not prosper, but whoever confesses and renounces them finds mercy* (Prov 28:13).

Achan could have quietly approached Joshua, Phinehas or someone else in authority with the humble acknowledgment that he took some of the firstfruits for himself. If he had, the account in the Book of Joshua would have read much differently. But as it was, he jeopardized the fate of the entire nation.

King David, when he saw Bathsheba, had a similar problem with lust. His coveting led him to make two crucial mistakes: an adulterous affair and the death of an innocent man. Afterwards, David wrote:

> *Then I acknowledged my sin to you and did not cover up my iniquity. I said, "I will confess my transgressions to the LORD"* – *and you forgave the guilt of my sin* (Ps 32:5).

At the end of that same Psalm, David wrote *"Sing, all you who are upright in heart!"* (Ps 32:11). In other words, David included himself among the upright. The foothold of lust had been defeated.

> **By confessing and turning from our sins, we prevent the footholds from becoming strongholds.**

Punishment

A question I have been occasionally asked is "Why was the entire family of Achan killed?" in Joshua 7:24,25. Two possible answers come to mind regarding this seemingly unfair practice:

- In *Antiquities of the Jews*, Josephus wrote that Achan *"made a deep ditch in his own tent"* to store the plunder. [34] One might ask "How do you make a deep ditch in your tent without your family knowing about it?" In other words, they might be considered accomplices to the deception.
- Another answer might be found in the spiritual realm. If the husband is infected by the spirits of coveting, lying and

---

[34] Josephus, 5.1.10.

deception, possibly the entire family was infected and therefore had to be dealt with.

My wife heard a story on the radio this morning about a seven-year old girl that called the police on her grandfather. The girl explained to the officer that her grandfather had been cheating at a card game they were playing. To that little girl, she wanted fairness and justice. Possibly she did not want her entire family to be judged for what was clearly his sin.

Chapter 8 – Achan's Sin is Resolved

*Then the LORD said to Joshua, "Do not be afraid; do not be discouraged. Take the whole army with you, and go up and attack Ai. For I have **delivered** into your hands the king of Ai, his people, his city and his land"* (Josh 8:1).

The liberation of Ai is similar in purpose and structure to how believers are delivered from the powers of the devil today. **Nātan** (naw-than') is the Hebrew word for 'give' or 'delivered'. On page 68, we saw where the two spies assured Joshua that the Lord has given **(nātan)** Jericho to the Jews. The same word is used twice in Joshua 6: the Lord assured Joshua that Jericho has been delivered (Josh 6:2), and then in verse 6:16 Joshua assured the people that Jericho has been given to the Jews. In this chapter, Ai is delivered from the strongholds that have had power over it (Josh 8:1, 7 and 18).

Nātan means more than just delivered. According to the *Vine's Dictionary*, some of the other meanings for the verb **nātan** are to "place, set up, lay, make, do." [35] The word **nātan** is frequently used in the Old Testament in a variety of ways to somehow denote the handing over of something. Of the many examples are:

*"All the land that you see I will **give** to you and your offspring forever"* (Gen 13:15).

*"And blessed be God Most High, who **delivered** your enemies into your hand"* (Gen 14:20).

*"Then Jacob **gave** Esau some bread and some lentil stew"* (Gen 25:34).

The King James Version translates Joshua 8:1 in a similar way: *"I have **given** into thy hand ..."* In this sense, "delivered" is not a deliverance session so much as it is the transfer of ownership or responsibility. In that way, the city was restored to the state that God had intended.

At Ai, the Lord was freeing the land, and the ultimate purpose was to give this land to Israel and to restore/cleanse it. We can see this in

---

[35] W. E. Vine, Merrill F. Unger, William White Jr., *Vine's Complete Expository Dictionary of Old and New Testament Words*, 1985, Thomas Nelson Inc., Publishers, Electronic database from PC Study Bible 2007

Joshua 8:28 when the city of Ai was burned and made desolate, thereby cleansing it of the previous tenants. The people of Ai worshipped false gods. The Israelite army was the liberator that the Lord commissioned to remove those false worshippers.

In this chapter, we will look at a series of analogies that compare the physical world with the spiritual world. This typology is a comparison to help us see the extent and implication of the spiritual warfare.

Ai achieved its freedom, just as people today are freed when delivered from oppression. The false worshippers are the demonic spirits that hold a person in bondage. The liberators are the people commissioned by the Lord to set the individual free.

When Ai was delivered in Joshua 8:1 (above), we see that the first to be listed was the king of Ai. As shown in the chart below, the king of Ai is the person that oversees the people of the city. In a spiritual sense, the king is analogous to the ruling spirit that controls the other demons.

Joshua 8:1 also states that the Lord delivered the king's people, city and land. These are the subjects of the analogy:

King of Ai - The person that controlled the people of the Ai	←→	**Ruling spirit** - One of the devil's angels that controls the other demons
People of Ai - Those 12,000 people that lived in Ai	←→	**Demons** - Those angels of the devil that have names like fear, anger and jealousy
City of Ai - A location on top of a hill where the people lived	←→	**Born again believer** - Person plagued with demonic spirits
The king's land - The physical jurisdiction where the king's crops were grown and animals were raised	←→	**Area of influence** - Believers have other people that they influence either for the better or for the worse

In reading this chapter, see if the analogy of the king, people, city and land holds up. In addition to the topic of deliverance, we will also look at two more geography lessons, study some more chiasms and then finish with the renewal of covenant vows.

Structure of Chapter 8

There are two parts to chapter 8: Ai is delivered (**nātan**) based on the instruction of the Lord, followed by a twenty-five mile trip to Shechem for the Israelites to renew their covenant with the Lord. The middle tier chiasm for this chapter covers most but not all of Joshua 8, extending only to Joshua 8:29. Within this middle tier chiasm, there are four inner tier chiasms, all of which are related to deliverance. Then the remainder of this chapter, Joshua 8:30-35, details the renewal of their covenants as another inner tier chiasm.

Level	First presentation	Inversion	Theme
A - A'	The Lord promises Ai is delivered (Josh 8:1)	Ai is burned and the King is killed (Josh 8:28,29)	Ai is delivered because ruling spirit is gone
B - B'	Lord says they can take the plunder (Josh 8:2)	Plunder is taken (Josh 8:27)	Plunder, not firstfruits
C - C'	The ambush is planned (Josh 8:3-8)	Ambush is executed (Josh 8:18-25)	Ambush
D - D'	Israelites assume their positions (Josh 8:9-13a)	Men of Ai assume their positions (Josh 8:14-17)	Armies assume their positions
E	Joshua went into the valley (Josh 8:13b)	No related verse	Listening to the voice of Lord

We have seen that the center point of the chiasm is where the reader's attention should normally be focused. In this chiasm, however, there are several stopping points that merit discussion.

Removal of the Ruling Spirit (A – A' level)

On the A – A' level, the Lord's promise of delivering Ai was related to the death of the king. In a spiritual sense, this has profound implications. Tim Mather has noted that the deliverance of an individual is complete only when the ruling spirit (king) is removed.[36] As born again believers in Jesus Christ, we have the authority to cast out demons. But if we do not remove the ruling spirit, we have only made things worse. Look with me at the following from Luke 11:24-26:

> *When an evil spirit comes out of a man, it goes through arid places seeking rest and does not find it. Then it says, "I will return to the house I left." When it arrives, it finds the house swept clean and put in order. Then it goes and takes seven other spirits more wicked than itself, and they go in and live there. And the final condition of that man is worse than the first.*

These verses are normally applied to a person who has been delivered but does not keep the door closed by following good counsel. Another way to interpret these verses is to see the *"evil spirit"* as a lesser demon. If the ruling spirit has not been removed, then when the evil spirit stops

---

[36] Mather, 175.

by to see if it can get back in (and it will), the door is opened by the ruling spirit. Because the ownership of the house has not been transferred, the children return home and bring some of their wicked cousins.

Here is what the apostle Paul wrote about how to deal with this:

> *The weapons we fight with are not the weapons of the world. On the contrary, they have divine power to demolish strongholds. We demolish arguments and every pretension that sets itself up against the knowledge of God, and we take captive every thought to make it obedient to Christ* (2 Cor 10:4,5).

The king of Ai is analogous to a stronghold; he was demolished at Ai.

> **The removal of the ruling spirit (king) brings deliverance to an individual.**

Plunder (B – B' level)

The B – B' level allows the Israelites to do what had been prohibited earlier. In Joshua 6, the army was not allowed to take any plunder, but now they were encouraged to do so. Why? See the firstfruits principle mentioned on page 121. The Lord was now allowing what had only a few days earlier been prohibited. Jericho was the first to be defeated and Ai was the second.

Listening to the Lord (E level)

The E level is to be open to interpretation: *"That night Joshua went into the valley"* (Josh 8:13b). We may never know why Joshua went into the valley, but here is one interpretation: on that night, Joshua may have left the soldiers so that he could hear if the Lord had any further directions. Remember that the physical often represents what is going on in the spiritual. At the end of Joshua 8:9, Joshua had spent the night with the people in Gilgal. The next night, however, Joshua appears to have taken time to listen to the Lord.

Joshua may have had considerable concern about the next day's events. That heaviness on his heart would explain the use of the word valley (`**emeq**), which can mean a 'depression' or 'flat low place'. This might have led to a Psalm 23 type of experience: *"Even though I walk through the valley of the shadow of death, I will fear no evil for you are* *with me ..."* (Ps 23:4). Because of his deeper intimacy with the Lord, he may well have taken time to hear the voice of the Lord.

In deliverance, we identify and cast out demons. However, if the Holy Spirit has not revealed all that He intends or if we have not heard correctly, we can easily miss the removal of the ruling spirit.

> As we are about to take authority over the devil, we need to be sure we have heard correctly from the Lord.

Geography: In Search of Ancient Ai (Part II)

The traditional location of Ai is three miles east of the modern day city of Bethel at a site called et-Tell. Dr. David Livingstone disputed this claim in 1970 for a variety of reasons, pointing to two other possible locations: Khirbet Maqatir and Khirbet Nisya. [37] Other archaeologists have also questioned whether et-Tell is that ancient site. No one knows for certain which of these three sites was Ai.

Naively, my wife and I had not heard about any of the three possible sites for ancient Ai. We only knew that the *Atlas of the Bible* showed Ai to be located north of a certain road near Bethel. [38] Apparently et-Tell was used in that book to identify the site of Ai.

As stated in Chapter 7, our search for Ai found two long and narrow hills with steep sides. The two hills were in the vicinity of the spot marked in the *Atlas of the Bible*, but they were on the south side of the road. We did not find et-Tell, but to us, there was nothing on the north side that resembled the description in Joshua 8.

Both hills that we found ran in an east-west direction, and to the novice, either one could have qualified as ancient Ai. We concentrated our thoughts on the northern hill. Both hills meet these criteria:

- Ai must be east of Bethel (Josh 7:2).
- A stone quarry must be located somewhere along the valley (Josh 7:5).
- A valley is to be on the north side (Josh 8:11).
- An ambush must be able to be hidden to the west of Ai (Josh 8:9,13).

---

[37] Dr. David Livingstone, *Locating Biblical Ai Correctly*, (Westminister Theological Journal, 1970)
[38] Rogerson, 148

- The valley must lead to the desert in the vicinity of Gilgal and Jericho (Josh 8:15).
- The city must be able to have twelve thousand people live there (Josh 8:25).

The last of the criteria is the ability to see the Arabah (Josh 8:14), which is the Jordan Valley, from the top of the hill. We did not hike up either hill; if we had, we should have ruled out the northern hill.

The Google Earth software, previously mentioned on page 7, has since revealed that part of the Jordan Valley can be seen from the southern hill. If you have found a computer that has Google Earth installed, I invite you to type the following longitude and latitude exactly as listed here:

31 54.4'N, 35 13.85'E

This site is Khirbet Nisya which Dr. Livingstone identified as a possible site for Ai and is his preferred site.

Once you have located this, use the controls to look at the site from the south in 3D: the two hills can be seen, one behind the other. If this is ancient Ai, Joshua would have brought his men to the valley between the two hills. The ambush would have hidden on the western slopes of the southern hill, and the people of Ai would have chased the Israelites down the valley between the two hills. If you are clever with Google Earth, you may be able to 'fly' your computer right down the valley back to the vicinity of Gilgal and Jericho. I invite you to try it.

Joshua's Directions for the Ambush

The next inner tier chiasm from Joshua 8:3-8 focuses on the decoys:

Level	First presentation	Inversion	Theme
A - A'	Sent them out with orders (Josh 8:3,4a)	Follow these orders (Josh 8:8c)	Directions from the Lord are to be followed
B - B'	Set up the ambush behind the city (Josh 8:4b,4c)	Ambush is to take the city and set it on fire (Josh 8:7,8a)	Positional changes of the ambush
C - C'	Decoy is to tempt the men (Josh 8:5)	Men of Ai will be lured from their stronghold (Josh 8:6)	Captives lured away from the city by the decoy

In this chiasm, we see Joshua giving directions to the thirty thousand men who had been chosen to be part of the ambush. How do you hide thirty thousand men? I have trouble enough hiding the Christmas presents for my wife. Maybe I need a decoy.

The C – C' level emphasizes the importance of the decoys. Joshua's spirit of wisdom must have shown him to set up the ambush and decoy. It was unexpected and the decoy got the people to leave the stronghold of their walled city.

When removing demonic spirits from a person, these spirits need to be dislodged from their stronghold. If a weak voice asks them to leave, they can easily hide. Reading God's Word, fervent prayer, fasting, worship music and purity of environment should also help.

> **When attempting to liberate an individual, the demons must be removed from their place of safety.**

Positions are Taken

There are two ambush parties mentioned in this narrative. In Joshua 8:3, there are 30,000 men sent at night to be part of the ambush. During the daylight of the following day, an additional 5,000 men were sent to the west of the city as an ambush (Josh 8:12). From Joshua 4:13 we know that there were 40,000 men in the armed guard. Therefore, by subtraction, the decoy is computed to be 5,000 men.

⟵──────── 40,000 armed men (Josh 4:13) ────────⟶

30,000 ambush (sent at night) (Josh 8:3)	5,000 ambush (Josh 8:12)	5,000 decoy (computed)

This 5,000 number is relevant to the B – B' level of this chiasm:

Level	First presentation	Inversion	Theme
A - A'	Joshua's army of 5,000 march from Gilgal to Ai (Josh 8:10,11)	The men of Ai march out of their city (Josh 8:16,17)	March out from their locations for battle
B - B'	5,000 set up ambush west of the city (Josh 8:12)	5,000 let themselves be pursued east of the city (Josh 8:14b,15)	Two brigades of 5,000 men
C - C'	The 10,000 take their positions (Josh 8:13)	The men of Ai assume their position at the top of the hill (Josh 8:14)	Armies are moved into position

If you have been involved with any deliverance sessions, you no doubt experienced some protocol as you prepared for each session. Many times there is a period of prayer and fasting. There may be a time of studying the Word of God. Possibly there is solitude so you can hear the voice of the Lord. This also holds true for any other ministries where spiritual warfare is involved. In the first attack on Ai, the forces were not prepared; in this attack, they were more prepared.

Whatever methodology is used in your deliverance session, we see that all three levels in this chiasm are showing that it is a mistake to begin the attack without proper preparation. In the same way, the enemy prepared for an early attack:

> When the king of Ai saw this, he and all the men of the city **hurried** out early in the morning to meet Israel in battle ... (Josh 8:14).

God help us if we are not properly prepared.

> **When attempting to intentionally deliver a person of demonic spirits, be well prepared.**

Ai is Delivered

In Joshua 8:18, Joshua raised his javelin in a manner similar to Exodus 17:8-13, when Moses raised his staff over his hand to defeat the Amalekites. In the Exodus story, Joshua was the commanding officer while Moses raised his hands. So Joshua, as the 'new Moses', demonstrates that he had the same power as Moses.

Level	First presentation	Inversion	Theme
A - A'	Deliverance begins with Joshua holding the javelin (Josh 8:18)	Deliverance ends when Joshua draws back the javelin (Josh 8:26)	Javelin signals the beginning and end
B - B'	Men of the ambush enter the city (Josh 8:19)	All of the Israelites return to the city (Josh 8:24,25)	City is occupied by Israelites
C - C'	The men of Ai are not able to escape (Josh 8:20)	The men of Ai are surrounded on all sides (Josh 8:22,23)	Men of Ai are surrounded
D - D'	Decoy army sees the city on fire (Josh 8:21a)	Decoy attacks the city (Josh 8:21b)	Decoy also destroys

Chapter 8 – Achan's Sin is Resolved

The javelin, while similar in some respects to the sword, is not the same instrument. In this case, it was the device that signaled the beginning of the battle. The javelin also kept Joshua's hands raised in the same way that Christians today lift their hands in praise and worship to the Lord: the battle is won by worshipping our Lord.

In the chiasm for Joshua 8:3-8, the decoy lured the captives out of their comfort zone. These 5,000 men lured the king and his army to leave the city on top of the hill. Here in the chiasm for Joshua 8:18-26, we see the decoy attacked the men of Ai.

When the Israelite army first attacked Ai (Josh 7:4,5), a spirit of fear came over the army first and the Israelites as a whole. This was because of the sin that was in the camp. On their second campaign to capture Ai, there was no fear: as the men of Ai attacked from their uphill positions, the decoy army had boldness instead of fear. An ambush came from a location south of the city, while another ambush came from the west, and the decoy force turned to attack from the east. The men of Ai were completely surrounded by the Israelites (Josh 8:22). Everybody did their part, including the decoy.

The men of Ai (demons) were completely surrounded and were dealt with by the Lord's prepared people. Ladies and gentlemen, as part of the Lord's army, we are all commissioned to fight. If the devil sees a weak body of Christ, how can we win this battle for our minds?

> **When preparing to be freed from demonic spirits, each and every area of our lives must be strong in the Lord so that we can withstand any attacks.**

Destruction of the Ruling Spirit

What makes the ambush particularly clever is that it cuts the men of Ai off from their king.

Level	First presentation	Inversion	Theme
A - A'	Ai is burned into a permanent heap of ruins (Josh 8:28)	A heap of rocks is built as a remembrance (Josh 8:29c)	Ruins are a reminder of the destruction
B - B'	King of Ai is hung on a tree (Josh 8:29)	King of Ai is removed from the tree (Josh 8:29a,29b)	Ruling spirit is cast away (deliverance)

In modern day military tactics, one of the objectives is to divide and conquer by separating the enemy into smaller groups. Another military tactic is to get the enemy to be in a position that is not easily defendable. Once the smaller groups are defeated, then the king can be removed from his high position.

On the B – B' level, we see that the king (ruling spirit) is cast away. The men of Ai were separated from their king, they were defeated, the king was defeated and the city was destroyed. In a spiritual sense, the victory at Ai was not complete until the ruling spirit was removed and the remains of the previous inhabitants were burned and destroyed.

Just as the king of Ai was hung on a tree to die, so was our Christ. The king's death brought the removal of the ruling spirit over Ai. In the same way, the death and resurrection of Jesus Christ, our King, took authority over all principalities, powers, ruling spirits and demons. With both kings, the death on a tree led to freedom from demonic spirits.

> **Through the death and resurrection of Christ, He took authority over all principalities, powers, ruling spirits and demons.**

Geography: Mount Ebal and Mount Gerizim

Once Ai was defeated, the scene shifts to Shechem, which is twenty-five miles north of Ai. The modern day city of Nablus is the ancient city of Shechem. The city is nestled between two large mountains: Mount Ebal and Mount Gerizim. It can be located on Google Earth by entering the following longitude and latitude:

32 12.9'N, 35 16.55'E

The location shown in Google Earth is in the valley floor where the two mountains are the closest. Here, the valley is roughly one-eighth of a mile wide and the mountain tops are one mile apart. Joshua would have stood in the middle of this valley with all of the people standing or sitting on one of the two mountains (Josh 8:33).

On both Mount Ebal and Mount Gerizim, there are natural amphitheaters that are opposite each other. The amphitheaters are located just west of the longitude and latitude that are listed above. Possibly the tribes were in the natural amphitheaters, or possibly they were where the two mountains were closest.

As my wife and I drove through the city of Nablus in 1999, we wondered how Joshua could have been heard over the sound of the taxis and buses. It was certainly a noisy city.

Chapter 8 – Achan's Sin is Resolved

When traveling by car, this predominantly Muslim city is located one hour north of Jerusalem in the West Bank. The population of Nablus has grown from 5,100 residents in 1950 to 130,000 in 2005. [39]

There is a small Jewish community named Elon Moreh that is situated on Mount Gerizim; Jews can walk from there to a nearby temple site to pray. (Remember that the people of Samaria had worshipped on Mount Gerizim in John 4:20.) In recent years, some Muslim forces have been trying very hard to remove these Jewish people from this area.

Just before Moses died, he gave instructions to Joshua to go to the locations of Mounts Ebal and Gerizim after they crossed the Jordan:

> *When you have crossed the Jordan into the land the LORD your God is giving you, set up some large stones and coat them with plaster. Write on them all the words of this law when you have crossed over to enter the land the LORD your God is giving you, a land flowing with milk and honey, just as the LORD, the God of your fathers, promised you. And when you have crossed the Jordan, set up these stones on **Mount Ebal**, as I command you today, and coat them with plaster. Build there an altar to the LORD your God, an altar of stones. Do not use any iron tool upon them. Build the altar of the LORD your God with fieldstones and offer burnt offerings on it to the LORD your God. Sacrifice fellowship offerings there, eating them and rejoicing in the presence of the LORD your God. And you shall write very clearly all the words of this law on these stones you have set up* (Deut 27:2-8).

These commands from Moses describe the altar as an altar of remembrance. It was not intended for the regular sacrifice of burnt offerings, but for the renewal of their vows. Notice the emphasis on the purity of the stones: coated with plaster, no iron tool, and all the words of the law written on these stones. The phrase *"all of the word of this law"* (Deut 27:8) likely referred to some or all of the Book of Deuteronomy.

After Moses gave instructions to obey the commands and decrees that the Lord has passed on to them, he gave these instructions to the twelve tribes:

> *When you have crossed the Jordan, these tribes shall stand on **Mount Gerizim** to bless the people: Simeon, Levi, Judah, Issachar, Joseph and Benjamin. And these*

---

[39] Palestinian Central Bureau of Statistics, Online: http://www.pcbs.gov.ps/Portals/_pcbs/populati/pop06.aspx, [7 June 2007]

*tribes shall stand on **Mount Ebal** to pronounce curses: Reuben, Gad, Asher, Zebulun, Dan and Naphtali* (Deut 27:12,13).

Therefore, based on the census of men given in Numbers 26:51, there would have been one million men, women and children standing on Mount Gerizim, and one million standing on Mount Ebal. As shown above in Deuteronomy 27:12,13, Mount Gerizim was to represent the blessings that the people would receive, while Mount Ebal was to represent the curses resulting from disobedience.

The Covenant is Renewed

We remember that in Joshua 7, Achan and his family had just been found guilty and sentenced to death because of their disobedience. Then in Joshua 8, the Lord blessed the people by conquering Ai using the supernatural wisdom that was poured into Joshua.

With the reminder of Achan's sin and the Lord's hand in conquering Ai, let's now look at the renewal of the covenant. As we see from this chiasm, it was time for an object lesson: Mount Gerizim and Mount Ebal.

Level	First presentation	Inversion	Theme
A - A'	Altar is built according to the Book of the Law (Josh 8:30,31a)	The entire Book of the Law is read (Josh 8:34,35)	Importance of the Book of the Law
B - B'	Law is copied onto uncut field stone (Josh 8:31b,32)	Law is read between uncut mountains of Gerizim and Ebal (Josh 8:33b)	Law, like the rock, is not changeable
C - C'	Ark of the covenant is in the center of the people (Josh 8:33a)	No inverted verse	The ark of the presence

Surprisingly, the center point of this chiasm is not the Book of the Law but the ark of the covenant. That is because the presence of God was between the cherubim that were on top of the ark of the covenant (Num 7:89 and 1 Chron 13:6). Therefore, the purpose of this renewal was an object lesson: by putting the Lord at the center of their lives, sin and its consequences would be avoided and the blessings of the Lord would flow.

When my wife Nancy and I were in Nablus (Shechem), we drove up the side of Mount Ebal to understand how well the people could understand what was being spoken in the valley. Houses have been built up the first third of the mountain. We drove up a very narrow street to a spot in the amphitheater where we could look out. Down below we could faintly hear the buses and taxis in the distance because they were quite a ways away. Across the way, we could see that a road goes to the top of Mount Gerizim and there were some buildings on top, but that was nearly a mile from where we stood.

Some theologians have proposed that Joshua's voice would have been able to be easily heard from either side of the natural amphitheaters. For example, Alan Redpath wrote these words in 1955, well before the population explosion in Nablus:

> *Any traveler to the land of Palestine today can tell you that you can stand on the top of Mount Ebal and talk with someone on the top of Mount Gerizim, almost without raising your voice, so perfect are the natural acoustics. The amphitheater provided by the valley is utterly natural and complete, and voices ring across it from peak to peak.* [40]

Possibly, but in Redpath's 254 page book about the Book of Joshua, he never indicates a personal knowledge of this land.

Look with me once again at Nablus on Google Earth: to seat one million people on each mountain side, how close could they have been to a place of perfect acoustics? Might the people have been a bit noisy? Having been there, I truly wonder if a person's voice would project a half a mile away.

All two million people may or may not have been able to hear words of the Law that Joshua spoke, but they were able to understand the object lesson very clearly. Their focus, as they stood on Mounts Ebal and Gerizim, was not to be on Joshua but on the ark of the covenant. That is what the center point of chiasm (C – C' level) is showing:

> *All Israel, aliens and citizens alike, with their elders, officials and judges, were standing on both sides of the ark of the covenant of the* LORD*, facing those who carried it ...* (Josh 8:33).

The ark of the Lord was before them, and the consequences of Achan's sin were behind them. Righteousness was being called from the throne. God was to be the center of their entire lives.

Some people may feel they are going through a time of blessings. Great: focus on the Lord. Others may know that they are going through some discipline or curse. Again: focus on the Lord. He is to be the

---

[40] Alan Redpath, *Victorious Christian Living: Studies in the Book of Joshua* (Fleming H. Revell Co., 1955), 126.

center of our existence. Then, the Lord will provide His power and wisdom to set the people in the land they were promised.

> **Success in spiritual warfare requires Christ to be at the center of our lives.**

Chapter 9 – Gibeonites are Grafted-In to God's Community

> *They answered Joshua, "Your servants were clearly told how the LORD your God had commanded His servant Moses to give you the whole land and to wipe out all its inhabitants from before you. So we feared for our lives because of you, and that is why we did this. We are now in your hands. Do to us whatever seems good and right to you"* (Josh 9:24,25).

The structure of the first twelve chapters of Joshua was outlined on page 42 and is repeated below. May I share that this story of the Gibeonites gave me a chiastic fit (that's when we say "Lord, I'm confused" twice as it becomes the center of our attention)? I knew there was a chiasm in these twelve chapters yet some of the levels did not seem to match up properly. In particular, the C – C' level did not make sense to me for the longest time.

Level	First presentation	Inversion	Theme
A - A'	Assurance that the Lord has given the whole land to the Israelites (Josh 1 - 2)	Remainder of the land is given to the Israelites (Josh 10:16 - 12:24)	The Lord has given the whole land to the Israelites
B - B'	Jordan River stands still (Josh 3)	Sun stands still (Josh 10:1-15)	Nature itself stands still
C - C'	Hebrews build piles of stones to show they are transformed to God's community (Josh 4)	Gibeonites fear the Lord God and so are grafted in to God's community (Josh 9)	Israelites and Gentiles can be part of God's community
D - D'	Failure to circumcise is revealed and dealt with (Josh 5)	Achan's sin is revealed and resolved (Josh 7 - 8)	Sin is exposed and is dealt with
E - E'	Jericho's king and it's people are destroyed (Josh 6:1-21)	Rahab and her family are saved (Josh 6:22-25)	Judgment of good and evil

Hearing the Voice of the Lord

Possibly you have been reading elsewhere in your Bible and have wondered if a particular set of verses is a chiasm. As you have analyzed the verses, part of it did not make sense. I am writing this section to help you understand that you are not alone with struggling over some chiasms. My hope is that if I reveal the events and my thought processes, you will see how I arrived at each theme.

My first clue that there is a potential chiasm for chapters 1 - 12 was when I saw the similarity between the Jordan River standing still and the sun standing still. This pairing eventually became the B – B' level.

My second clue was the realization that at Jericho, most of the people were destroyed and some were saved. This was the apparent center point of the chiasm (E – E' level).

The first and second clues were both fairly easy. The **rhema** word of God was necessary from here on. With each successive step, I asked the Lord for help and He provided.

As I was analyzing chapter 5, the Lord asked me why that generation was not circumcised. This pointed me to the sins of the fathers and how truly rebellious they were. This then was similar to the sin of Achan, which became the D – D' level.

The inclusion of chapter 2 with chapter 1 as an "Assurance from the Lord" came as I was reading Joshua 2:24: *"The LORD has surely given the whole land into our hands ..."* It was like a light bulb turned on as I saw this verse concluding the thoughts of Joshua 1:6-9: it was an illumination from the Lord. Previously I had been speculating that the story of the two spies was somehow related to Joshua 10:16-28, but it just did not make any sense. But I had been attentive to His voice and it came as revelation. The comparison of Joshua 1 - 2 to Joshua 10:16 - 12:24 was then obvious, which was the A – A' level.

But now I had a problem with comparing the construction of a pile of stones (Joshua 4) with the failure of Joshua to seek the Lord with regard to Gibeon (Joshua 9). There seemed to be no apparent similarity. Once again I had another chiastic fit and sought the Lord, but He seemed to be a long time in answering.

Several days later, as I was attempting to break through this apparent dichotomy, the Lord spoke the nearly audible word 'transformed' to me. I knew that the Jordan River had been transformed from wet to dry, so I went back to read chapters 3 - 4 once again. The writing on page 79 entitled "Transformed at the Jordan" was the result. The revelation on how Christ was transformed from manna to the Commander of the Army of the Lord, as described on page 96, also came at that time. God is so good!

Finally, the Lord had me read chapter 9 about the Gibeonites once again. My search, as I read about the Gibeonites, was to look for some type of transformation. The center point of the second chiasm in chapter 9 revealed the answer (page 151). By analyzing Joshua 9:23, I saw that the Gibeonites were transformed from a foreign nation to servants of Israel: "... *you will never cease to **serve** as woodcutters and water carriers for the house of my God.*" The rhema word 'transformed' literally changed my understanding of these chapters.

Then it made sense. In chapter 4, the Israelites showed how they were transformed from a rebellious generation to a faithful generation. In chapter 9, the Gibeonites revealed their desire for transformation by showing how they wanted to become part of the nation of Israel. Then the Gibeonites were grafted in.

I wrote this sequence of events to help you understand the art of identifying chiasms and to encourage you in your own walk. To hear the voice of the Lord, that is the **rhema** word, is a very important step in the walk of a Christian believer. Allow your imagination to run; the Holy Spirit generally speaks to the imaginative side of our brain, as opposed to the mathematical and organized portions of our brain. As the prophet Joel wrote:

> *And afterward, I will pour out my Spirit on all people. Your sons and daughters will prophesy, your old men will dream dreams, your young men will see visions* (Joel 2:28).

> **Allow our thoughts to wander and dreams to be dreamt so that we can hear from the Lord, and truly see and understand the spiritual warfare that is taking place.**

Structure of Chapter 9

In this story of Gibeon, many people catch the idea that no one inquired of the Lord, and so the Israelite community fell into the ruse. The following middle tier chiasm shows the overall structure of the story of the Gibeonites. The center point of the chiasm (D – D' level) states: *"The men of Israel ...did not inquire of the LORD"* (Josh 9:14). The inference generally is that because Joshua and Israel did not do the right thing, their weakness allowed Gibeon to be part of Israel. After all, Moses directed them to completely destroy all of these nations and make no treaty with them (Deut 7:1,2; 20:16-18).

Level	First presentation	Inversion	Theme
A - A'	Gibeonites decide to separate from the rest of the nations (Josh 9:3,4a)	Gibeonites become slaves to Israel (Josh 9:26,27)	Separation from past, attachment to new
B - B'	"We are your servants" (Josh 9:4-8)	"Your servants were clearly told ..." (Josh 9:24,25)	Gibeonites have attitude of a servant
C - C'	The ruse is completed (Josh 9:9-13)	The ruse is exposed (Josh 9:16-23)	Deception and the exposure
D - D'	Joshua and the others did not inquire of the Lord (Josh 9:14)	Treaty was naively made because of failure to inquire (Josh 9:15)	Importance of inquiring of the Lord

This chiasm reveals the Lord's purpose with this story – He allowed the Gibeonites to be their servants. He was trying to convince Joshua that he must inquire of the Lord in all circumstances.

I propose that the higher purpose may have been to show that the Lord is in control, and despite how we may mess things up, He will do His perfect will. Possibly the Lord would have said "Allow the Gibeonites to be part of My community because they fear Me. I will transform them just as I did you when you crossed the Jordan." We will see in Joshua 10:12,13 that the sun stood still over Gibeon. If Joshua would have inquired of the Lord, he would have known His perfect will.

Let's look at another verse from Deuteronomy:

> *When you march up to attack a city, make its people an offer of peace. If they accept and open their gates, all the people in it shall be subject to forced labor and shall work for you* (Deut 20:10,11).

The peace treaty allowed aliens to be servants of the Israelites.

In Deuteronomy 29:11, the aliens were given the responsibility to "*... chop your wood and carry your water.*" This was the same responsibility that was given to the Gibeonites. Deuteronomy 29 continues by requiring all of the people, including all of the aliens, to enter into a covenant with the Lord (Deut 29:12).

The next question might be: "If the Gibeonites were truly grafted in, how did they do?" By studying the various passages where Gibeon is mentioned in the Bible, we see that for a period during King David's reign, the altar of burnt offerings was at Gibeon (1 Chron 21:29). King Solomon is recorded as having sacrificed one-thousand burnt offerings in one day at Gibeon because God's Tent of Meeting was there (2 Chron 1:3). The Gibeonites were grafted in.

Geography: In Search for Ancient Gibeon

The *Atlas of the Bible* clearly identifies Gibeon on a map and provides a two-page aerial photograph of the ancient city.[41] So off my wife Nancy and I went, driving our rental car through the West Bank in search for a hill with a small community of houses on the north side. The ancient roads on the *Atlas of the Bible* did not match the road map that had been provided, there was no identification of Gibeon on the road map, and again there were no signs to assist us. Yet I knew we were within 5 miles of the location.

That day, the Lord provided as He did many times on our trip in 1999. We drove by a sign that said "Prophet Samuel's Tomb" in English, so we drove up. This ancient site of the Israelites was once, according to tradition, the home of the Prophet Samuel; his tomb is in the basement and is a sacred site to the Jewish people.

From the roof of the building, we looked in the valley to the north and saw the nearly identical view of Gideon that was in the *Atlas of the Bible*. Imagine our excitement – the Lord had drawn us to the Prophet Samuel's Tomb, altering our plans, so that we could find the ancient city of Gibeon.

You can see this same site in 3-D using Google Earth by typing this longitude and latitude:

31 50.87'N, 35 11.1'E

By rotating the view so that it is in more of a 3-D mode, you will be able to see the size of the hill.

Ancient Gibeon was built on top of the hill. The rock formations all around the hill are exposed because of the severe deforestation and resulting erosion. With the Tent of Meeting being located at Gibeon for some time, clearly all this animal sacrifice has had its toll on the landscape.

When we were done at the Prophet Samuel's house, we wound our way through the Muslim village of el-Jib to the top of the hill. No archaeological alterations had been made to Gibeon. We since learned that the Jewish authorities refer to el-Jib as Tel en Nasbeh. The only indication of any changes to the area was a barbed wire fence that had been built around a cistern. (During the hour that we were there, the sun did not stop so we had to move along.)

The Ruse

Joshua had to be taught the lesson of obtaining directions from the Lord twice. When the Achan sinned and Joshua set out to conquer Ai,

---

[41] John Rogerson, 162 and 166.

Joshua did not inquire of the Lord (Josh 7:3-5). Here with the Gibeonites, Joshua once again did not seek the Lord. The difference between the two events is that at Ai, the Lord apparently did not speak, whereas at Gibeon, Joshua did not ask.

This is the chiasm that is related to the ruse:

Level	First presentation	Inversion	Theme
A - A'	Delegation brings worn-out sacks, old wineskins, worn out clothes and stale bread (Josh 9:4b,5)	When left home, bread was warm, wineskins were new, but clothes/sandals are now worn out (Josh 9:13)	Wineskins, sacks and clothes
B - B'	From a distant country; make a treaty (Josh 9:6)	From a distant country; fear of the Lord; make a treaty (Josh 9:9-11)	Distant land; want a treaty
C - C'	We are your servants (Josh 9:7,8a)	Joshua: Who are you? (Josh 9:8b)	Attempts to identify the delegation

The center point of this chiasm deals with identification: the Gibeonites say they are servants, and Joshua asks for clarification. In a spiritual sense, Joshua was correct in asking for identification. His mistake was that he did not ask the Lord for discernment.

Let us suppose that one person is being particularly disrespectful to another. The Lord can identify the name of the spirit or spirits tormenting that first person when we ask. It might be a spirit of fear, a spirit of criticism, a spirit of deceit, etc. This is the discernment or rhema that the Lord freely gives. In this case, it was not a tormenting spirit.

> **When dealing with demonic spirits, understanding the name of the spirit or spirits will often identify how to deal with that spirit.**

A Humble Spirit

Is it so bad to have the responsibility as a servant? The Gibeonites did not complain. In fact, that is what they asked for: *"We are your servants"* (Josh 9:8). A servant's heart is a humble heart. Using Joshua 9:18-26 as a basis, this inner tier chiasm relates how the ruse was exposed:

Chapter 9 – Gibeonites are Grafted In

Level	First presentation	Inversion	Theme
A - A'	The Israelites do not attack Gibeon (Josh 9:18)	The Israelites do not kill the people of Gibeon (Josh 9:26)	Israelites could have attacked Gibeon
B - B'	Israel chooses to honor the oath so that wrath does not fall on them (Josh 9:19,20)	Gibeonites chose the ruse so that wrath does not fall on them (Josh 9:24,25)	Wrath of God motivates decisions
C - C'	Assembly says *"let them be woodcutters and water carriers ..."* (Josh 9:21)	Joshua states they will *" serve as woodcutters and water carriers ..."* (Josh 9:22,23)	Gibeonites are grafted in as woodcutters and water carriers

By looking at the B – B' level, we can see the ruse from the perspective of the Gibeonites. They chose a ruse because they feared the Lord (Josh 9:24,25). They were willing to humble themselves and become servants rather than expose themselves to the high likelihood that they would be annihilated. Proverbs 1:7 states *"The fear of the LORD is the beginning of knowledge, but fools despise wisdom and discipline."*

Regarding the ruse, Rahab had done something similar: she deceived her king by saying that the spies had left (Josh 2:5). Yet she was grafted in while the rest of the people of Jericho were killed.

Now I am not justifying a spirit of deceit or manipulation. The Lord is the judge of all circumstances. But I am saying that the humility the Gibeonites demonstrated by being willing to be servants was admirable.

At the C – C' level, we see the consequences of the decision: the Gibeonites are accepted into the community as servants. Therefore, their statement from Joshua 9:8 was fulfilled: *"We are your servants."*

Years later, King David would be honoring the Gibeonite relationship by asking them how to make amends for Saul attempting to annihilate them. Again, the Gibeonites responded with humility by stating that they had no rights (2 Sam 21:1-4). David pressed the Gibeonites for an answer, and seven of Saul's heirs were found and subsequently killed.

Why would David go to this effort? Because the Lord was displeased with how Saul had put some Gibeonites to death, resulting in a famine (2 Sam 21:1). The Gibeonites had lived up to their reputation as a people worthy of being grafted in, and so the Lord honored them.

> **When a large spiritual battle is on the horizon, a humble heart will often save the day and no battle will need to be fought.**

Chapter 10 – The Sun Stands Still

> *"O sun, stand still over Gibeon,*
> *O moon, over the Valley of Ajalon."*
> *So the sun stood still,*
> *and the moon stopped,*
> *till the nation avenged itself on its enemies*
> (Josh 10:12,13).

Our prayer to the Lord might ask Him to take control of the weather:

> "Oh dear Sovereign Lord of Heaven and Earth, my daughter is getting married tomorrow and I just heard the weather forecast. Lord, if You would be so kind, would You please hold off that band of thunderstorms until after the wedding reception? Thank you, Lord, for hearing my request. In the name of Jesus Christ, Amen."

Your prayer probably has more fervor than that, but I think you get the point. Then the Lord either honors your request or ignores it because He has a better plan.

We have no control over the weather in our own strength, just as Joshua had no control over the sun and moon in his own strength. Yet the Lord listened to and honored Joshua's request. There was power and authority in Joshua's command and that is why the sun stood still.

The incredible idea that the sun and the moon stood in one place for any period of time may have those with a scientific mind saying "No way." Yet,

> *Now faith is being sure of what we hope for and certain of what we do not see* (Heb 11:1).

Some things in our Christian faith must be accepted by faith alone.

In this chapter, we will look at the middle tier chiasm that extends from Joshua 10:1-28, three inner tier chiasms and the repetition of the Hebrew word **charam** in Joshua 10:29-43.

Structure of Chapter 10

The next middle tier chiasm extends from Joshua 10:1-28, which is not the entire chapter. There is no chiasm for Joshua 10:29-43.

Level	First presentation	Inversion	Theme
A - A'	Ai had been totally destroyed by Joshua's army (Josh 10:1)	Makkedah is totally destroyed by Joshua's army (Josh 10:28)	Two cities are totally destroyed (charam)
B - B'	Five Amorite kings attack Gibeon (Josh 10:2-6)	Five Amorite kings are killed (Josh 10:16-27)	Five Amorite kings
C - C'	The Lord defeats the king's army by confusion (Josh 10:7-10)	The Lord defeats the king's army by supernatural events (Josh 10:11-15)	Lord defeats the king's army

On the A – A' level, the Hebrew word **charam** (kwaw-ram') is used, which we will discuss later in this chapter. Notice the separation of the kings on the B – B' level from his army on the C – C' level. The emphasis of this chiasm is on how the army were surprised by the confusion and supernatural events (C – C' level).

We have discussed in regards to Ai (page 140) how the king is the most powerful person, and he represents the ruling spirit that attempts to control our lives. We have also discussed how the people of these foreign nations are similar to the demons that plague a person. In this case, the believer to be liberated would be Gibeon.

Physical battle		Analogous to
City	←→	Believer to be liberated
King	←→	Ruling spirit
Army of the king	←→	Demons
Israelite army	←→	Warrior angels

With this hierarchy, when there is no army, the kings must flee their positions. That is to say: the demons must be quieted and put in their places before removing the ruling spirit. The demons should be ordered, in the name of Jesus Christ, to be still and not manifest in some way. For example, if a spirit of anger were to suddenly show itself when dealing with the ruling spirit, the anger is protecting the ruling spirit.

> **The demons must be brought under control before removing the ruling spirit.**

Five Amorite Kings Attack Gibeon

Just as peace was achieved between the Israelites and Gibeon in Joshua 9, an attack came from five kings. The chiasm for Joshua 10:1-6 shows the progression from alarm to attack:

Level	First presentation	Inversion	Theme
A - A'	King of Jerusalem is alarmed at what happened at Jericho, Ai and Gibeon (Josh 10:1,2)	Gibeonites are alarmed at the attack by the five kings (Josh 10:6)	Alarm
B - B'	Jerusalem appeals to Hebron, Jarmuth, Lachish and Eglon kings to attack Gibeon (Josh 10:3,4)	Forces of Jerusalem, Hebron, Jarmuth, Lachish and Eglon attack Gibeon (Josh 10:5)	Attack on Gibeon

Attacks can come at any time, but it seems that they often come just after a significant battle has been won:

- We get a 90 on an exam in a subject that we have been struggling with, and shortly afterwards BAM!
- Our boss congratulates us on some hard work by taking us to lunch, and shortly afterwards BAM!
- We experience a tremendous anointing of God at a special church service, and shortly afterwards BAM!
- We sense God lifting burdens that we have been carrying, and shortly afterwards BAM!

It doesn't always happen, thank God. But when it does, we feel suddenly more exhausted than if the attack had come during tough times. I can't explain it, but I don't think I am alone in this experience.

The devil seems to somehow know that we can be weakest when things are going particularly well. That was the case with Gibeon. They had just had an oath sworn by the Israelites that would have given them a servant position as well as protection from destruction. BAM!

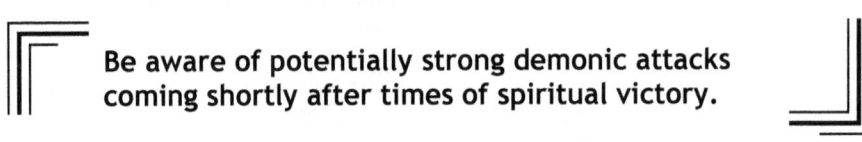

Be aware of potentially strong demonic attacks coming shortly after times of spiritual victory.

Gibeonites are Liberated

Even though we can be attacked after a victory, that does not mean we are defeated. In Joshua 10:7-15, the Lord fights for Israel:

Level	First presentation	Inversion	Theme
A - A'	Joshua marches from Gilgal to Gibeon (Josh 10:7)	Joshua returns from Gibeon to Gilgal (Josh 10:15)	Joshua considers Gilgal his home base
B - B'	Lord says to Joshua: "*I have given (nātan) them into your hand*" (Josh 10:8)	Lord showed He was fighting for Israel (Josh 10:14)	**Nātan** (Lord delivers them by fighting for Israel)
C - C'	Lord sends a spirit of confusion and hailstones, killing many (Josh 10:9-11)	Lord stops the sun and moon in response to Joshua's request (Josh 10:12,13)	Lord provides and defeats by using miracles of nature

The C – C' level of this chiasm was used to emphasize how the Lord responded to the attack on the Gibeonites:

- On the road between Beth Horon and Azekah, the Lord saw their plight and sent hailstones.
- In the vicinity of Gibeon and the Aijalon Valley, the Lord heard Joshua and caused the sun and moon to stop still.

Both events were supernatural events that only the Lord could have performed. Man cannot make hailstones or cause the sun or moon to stand still; only the Lord can. As the angel said to Mary regarding her conceiving a baby: *"For nothing is impossible with God"* (Luke 1:37).

Joshua 3	Joshua 10
The priests stand in faith where the water once was, allowing the people to pass by (Josh 3:14-17)	The Israelites stood in faith knowing that the Lord was fighting with them (Josh 10:8)
The water stood (`**amad**) in obedience (Josh 3:16)	The moon and sun stood (`**amad**) in obedience (Josh 10:13)

In the explanation of why the Jordan River stood still from Joshua 3 (page 72), it was that the Jordan River stood (`**amad**) because the priests stood (`**amad**). The same Hebrew phrases are present in this story of the sun and moon. In Joshua 10:8, the Lord says that "*... not one will be able to withstand* (`**amad**) *you."* The NKJV presents this as: *"... not a man of them shall stand before you."* Then in Joshua 10:13,

Chapter 10 – The Sun Stands Still

the word `**amad** is used twice: the moon stopped (`**amad**) and the sun stopped (`**amad**). Therefore, the message from Joshua 10 has the same pattern that was presented in Joshua 3.

 The Lord is waiting for us to take our stand first.

Five Amorite Kings are Killed

My wife and I did not attempt to locate the cave at Makkedah in 1999, so we cannot relay anything about that location except to note that the *Atlas of the Bible* places it twenty-five miles southwest of Gibeon. [42] Here is the next inner tier chiasm:

Level	First presentation	Inversion	Theme
A - A'	Five kings hide at Makkedah (Josh 10:16)	Joshua strikes down the king at Makkedah (Josh 10:28)	Hiding place at Makkedah becomes a place of destruction
B - B'	Large rocks are moved at mouth of the cave, locking in the five kings (Josh 10:17,18)	Large rocks are moved at the mouth of the cave where five kings were placed (Josh 10:27)	Rocks symbolize the sealed death fate given to the kings
C - C'	The people from five fortified cities are destroyed (Josh 10:19-21)	The kings are hung on five trees (Josh 10:26)	People and kings are destroyed
D - D'	The five kings are brought to Joshua for placing feet on their necks (Josh 10:22-24)	Fear is to be replaced with courage for you will stomp on your enemies in the same way (Josh 10:25)	Be strong and courageous because the power of the Lord will be with us

The illustration of the army commanders placing their feet on the necks of the five kings was a vivid picture of the future successes that they will have. As Romans 16:20 states: *"The God of peace will soon crush Satan under your feet."* Words like this are intended to bring boldness, strength and courage into His people with what the Lord is about to do. That is why Joshua stated in the second part of Joshua 10:25 that this is what they will do to their enemies.

---

[42] John Rogerson, 85.

Joshua 10:25 starts with Joshua stating *"do not be afraid; do not be discouraged."* The metaphor of placing feet on the necks of the kings is intended to give courage. The metaphor also says that we should not expect success when filled with doubt, fear or discouragement. These spirits bring defeat, but the Lord's strength conquers.

> **Have strength and courage when going after the ruling spirits because the power of the Lord accompanies us.**

Totally Destroyed

There is no chiasm in Joshua 10:29-43, but the emphasis on "totally destroyed" is unmistakable. Linguistically, repetition of words is often a way of emphasizing importance. People will repeat to their puppy not to chew the furniture and repeatedly tell their kitty to get off the kitchen table. Repetition emphasizes importance.

Repetition of words is often used to emphasize the importance of a topic. Isn't that what a chiasm is: a structured repetition of words and topics for the purpose of emphasis on a central theme?

The word **charam** (khaw-ram') is presented four times in Joshua 10:29-43, although it appears fourteen times throughout the Book of Joshua. The NIV translated **charam** in these verses as *"totally destroyed,"* and the KJV use the words *"utterly destroyed."* Here are the four occurrences in Joshua 10:29-43:

Verse	Location
Josh 10:35	Eglon
Josh 10:37	Hebron
Josh 10:39	Debir
Josh 10:40	Hill country, Negev, western foothills and mountain slopes

Other occurrences of the word **charam** are in regard to Sihon and Og, Jericho (two times), Ai (two times), Makkedah, Hazor, and the northern cities (three times). Moses instructed Joshua to totally destroy the cities of the inheritance (Deut 20:17), using the words **charam charam** for emphasis.

In Joshua 6, the related word **cherem** (kheh'-rem) was used to refer to a devoted thing or banned thing. If you have access to an NIV Bible, please turn with me to Joshua 6:17. After the word *"devoted"* you should see a small letter which indicates a footnote at the bottom of the

Chapter 10 – The Sun Stands Still

page. This footnote reads "the irrevocable giving over of things or persons to the Lord, often by totally destroying them." This is the word **cherem**.

Now please turn in your NIV Bible to Joshua 10:1 where you should see a small letter for the footnote after the words *"totally destroyed"*. This is the word **charam**. The footnote should read the same as in Joshua 6:17.

Does it seem peculiar to you that the silver, gold, bronze and iron items (which were to be placed in the treasury of the Lord's house in Joshua 6) are treated in the same sense as these cities (which were totally destroyed in Joshua 10)? After all, the treasury items would be sacred whereas the Lord instructed that the cities were to be demolished.

Regarding the words **charam** and **cherem**, the *Theological Workbook of the Old Testament* defines these words this way:

> The basic meaning is the exclusion of an object from the use or abuse of man and its irrevocable surrender to God. ... Surrendering something to God meant devoting it to the service of God or putting it under a ban for utter destruction. [43]

The common theme of these two Hebrew words is "surrender to God and service for God." In other words, the devoted things (**cherem**) in Jericho were to be set aside as firstfruits so that they may be used exclusively for the service to God. The devoted things were to be used for the support of ceremonies that worshipped the Lord. On the other hand, the cities were to be totally cleansed (**charam**) so that they may be used exclusively for the service to God. The cities were to be dwelling places where the people would abide and worship the Lord. The temple was to be a place of worship, but so were the places where they would live.

Now let us apply the analogy that we have used with Jericho and Ai: the cities represent believers and the people who lived in the cities represent demonic forces. The cities (believers) wanted the people of the city (demons) to be totally destroyed. The message should be very clear that the Lord wants to totally destroy those forces within every person that would not be dedicated for the service and worship to the Lord. The resistance by the demons to that purpose is called spiritual warfare.

The commandments that Moses passed down included the putting to death any person that was disobedient to the Lord. Many of those

---

[43] R. Laird Harris, *Theological Workbook of the Old Testament*, 1980, The Moody Bible Institute of Chicago

statements are hard to take as New Testament believers; for example, if we curse our mother or father, we were to be stoned to death (Lev 20:9). The harshness of these consequences seems hard to justify. Yet Achan's problem was not just that he was stealing what was intended for the Lord, but that his heart was self-centered and devoted to himself. In the same way, the total annihilation of a city seems hard to justify as a New Testament believer. The Lord was looking for devotion to Himself.

Unfortunately, there were two occasions where Joshua and the Israelites missed their opportunity to **charam** (totally destroy) the enemy. In Joshua 10:20, there is reference that some of the enemy escaped to the fortified cities. Then in Joshua 11:13, those cities that were built on mounds were not destroyed, with the exception of Hazor. Josephus, in the *Antiquities of the Jews*, explained that the reason they were not destroyed was because they had made their walls exceptionally strong. These cities had heard of the reputation of the Israelite army, and so they fortified them by taking advantage of their being built on mounds. [44]

> **Deliverance requires the total removal of the demonic forces.**

---

[44] Josephus, 5.1.20

Chapters 11 and 12 – More Kings are Defeated

> *Joshua took all these royal cities and their kings and put them to the **sword*** (Josh 11:12).

The word "sword" is the Hebrew word **chereb** which was discussed in some depth on page 17. **Chereb** appears twenty times in the Book of Joshua, including four times in Joshua 11. The sword was used in Joshua 5 for the circumcision, and the Commander of the Army of the Lord carried a sword. The sword was used at Jericho (Josh 6:21) and at Ai (twice in Josh 8:24). When the five armies fled from Gibeon, the **chereb** was used (Josh 10:11). In Joshua 10 and 11, the sword was mentioned eleven times in regard to the destruction of the kingdoms.

When Joshua stated *"You did not do it with your own sword or bow"* (Josh 24:12), he knew that the sword was wielded by the Commander of the Army of the Lord. The sword indicates the presence of Christ. At the end of Joshua 10, we again see the force that was behind the sword:

> *All these kings and their lands Joshua conquered in one campaign, because the LORD, the God of Israel, fought for Israel* (Josh 10:42).

Joshua could have taken credit for the many defeats throughout Israel, but he remembered how Moses fell into that trap. The Lord instructed Moses to speak to the rock (Num 20:8), but instead he struck it. Before he struck it, Moses said he and Aaron could provide water:

> *... Moses said to them, "Listen, you rebels, must **we** bring you water out of this rock?"* (Num 20:10).

Moses should have said "Listen, you rebels, must the Lord bring you water from this rock?" Moses failed to give credit to the Lord. Even so, the water gushed out and everyone drank the water. But then the Lord had to speak to Moses about failure to honor the Lord:

> *But the LORD said to Moses and Aaron, "Because you did not trust in me enough to honor me as holy in the sight of the Israelites, you will not bring this community into the land I give them"* (Num 20:12).

If Moses can fall in that trap, so we can also. Neither Joshua nor the Israelites took credit for the miracle at Jericho for themselves. They knew the Lord's hand was in charge. It was the sword of the Lord.

When a surgeon successfully performs a delicate surgery, he should not be overconfident, but instead be dependent on the Lord. When a worship leader experiences a strong touch from the Lord, that leader should be humble. When an author writes a book on Biblical truths, that author should be in awe at what the Lord is doing. And when we see the release of the Lord's hand in spiritual warfare, we should praise the Lord.

> In spiritual warfare, thank the Lord that we are able to witness His successes; do not give any credit to ourselves.

Structure of Chapters 11 and 12

The outer tier chiasm, which is the dominant structure of first twelve chapters of Joshua, indicates that the A – A' level has Joshua 1 - 2 paired with Joshua 10:16 - 12:24 (see page 42):

Level	First presentation	Inversion	Theme
A - A'	Assurance that the Lord has given the whole land to the Israelites (Josh 1 - 2)	Remainder of the land is given to the Israelites (Josh 10:16-12:24)	The Lord has given the whole land to the Israelites

This pairing makes sense for three reasons. First, Joshua 1:3,4 states that the Lord will give Joshua the entire land from the desert to Lebanon, from the Euphrates to the Mediterranean. In Joshua 10:16 - 12:24, that promise is fulfilled.

Secondly, in Joshua 2, the people of Jericho melted in fear because of what happened to Sihon and Og. In Joshua 12:1-6, we are reminded of how Sihon and Og were totally defeated.

Thirdly, at the end of Joshua 2, the two spies reported their confidence that "... *the LORD has surely given the whole land into our hands ...*"(Josh 2:24). The parallel verse from Josh 11:23 reads: *"So Joshua took the entire land, just as the LORD had directed Moses, and he gave it as an inheritance to Israel ..."*

Joshua was successful in conquering this land because of his total obedience to the Lord's commands. The Lord honored Joshua's obedience by taking authority over the land by use of the sword. The next middle tier chiasm, which covers Josh 10:29 - 12:24, emphasizes how Joshua was so very obedient:

Chapters 11 and 12 – More Kings are Defeated

Level	First presentation	Inversion	Theme
A - A'	Southern and northern kings are defeated (Josh 10:29 - 11:14)	The defeated kings are listed (Josh 12:1-24)	Kings who have been defeated
B - B'	Joshua did everything the Lord had commanded through Moses, destroying the royal cities (Josh 11:12-15)	Joshua took all the land as the Lord directed Moses, destroying the cities (Josh 11:16-23)	Royal cities and other cities are destroyed by Joshua as per Lord's command through Moses

The center point of this chiasm (B – B' level) emphasizes Joshua's obedience in destroying the cities. In the summarization of the Deuteronomic Covenant, the importance of obedience was strongly emphasized (page 63). Joshua models obedience in this war against the kings and kingdoms.

> **Total obedience is a prerequisite for the complete defeat of the enemy's powers and rulers in our lives.**

Kings and Kingdoms

In Joshua 10:16 - 12:24, there is a summary of the kings that were defeated both west and east of the Jordan River:

Verses	Cities where kings were killed
Josh 10:16-27	Jerusalem, Hebron, Jarmuth, Lachish, Eglon
Josh 10:28-42	Makkedah, Libnah, Debir, Gezer
Josh 11:1-11	Hazor and all of the kings of Shimron, Acshaph, the northern kings, Canaanites, Amorites, Hittites, Perizzites, Jebusites, Hitivites
Josh 11:12-23	Anakites
Josh 12:1-6	Heshbon, Bashan
Josh 12:7-24	Summary of thirty-one kings

Going back to the analogy of kingdoms, kings and the people, the kingdom kings (such as Sihon and Og) are the powers, the kings (such as the kings of Jericho and Ai) are the rulers and the people of the city are the demonic or evil spirits.

On the east side of the Jordan, we saw that Sihon and Og were powers over their kingdoms (see page 50), and they were destroyed by Moses. In the same way, Jabin king of Hazor was a power because he had authority over other kings and nations: *"Hazor had been the head of all these kingdoms"* (Josh 11:10b). In Joshua 11:1-4, Jabin sent word to a number of the other kings. The kingdoms that Jabin had influence over included the Canaanites, Amorites, Hittites, Perizzites, Jebusites and Hivites (Joshua 11:3). Those kings joined together to fight against the Israelites. Jabin apparently had the authority to call all of these kings together and instructed them to fight a large battle against the Israelites.

Notice also the two types of kings that were destroyed in the B – B' level of the previous chiasm. In Joshua 11:12-15, it was the royal cities, whereas in Joshua 11:16-23 it was the cities and countryside areas. The royal cities would represent the kingdoms or powers, and the lesser cities would represent the kings or rulers. Joshua was obedient to destroy both.

Total Destruction of Jabin's Kingdom

Now that we have seen that Jabin king of Hazor was similar to a power, having authority over these various kingdoms, let us look at the chiasm for Joshua 11:1-11:

Level	First presentation	Inversion	Theme
A - A'	Jabin, king of Hazor, calls his kingdom to battle (Josh 11:1-5)	Hazor, as head of the kingdom, is totally destroyed by the sword (Josh 11:10,11)	Hazor's authority and his destruction
B - B'	The Lord instructs Joshua to hamstring their horses and burn their chariots (Josh 11:6)	Joshua hamstrung their horses and burned their chariots (Josh 11:9)	Hamstrung horses, burned chariots
C - C'	Lord delivers the kings and their forces into hand of Israel (Josh 11:7,8a)	No survivors are left (Josh 11:8b)	Kingdoms are defeated

Hopefully we see that the destruction of Hazor and all of the northern kingdoms was accomplished in the same way as the cities were destroyed in earlier chapters. Let us look at the words that have been identified for the destruction of the cities to see how they are applied to the destruction of the royal kingdoms:

- The Lord gave Joshua a plan, which was a **rhema** word given to him (Josh 11:6).
- The Lord delivered (**nātan**) the nations into the hand of Israel (Josh 11:8).
- The sword (**chereb**) was used for the destruction (Josh 11:11).
- They were totally destroyed (**charam**) (Josh 11:11).

Therefore, the method for destroying the powers is similar to the destruction of the rulers.

People might think "That's what we need, a deliverance from the powers over our city." Before we get out our Bibles and our running shoes, consider this: the cities wanted to be liberated.

In Jericho, the walls of the city fell down in worship (see page 112). The city had been inhabited by the king and the people that did not belong in a city that truly worshipped the Lord. The city had spirits that controlled Jericho and had it tied up. The city desired, possibly even craved, to be liberated, but it needed an external force to help liberate it.

The deliverance that is being described with Jabin, king of Hazor, is the process of freeing a church or possibly a set of churches from the strong demonic forces that have been holding it down. Possibly a previous pastor led the congregation improperly, leaving a wrong spirit. Possibly some people had to be removed from the church. Possibly some people had been actively tormenting certain people but are no longer around. Possibly there were some church practices or doctrines that were contrary to the Lord's will. Possibly there were some problems in corporate worship.

Whatever the cause of the powers to come over the church, a repentant heart is necessary for the church as a whole. If the church is not truly repentant, then it would be like going into any city that is full of non-believers. Those evil spirits have every right to be there because they have been invited to stay.

Church-wide participation is essential to removing these principalities and ruling spirits. Otherwise, we have not accomplished **charam** – total destruction. The revivals led by John Wesley, Charles Finney and others were long lasting because the people truly repented.

Hardened Hearts

In Joshua 11:12-23, a summary of the accomplishments is given in the next chiasm. On the A – A' level, the credit is given to the Lord for commanding Moses, and for Moses for commanding Joshua. Then the credit is given to Joshua for being obedient (B – B' level) which led to the Lord's faithfulness in hardening the hearts of the nations (C – C' level).

Level	First presentation	Inversion	Theme
A - A'	Joshua did everything the Lord had commanded through Moses, destroying the royal cities (Josh 11:12-15)	Joshua took the entire land as commanded by the Lord through Moses (Josh 11:23)	Joshua's obedience in what he did
B - B'	Joshua took large areas of Israel, destroying their kings (Josh 11:16-18)	Joshua took the area of the Anakites, killing their kings (Josh 11:21,22)	Joshua totally destroyed and killed their kings
C - C'	Gibeonites made a peace treaty with Israel (Josh 11:19)	The Lord hardened the hearts of all other cities so that they might be destroyed (Josh 11:20)	Contrast between those favorable to the Lord and those who are not

The C – C' level also contrasts Gibeon, whose heart was yielded to the Lord in fear, with all of the other cities where the Lord hardened their hearts. The emphasis is not so much on Gibeon as it is on the other cities: *"For it was the LORD himself who hardened their hearts to wage war against Israel ..."* (Josh 11:20). This is the same Hebrew wording as Exodus 4 - 14, where the Lord hardened Pharaoh's heart to accomplish the Lord's will in releasing the Israelites.

How did the Lord harden their hearts? Let's look at the following:

> *I sent the **hornet** ahead of you, which drove them out before you ...* (Josh 24:12).

In the discussion of the hornet (page 92), the statement was made that the purpose of the hornet was to drive out evil using terror and confusion based on Exodus 23:27,28.

The Bible does not state this directly, but I wonder if the way that the Lord hardened the hearts of the nations was to send the hornet to spread a spirit of fear and terror into their inner most being. If that is the case, then the Lord used the hornet to release the spirits of terror and confusion. For a moment, open your spiritual eyes and look if you can see the hornet goading the spirits of terror and confusion with His stinger.

> **In spiritual warfare, we may not be able to see what the Lord is doing with our natural eyes.**

The Eastern and Western Tribes

In Joshua 12, we see a summary of the kings that were defeated and the land given as an inheritance to their respective tribes:

Level	First presentation	Inversion	Theme
A - A'	Kings Sihon and Og were defeated (Josh 12:1-5)	Thirty one kings are listed that have been defeated (Josh 12:8-24)	Kings east and west of the Jordan are defeated
B - B'	Moses gave the land east of the Jordan to the 2 ½ tribes (Josh 12:6)	Joshua gave the land west of the Jordan to the other tribes of Israel (Josh 12:7,8)	Land east and west of the Jordan is given as an inheritance

The center point of this chiasm emphasizes the equal treatment of the lands east and west of the Jordan. In the Lord's eyes, they were both just as important. This is important as it relates to Joshua 22 where a dispute arose over the eastern territory, as further described on page 183.

The Lord can give one church a small congregation that struggles to make ends meet from week to week. Another church might have a congregation of tens of thousands of people, and be well endowed and be apparently ever-growing. If the Lord has given that smaller church its ministry, it is equally important in the eyes of the Lord. The size, economic status and church growth are not what matters to the Lord. What does matter is how our hearts are towards the Lord.

> **The Lord is not interested in the external; He is interested in our hearts.**

Part Three – The Allotments

Second Outer Tier Chiasm

The whole assembly of the Israelites gathered at Shiloh and set up the Tent of Meeting there (Josh 18:1).

The first outer tier chiasm covered the first half of the Book of Joshua, namely Joshua 1 - 12 (see page 42). It described the activities prior to the invasion of the Promised Land as well as the events of the invasion. The center point of that chiasm was the presence of the Lord Jesus Christ in Jericho, where He judged the destruction of most of the people but saved Rahab and her family.

This second outer tier chiasm covers Joshua 13 - 24. The majority of these chapters are devoted to the allocation of the land to the various tribes. Also in these chapters is the contention by some of the Israelites that the tribes east of the Jordan should not have constructed an altar. The last two chapters record Joshua's farewell address to the Israelites at Shechem.

The spirits of discontent and complacency are near the center point of this outer tier chiasm (F – F' level). They are discussed on pages 177 and 178 respectively. But first, look at Joshua 18:1, which is in the center between the discontent of Manasseh and the complacency of the remaining seven tribes. In that verse, which is shown at the beginning of this chapter, we see that all of Israel gathered around the presence of the Lord. Therefore, the center point of this chiasm emphasizes the whole assembly showing up at the dwelling place of the Lord.

The Lord wants the whole assembly to show up when He appears in His glory.

Level	First presentation	Inversion	Theme
A - A'	The Lord says Joshua is old; the land that has not yet been conquered is identified (Josh 13:1-7)	Joshua says he is old; Israel agrees to serve the Lord so that the remaining land will be conquered (Josh 23:1 - 24:27)	Joshua is old; a commitment to conquer the remaining land is established
B - B'	Land east of the Jordan is defined for the tribes of Reuben, Gad and ½ tribe of Manasseh (Josh 13:8-32)	Land east of the Jordan is affirmed (Josh 22:1-34)	Land east of the Jordan
C - C'	Levites received towns to live in (Josh 13:33 - 14:5)	Towns are allocated to the Levites to live in (Josh 21:1-45)	Levites are given towns to live in
D - D'	Caleb is given Hebron, which is a city of refuge (Josh 14:6-15)	Joshua is given a city, and cities of refuge are designated (Josh 19:49 - 20:9)	Caleb and Joshua are given cities, and cities of refuge
E - E'	Judah, Ephraim and ½ tribe of Manasseh are allotted land (Josh 15:1- 17:18)	Seven tribes are allotted land (Josh 18:11 - 19:48)	All of the tribes west of the Jordan are allotted their land
F - F'	Spirit of discontent is revealed in Manasseh and dealt with (Josh 17:12-18)	Seven tribes show the spirit of complacency, and it is dealt with (Josh 18:2-10)	Two spirits that hold back people from the presence of the Lord
G - G'	The Tent of Meeting was set up at Shiloh with all the Israelites in attendance (Josh 18:1)	No inverted verse	Israelites surround the Tent of Meeting

Chapters 13 to 21 – Allotments of the Land

> *When Joshua was old and well advanced in years, the LORD said to him, "You are very old, and there are still very large areas of land to be taken over"* (Josh 13:1).

Even though thirty-one cities and their kings had been conquered by Joshua's army during their invasion of the land of Canaan (Josh 12:24), the verse above shows that there was much land to be taken. According to Joshua 13:2-5, the two major remaining areas were the lands along the Mediterranean to the west including what is known as Gaza, and the lands to the north which is today in southern Lebanon. In addition, there were individual cities that eluded control by the Israelites, the most notable being Jerusalem (Josh 15:63).

In these chapters, the land east and west of the Jordan was allotted to the various tribes. Joshua 13 focuses on the land east of the Jordan, Joshua 14 - 20 are the allotments of the land west of the Jordan, and then the distribution for the Levites is described in Joshua 21. Unlike other sections of the Book of Joshua, there does not appear to be a middle tier chiasm that covers Joshua 13 - 21.

Admittedly, Joshua 13 - 21 is tedious to most readers, although it is historically important. The fighting to conquer the land was described in detail in Joshua 6 - 12. But now, the emphasis turns to the internal process of taking over the land rather than the external battle. We will briefly cover the land allotments, focusing most of our attention instead on four inner tier chiasms that emphasize the spiritual battle that accompanied these allotments.

Geography: Hebron and Debir

Hebron is twenty miles south of Jerusalem towards the Negev. Abraham lived there for a number of years as did Isaac and Jacob. Near Hebron was a hamlet named Mamre and the cave at Machpelah was located nearby. Jacob spoke these words to his sons regarding the cave at Machpelah:

> *There Abraham and his wife Sarah were buried, there Isaac and his wife Rebekah were buried, and there I buried Leah.* (Gen 49:31)

Jacob was also buried at the cave at Machpelah several years later (Gen 50:13).

To the Jewish people of Israel today, the cave at Machpelah is their second most sacred site because their father Abraham was buried there. The Temple Mount in Jerusalem is their most sacred site. Using Google Earth, the cave at Machpelah can be located at:

31 31.48'N, 35 06.64'E

Somewhere in the last 2,400 years, a temple was built above the cave, allowing the Lord to be worshipped in that temple. The tombs were moved from the cave to the temple. When my wife and I visited Israel in 1999, we went to the temple that is constructed over the cave at Machpelah. Mamre and the cave are now within the city of Hebron.

We saw the tombs of Sarah, Isaac, Rebekah, Leah and Jacob, which are each six feet tall, four feet wide, and covered with a very faded tapestry that may have been gold and crimson in their time. We stood within three or four feet of their tombs. The air in Hebron is very dry so that tapestry on these tombs would have been preserved for many years. We wondered if it was the original tapestry.

Next to the temple is a Muslim mosque which shares the site with the Jews. For this reason, we were not permitted to visit Abraham's tomb. Abraham is also a patriarch of the people of Muslim religion because his son Ishmael is an ancestor of the Islamic people. The mosque had speakers blasting their prayers over the temple. Hebron is within the West Bank, and the Jewish community in Hebron is a distinct minority. At the cave at Machpelah, there is a disturbing contrast of the people who worship the Lord and those who worship Allah.

As we will see, Joshua allocated Hebron to Caleb, and in turn, Caleb conquered Debir. The city of Debir is ten miles southwest of Hebron on the main road between Hebron and Beersheba.

Joshua had attacked and totally destroyed Debir in his earlier southern campaign (Josh 10:38,39). Apparently the city had slipped back into the hands of the Anakites. When Caleb conquered Debir, he must have known that Debir needed the long-term presence of the Israelites.

Caleb's Strength

The first inner tier chiasm within Joshua 13 - 21 is found in Joshua 14. In this simply organized chiasm, we see the flow transitioning from wholehearted service (A – A' level) to the blessings of his inheritance (B – B' level) to Caleb's strength which comes from the Lord (C – C' level). The emphasis is not so much on the inheritance of Hebron as it is on the apparent boasting by Caleb of his strength and vigor. Caleb was now eighty-five years old. Yet Caleb was still practicing the words given to both Moses and Joshua many years earlier: *"Be strong and courageous".*

Level	First presentation	Inversion	Theme
A - A'	Caleb states he has followed the Lord wholeheartedly (Josh 14:8b)	Joshua attests that Caleb has followed the Lord wholeheartedly (Josh 14:14b)	Caleb follows the Lord wholeheartedly
B - B'	Caleb reminds Joshua of Moses' promise of an inheritance (Josh 14:9)	Joshua blesses Caleb with his inheritance at Hebron (Josh 14:13,14a)	Inheritance is promised and fulfilled
C - C'	Even though Caleb is 85 years old, he is ready for battle (Josh 14:10,11)	Caleb knows that the Lord's strength will drive out the Anakites (Josh 14:12)	Caleb is strong but knows his true strength is from the Lord

At the central point of this chiasm, we see the real reason that Caleb can confidently boast about defeating the large and fortified Anakites:

> ... the LORD helping me, I will drive them out just as he said (Josh 14:12).

Caleb's secret to his strength was his faithful obedience to the Lord. He served the Lord wholeheartedly and he was confident in the Lord's help.

> **No matter how large the enemy appears, the Lord is to be our strength in overcoming obstacles.**

A Servant's Heart

Caleb's zeal for the Lord is shown in the next inner tier chiasm which is presented in Joshua 15. Caleb was given just Hebron, but he does more than he was asked to do.

Level	First presentation	Inversion	Theme
A - A'	Joshua gives Hebron to Caleb (Josh 15:13)	Caleb gives spring to his daughter Acsah (Josh 15:19)	Giving land to one another
B - B'	Caleb drives Anakites out of Hebron (Josh 15:14,15)	Othniel drives Anakites out of Debir (Josh 15:16,17)	Enemy is driven out

The Lord was generous to the Israelites in giving them the land. Joshua was generous to Caleb because of his faithfulness and wholehearted service. Caleb in turn was generous to his daughter

Acsah. This spirit of obedience, faithfulness and generosity was passed on to Othniel, Caleb's son-in-law, who became a good judge and leader over Israel (Judg 3:7-11).

Back in Joshua 14:6-12, Caleb spoke to Joshua when he was in Gilgal:

> *Now therefore, give me this mountain of which the LORD spoke in that day ...* (Josh 14:12 NKJV).

When Caleb made this request at Gilgal near the Jordan, he would have been looking at a ridge of mountains directly to the west. Depending on which part of the mountain range he was looking at, this land was eventually allocated to the tribe of Benjamin, Manasseh or Ephraim.

Joshua gave Caleb the land of Hebron which was many miles to the southwest. The vicinity of Hebron is not mountainous, being more akin to gently rolling hills. Clearly Joshua did not honor Caleb's request.

When Joshua made his allotments, the first piece of land was given to Caleb. Joshua could have given Caleb, his accomplice, any land that he wanted. But instead, Caleb was given Hebron which is a more arid land south of Jerusalem. Hebron is on a road from Jerusalem that heads towards the Negev and Kadesh Barnea, which are parts of the desert.

Why didn't Joshua give Caleb better land? It was because he knew that Caleb could be trusted to take the land of Hebron, where the patriarchs were buried. Joshua understood that the burial places of Abraham, Isaac, Jacob and wives would be important to future generations. Joshua knew that Caleb had the responsibility to adequately capture and protect this holy location.

The other tribes had difficulty conquering all of their land: Judah did not conquer Jerusalem (Josh 15:63); Ephraim was not able to dislodge the people of Gezer (Josh 16:10); Manasseh was not able to occupy a number of towns in their territory (Josh 17:11,12), etc. But Caleb not only completely conquered the land he was given, but he took on additional responsibilities in conquering Debir. That is the central point of this chiasm: Caleb did what he was told to do and then even more.

Caleb was not a leader; Joshua was. Caleb was not filled with a spirit of wisdom; that was given to Joshua. What Caleb did have was zeal and passion, and he served the Lord wholeheartedly.

> **The Lord is looking for consistent, faithful servants who will do their part wholeheartedly in spiritual warfare.**

The Full Inheritance

Alan Redpath, in his book entitled *Victorious Christian Living*, observed that the word "lot" was used twenty-two times between Joshua 13 and 21. [45] The Hebrew word for "lot", **gowral** (go-rawl'), is actually repeated twenty-six times, but it makes little difference. [46] Each tribe was given their "lot" or "allotment" such as *"The **allotment** for the tribe of Judah ..."* (Josh 15:1) or *"The **allotment** for Joseph ..."* (Josh 16:1).

Redpath's point is that the Israelites, like many Christians today, did not fully walk in the allotment that they were given. For whatever reason, they did not take certain cities even though the Lord designated these cities as theirs. In speaking to born again believers in Jesus Christ, Redpath encourages us to reach toward the full potential that we have been given.

For some, this means complete surrender and dedication to our Lord Jesus Christ. For others, it may mean stepping into the full anointing that is available through the Holy Spirit. For still others, it may mean giving up certain lifestyle choices.

> We should each step into the full anointing that is available through the Holy Spirit.

Geography: Shiloh and the Territory of Joseph

According to the *Atlas of the Bible,* ancient Shiloh is located eight miles north of Bethel and ten miles south of Shechem. [47] My wife and I arrived at Tel Shiloh at dusk in 1999; it was too late to tour more than the parking lot. Shiloh can be located in Google Earth by typing the following:

32 03.38'N, 35 17.375'E

Located in the territory of Ephraim, Shiloh is at the approximate center of the populated areas of Israel. As the eagle flies, the Mediterranean Sea is thirty-five miles to the west, and the eastern edge of the tribe of Gad is the same distance to the east. Beersheba is near the Negev approximately sixty miles to the south, and Kedesh in Galilee is sixty miles to the north.

The Tent of Meeting, which housed the ark of the Lord, was set up in Shiloh (Josh 18:1); it probably had been set up at Gilgal prior to this

---

[45] Redpath, 186.
[46] Englishman's Search on Strong's Number 1486, *PC Study Bible*
[47] Rogerson, 148, 152.

verse. The Tent of Meeting remained in Shiloh for nearly 400 years through the period of the Judges. Hannah, the mother of Samuel, prayed for a son at Shiloh (1 Sam 1:9-11). Later, after her son was weaned, she took her son Samuel to Shiloh to be brought up in the house of the Lord (1 Sam 1:24). Samuel received his calling from the Lord at the temple in Shiloh where the ark of the covenant was located (1 Sam 3:3).

North of Shiloh, the mountains become more pronounced. For example, Mount Ebal and Mount Gerizim are in that vicinity. The tribes of Joseph (Ephraim and Manasseh) were given that territory as part of their allotment. The northern portion of this mountainous region was the forested area where the Perizzites lived.

At the northeast corner of this mountain range is Mount Gilboa, and Mount Carmel is at the northwest corner of the range. In the middle between these two mountains, iron quarries are to be found.

Beyond this mountainous territory is the Jezreel Valley which is very fertile land. This valley extends from the plains near the northern part of the Jordan River to the Mediterranean.

Spirit of Discontentedness

The following chiasm from Joshua 17 illustrates the spirit of discontentedness:

Level	First presentation	Inversion	Theme
A - A'	Israelites have grown strong but did not completely drive out the Canaanites (Josh 17:13)	Canaanites are strong, yet Ephraim and Manasseh can drive them out (Josh 17:18b)	Perception of strength, driving out the Canaanites
B - B'	The two tribes ask for more than one lot and one portion because they are numerous; Joshua says to cut wood in forested land of the Perizzites and Rephaites (Josh 17:14,15)	Ephraim and Manasseh are numerous so they will not have only one lot; their portion is a forested land (Josh 17:17,18a)	Children of Joseph are numerous, want more territory, and are to cut wood in their forested mountain region
C - C'	Children of Joseph ask for more than the forested mountain region (Josh 17:16a)	Children of Joseph have fear of the iron chariots in the plains below the mountain region (Josh 17:16b)	Discontent with the mountain region is motivated by fear of the plains people

The spirit of discontentment had been around for a long time prior to the invasion of the Promised Land. It had haunted the Israelites for the forty years that they wandered in the desert. Even before that, it showed its ugly head in the Garden of Eden (Gen 3:6).

Ephraim and Manasseh, the two sons of Joseph, had little to be discontented about. Back in Genesis 49, Jacob blessed each of his twelve sons to become a tribe with the exception of Joseph, who became two tribes: Ephraim and Manasseh. In this way, Joseph received a double blessing from his father Jacob.

On the B – B' level, we see the two tribes asking for more territory with the excuse that there are too many of them. Joshua knew better; he did not change the allotment that had been granted. Instead, Joshua gave them the challenge to move into the forested mountain regions where the Perizzites and Rephaites live. As mentioned on page 176, the Perizzites inhabited the forested portion of their western territory. The Rephaites lived in the mountainous area east of the Jordan that had been allotted to the other half of the tribe of Manasseh.

West of the Jordan		East of the Jordan	
Judah	76,500		
Dan	64,400		
Issachar	64,300		
Zebulun	60,500		
Ephraim + half of Manasseh	**58,850**		
Asher	53,400		
Benjamin	45,600		
Naphtali	45,400		
		Reuben	43,730
		Gad	40,500
		Half of Manasseh	26,350
Simeon	22,200		

The chart shown above, based on the census in Numbers 26, illustrates how Joshua knew that Ephraim and the half tribe of Manasseh were not as numerous as they contended. Just before the invasion of the Promised Land, the second census was taken which was presented in Numbers 26. The combined total between Ephraim and the other half tribe of Manasseh would have been 58,850 men (32,500 from Ephraim + 26,350 from half of Manasseh). Yet four other tribes (Judah, Dan, Issachar and Zebulun) had more men. Therefore, one would have to question why these people of Joseph asked Joshua:

> ... why have you given us only one allotment and one portion for an inheritance? We are a **numerous** people and the LORD has blessed us abundantly (Josh 17:14).

These other four tribes were more numerous than the houses of Joseph.

In the years after Solomon, Ephraim and Manasseh lead the northern kingdom to split from the southern kingdom and follow false gods. Eventually, they were conquered by the Assyrians because they were spiritually weak. They had become discontented with the one true God.

Joshua, when asked for a larger inheritance by Ephraim and Manasseh, used the spirit of wisdom that the Lord gave him to deal with their complaint. Paraphrasing Joshua 17:15, Joshua said:

"Go chop wood."

Joshua did not grant them additional territory, but instructed them to clear land within their own territories.

The Gibeonites, you may recall, were given the responsibility to chop wood for the temple and they were pleased to do so (Josh 9:23,24). For the two tribes of Joseph, Joshua was saying, in essence, "you are behaving like foreigners. Have a servant's heart: go chop wood."

On the C – C' level, discontent became a secondary issue to a greater concern: the Canaanites in the Jezreel Valley and the vicinity of Beth Shan were identified with having chariots with iron wheels. The true motive was fear of man's weapons rather than the weapons of the Lord. They lost their trust in the power of the Lord.

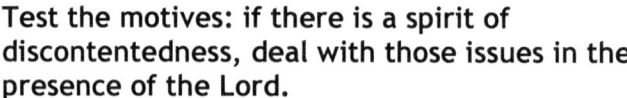

Test the motives: if there is a spirit of discontentedness, deal with those issues in the presence of the Lord.

Spirit of Complacency

Just as the spirit of discontentment haunted the tribes of Joseph, the spirit of complacency had immobilized the seven remaining tribes: Benjamin, Simeon, Zebulun, Issachar, Asher, Naphtali and Dan. Joshua had to ask these seven tribes:

> *How long will you wait before you begin to take possession of the land that the* LORD, *the God of your fathers, has given you?* (Josh 18:3).

These seven tribes consisted of nearly 60% of the people of Israel, based on Numbers 26. Yet Joshua had to shake them out of their self-satisfaction by having them survey the land.

Joshua's method of shaking them out of complacency was presented in a beautifully constructed double chiasm:

Chapters 13 to 21 – Allotments of the Land

Chiasm	Verses	A - A' level	C - C' level
First	Josh 18:4-8a	Seven part division	Presence of the Lord
Second	Josh 18:8b-10a	Presence of the Lord	Seven part division

If these verses were not divinely inspired, I can't imagine how many hours it would have taken to write this double chiasm.

For the first chiasm, on the A – A' level, the land was to be divided into seven parts; on the C – C' level, lots were being cast in the presence of the Lord. The first chiasm is:

Level	First presentation	Inversion	Theme
A - A'	Have seven tribes survey the land in seven parts and return to Joshua (Josh 18:4,5a)	Go make a survey of the land and return it to Joshua (Josh 18:8a)	Survey land in seven parts and return it to Joshua
B - B'	Judah and house of Joseph are already allotted (Josh 18:5b)	Levites didn't get any; Gad, Reuben and half-tribe of Manasseh are allotted (Josh 18:7)	Tribes that do not get allotments
C - C'	After conducting the survey, cast lots in the presence of the Lord (Josh 18:6)	No inverted verse	Cast lots in the presence of the Lord

For the second chiasm, on the A – A' level, lots were being cast; on the C – C' level, the land was divided into seven parts. The second chiasm that immediately follows is:

Level	First presentation	Inversion	Theme
A - A'	Lots will be cast in the presence of the Lord (Josh 18:8b)	Joshua cast lots in the presence of the Lord (Josh 18:10a)	Cast lots in the presence of the Lord
B - B'	Men went throughout the land (Josh 18:9a)	Men returned to Joshua (Josh 18:9c)	Men left and returned
C - C'	Description is prepared in seven parts (Josh 18:9b)	No inverted verse	A seven part description of boundaries

What is the application of this double chiasm? The seven part division of the land, which would shake up the spirit of complacency, was to be done in the presence of the Lord.

Test the motives: if there is a spirit of complacency, allow the presence of the Lord to help deal with those issues.

Chapter 22 – An Altar to Remember Us By

> *No! We did it for fear that some day your descendants might say to ours, "What do you have to do with the LORD, the God of Israel? The LORD has made the Jordan a boundary between us and you – you Reubenites and Gadites! You have no share in the LORD." So your descendants might cause ours to stop fearing the LORD* (Josh 22:24,25).

One of the controversial portions of the Book of Joshua is the true meaning of Joshua 22: were the Israelites correct in condemning the construction of the altar at the Jordan, or were those Eastern tribes correct in building that altar? I suspect that most people lean towards the idea that the Eastern tribes should not have built that altar. That was what I believed until I read a review of the chiasms of Joshua 22 by Ellie Assis. [48] Although Assis does not discuss spiritual warfare, hopefully you will see that these Eastern tribes had good reason to build this altar.

How easy it is to misinterpret the motives of another person. Something can happen in such circumstances where our imagination takes over, bitterness sets in, and pretty soon the devil has scored another victory. It is surprising how quickly these events can spread and catch on fire.

The misinterpretation happened this way:

> *When the Israelites heard that they had built the altar on the border of Canaan at Geliloth near the Jordan on the Israelite side, the whole assembly of Israel gathered at Shiloh to go to war against them* (Josh 22:11,12).

The story of Joshua 22 details another aspect of spiritual warfare: the spirits of pride and deception. Satan, the great deceiver, helped the Israelites change a misunderstanding into preparation for war. The remainder of this story focuses on the de-escalation of the confrontation by taking a strong stand for the Lord.

The land east of the Jordan was given by Moses to the tribes of Reuben, Gad and the half tribe of Manasseh. Theologians refer to those people as the "Transjordanian tribes." Some theologians refer to those on the western side of the Jordan as the "Cisjordanian tribes." For

---

[48] Ellie Assis, *For It Shall Be A Witness Between Us: A Literary Reading of Josh 22*, Scandinavian Journal of the Old Testament, Vol. 18, No. 2 (2004), 208-231.

simplicity, I have chosen to refer to them as the Eastern tribes and the Western tribes. That is, the two and one-half tribes allotted by Moses are the Eastern tribes, and the nine and one-half tribes allotted by Joshua are the Western tribes.

Structure of Chapter 22

In the first half of the Book of Joshua (chapters 1 - 12), there were nine middle tier chiasms with each middle tier chiasm typically extending over one or two chapters. In the second half of the Book of Joshua (chapters 13 - 24), there is no middle tier chiasm (or at least none that I have been able to discern) for chapters 13 - 21. The middle tier chiasms reappear starting in Joshua 22:1. The first of these is shown below, and the second which covers the remainder of the Book of Joshua is discussed in the next chapter.

Level	First presentation	Inversion	Theme
A - A'	Joshua sends the Eastern tribes home to receive their rest (Josh 22:1-9)	The Lord gives rest to all of Israel (Josh 23:1)	Rest is given to all of the people
B - B'	Eastern tribes build an altar which offends the Western tribes (Josh 22:10-12)	Western tribes are relieved of their offense by Phinehas (Josh 22:30-34)	Offense is taken and is resolved
C - C'	Western tribes accuse Eastern tribes of being rebels (Josh 22:13-20)	Eastern tribes refute that they would never rebel (Josh 22:29)	Rebellion is accused and denied
D - D'	Eastern tribes call for Lord to judge them if it is a rebellion (Josh 22:21-23)	Eastern tribes testify that they want a share of the Lord (Josh 22:27b,28)	Eastern tribes express fear of the Lord and desire to hold fast to the Lord
E - E'	Eastern tribes explain they do not want to be forgotten (Josh 22:24,25)	Eastern tribes will worship Lord at same place as Western tribes (Josh 22:26,27a)	Eastern tribes will not be severed from Western tribes

On the A – A' level, we see the Eastern tribes attaining the rest that Moses had promised in Deuteronomy 3:20. Joshua had reiterated that promise in Joshua 1:14,15. In the same way, "... *the LORD had given Israel rest from all their enemies around them ...*" (Josh 23:1).

As Christians, it is very easy to fall into Satan's trap of judging one another: "Shame on Brother Tom for doing such-and-such." In the same way, the B – B' level reveals a similar accusation. The Western tribes pass judgment on the Eastern tribes for their actions. They become self-appointed instruments to punish the Eastern tribes; presumably they were thinking that they were carrying out God's will. The accusation is that they have built an altar as an alternative to the one built at the temple for the purpose of sacrificing to the Lord. At the end of this story, Phinehas has absolved those Eastern tribes of this accusation.

The C – C' level focuses on rebellion as the likely cause of their actions. The Eastern tribes politely but firmly state that rebellion had no part in their decision to build an altar.

The Eastern tribes begin the heart of their response in Joshua 22:21-28, which is the D – D' and E – E' levels. It becomes apparent from their response that the Western tribes had completely misinterpreted the construction of this altar. More on these D – D' and E – E' levels later because they are the center point of this chapter.

Geography: The Land East of the Jordan (Part III)

A question can be asked for today's times: Is the land east of the Jordan River, which is the land given to the Eastern tribes, part of Israel? There is a tension in the Bible itself over that very question. For example, ponder this thought: Moses was not allowed to enter the Promised Land and therefore died in the territory given to the tribe of Reuben. Was the territory of Reuben within Israel, or was it outside?

The Lord permitted Moses to climb Mount Nebo to "... *view Canaan, the land I am giving the Israelites as their own possession*" (Deut 32:49). Through Moses, the Lord had given the land east of the Jordan to the Eastern tribes (Deut 3:12-20), and through Joshua the Lord gave the land west of the Jordan to the Western tribes (Joshua 14 - 21).

If you have access to colored maps of the land of Israel such as that which is often found in the back of Bibles, see if you have a map that shows the territories of the twelve tribes. Within the territory of Reuben, you should be able to find Mount Nebo. Hopefully you can see that Moses was permitted to die in this territory of Reuben.

Today, the territory of these Eastern tribes is not within the country of Israel with the exception of a barren area east of the Sea of Galilee known as the Golan Heights. The remainder of this territory is today within the country of Jordan.

Another example of this tension in the Bible can be seen with how the term *"Israelites"* is used in Joshua 22. Surprisingly, *"Israelites"* is referring to just the Western tribes: *"And when the **Israelites** heard that they had built the altar ... on the **Israelites** side ..."* (Josh 22:11). The KJV uses the term *"children of Israel"* which could imply that Gad and Reuben were not children of Israel; that is certainly not true.

This tension over the territory east of the Jordan is the focus of Joshua 22. For the Eastern tribes, they fought with their fellow Israelites to conquer the land. They were all sons of Jacob and all were part of the same heritage. The Lord had given each tribe their land. Yet for those that settled west of the Jordan River, there was a spirit of arrogance because their territory was "the Promised Land", whereas the territory east of the Jordan was where Moses was punished and died. Therefore, much of Joshua 22 is about a spirit of pride.

Commandments of the Deuteronomic Covenant are Repeated

The organization of Joshua 22:1-9 is a very good example of the chiastic approach, where the themes of each level are distinctly different from each other:

Level	First presentation	Inversion	Theme
A - A'	Eastern tribes have obeyed the commands of Moses (Josh 22:1-3)	Eastern tribes are to return as commanded by the Lord through Moses (Josh 22:9)	Eastern tribes have their promise fulfilled
B - B'	Joshua instructs the Eastern tribes to return to their land (Josh 22:4)	Joshua sends away the Eastern tribes to return with their plunder (Josh 22:6-8)	Joshua allows the Eastern tribes to return
C - C'	Joshua urges the Eastern tribes to: • Love the Lord your God • Walk in all His ways • Obey His commands • Cling to the Lord • Serve the Lord (Josh 22:5)	No inverted verse	Deuteronomic covenant commandments

At the center point of this chiasm, five of the seven commands of the Deuteronomic covenant are repeated and emphasized. Notice the order of presentation in Joshua 22:5. The center command is instructing us to be obedient. But notice also that the first command (love the Lord) is associated in a chiastic way with the last command (serve the Lord). This pairing of loving the Lord and serving the Lord becomes a major point of emphasis in Joshua 23 – 24, which we will see in the next chapter. Moses exhibited the command to listen to the Lord on the A – A' level.

Chapter 22 – An Altar to Remember Us By

A Spirit of Arrogance

The next inner tier chiasm begins and ends with the construction of the altar:

Level	First presentation	Inversion	Theme
A - A'	The Eastern tribes innocently build an extremely large altar (Josh 22:10)	The Western tribes state how they are offended by the altar (Josh 22:15,16)	Opposing views of innocence and offense
B - B'	Western tribes escalate the misunderstanding by gathering to go to war (Josh 22:10-12)	Ten men gather to approach the Eastern tribes in preparation for war (Josh 22:13,14)	Rapid escalation from misunderstanding to bitterness

The A – A' level of this chiasm presents two alternate views of this situation. The Eastern tribes, in their zeal, innocently build an altar, while the remaining tribes, in their zeal, confront the altar builders.

The altar was built at Geliloth near the Jordan River on the western side of the Jordan (Josh 22:11). Joshua 18:17 identifies Geliloth as a city facing the Pass of Adummim; the main road from Jerusalem to Jericho is constructed in the Pass of Adummim. Gilgal was between Jericho and the Jordan River, so possibly Geliloth was the same as Gilgal.

The memorial stones had been placed at Gilgal by Joshua after crossing the Jordan. Possibly the Eastern tribes chose the site where the twelve memorial stones were constructed (Josh 4:1-24). If they had, this new altar might also have been an altar of remembrance.

The altar that was associated with the Tent of Meeting was not the only altar in the Book of Joshua. After Achan's sin was exposed and they marched to Shechem to renew their vows, they set up at Mount Ebal *"an altar to the LORD"* (Josh 8:30), as Moses had commanded (Deut 27:4-6). At that altar, fellowship offerings were sacrificed, but it was not associated with the Tent of Meeting. To the Eastern tribes, the construction of that altar must have seemed like a natural thing to do.

The B – B' level reveals how a spirit of pride and arrogance leads to deception and religious zeal. The spirit of pride, which is an ailment of many in our modern times, can deceive us into thinking that we are within the will of the Lord when in fact we have completely missed His will. Arrogance puts us in that place of superiority, which the devil can turn into religiosity, and this is what happened to the Israelites.

In the following two dialogs from the historian Josephus, notice how Joshua's attitude is contrasted to those who were ready for war. The scenario is the ceremony where the Western tribes release the Eastern tribes. After thanking them for their hard work and recognizing that they may be called on again, Joshua stated:

> We therefore dismiss you joyful to your own inheritances; and we entreat you to suppose, that there is no limit to be set to the intimate relation that is between us; and that you will not imagine, because this river is interposed between us, that you are of a different race from us, and not Hebrews; **for we are all the posterity of Abraham, both we that inhabit here, and you that inhabit there**; and it is the same God that brought our forefathers and yours into the world, whose worship and form of government we are to take care of, which he has ordained, and are most carefully to observe; because while you continue in those laws, God will also show himself merciful and assisting to you; but if you imitate the other nations, and forsake those laws, he will reject your nation. [49]

Joshua recognized that the tribes were one, but that sentiment was not shared by all. Josephus records this reaction by an emotional, war hungry crowd:

> But when those on the other side heard that those who had been dismissed had built an altar, but did not hear with what intention they built it, but supposed it to be by way of innovation, and for the introduction of strange gods, they did not incline to disbelieve it; but **thinking** this defamatory report, as if it were built for divine worship, was credible, they appeared in arms, as though they would avenge themselves on those that built the altar; and they were about to pass over the river, and to punish them for their subversion of the laws of their country; for they did not think it fit to regard them on account of their kindred or the dignity of those that had given the occasion, but to regard the will of God, and the manner wherein he desired to be worshipped; so these men put themselves in array for war. **But Joshua, and Eleazar the high priest, and the senate, restrained them**; and persuaded them first to make trial by words of their intention, and afterwards, if

---

[49] Josephus, 5.1.25.

they found that their intention was evil, then only to proceed to make war upon them. [50]

The hotheads were ready for war, but Joshua, Eleazar and the others gave them wise counsel: go investigate first. Thankfully, Joshua had the presence of the Lord to know how to deal with these issues. Once again, we see in Joshua the spirit of wisdom that had been poured into him from the Lord.

> If we see a sudden change of attitude, suspect that the devil may be using a spirit of arrogance or pride to pull us down: gather the facts first.

Spirit of Obsession

We have seen several evil spirits rise up their ugly heads so far: fear, complaining, lust, discontent, complacency, and most recently pride or arrogance. In this next inner tier chiasm, we are taken back to the Book of Numbers to see a spirit of obsession.

Sin is sin, and to place the blame for an action on a demonic spirit is a huge mistake. We each have a choice in either allowing the adversity to have its way, or to allow God's will to have its way.

Level	First presentation	Inversion	Theme
A - A'	Sin of Peor (obsession) continues to plague the people (Josh 22:17,18a)	Sin of Achan (lust) caused others to die (Josh 22:20)	Two sins are contrasted: obsession and lust
B - B'	Rebellion leads to the Lord's anger (Josh 22:18b)	Building an altar is associated with rebellion (Josh 22:19)	Western tribes assume the altar was a form of rebellion

That being said, note how the A – A' level reveals a comparison between the sin of Peor and the sin of Achan. At Peor, the men first started indulging in sexual immorality which led them to sacrifice to false gods (Num 25:1-3). As we read about the sin of Peor in Joshua 22:17, the Israelites are confessing that this sin has continued for nearly forty years:

---

[50] Josephus, 5.1.26.

> *Up to this very day we have not cleansed ourselves from that sin ...* (Josh 22:17).

In other words, that first indulgence had become an obsession.

By comparing the sin of Peor with the sin of Achan on the A – A' level, the Lord is warning us of how obsessions cause us to loose our relationship with the Lord. At Ai, Achan's sin not only led to the defeat of the Israelites, but the presence of the Lord left them.

Whether the obsession is sexual immorality, alcohol, substance abuse, gambling, compulsive buying, soap operas, etc., the Lord is saying that this obsessive behavior is as repulsive to Him as lust, which He dealt with by stoning the instigators.

> **Obsessive and compulsive behaviors can cause us to loose our relationship with the Lord.**

Spirit of Self-Righteousness

In the last chiasm, the emphasis in the B – B' level was rebellion. The Western tribes suggested that constructing the altar was a form of rebellion. In this way, they were then inferring that building the altar opens the opportunity for the Lord to show His wrath on either side of the Jordan.

Phinehas and his ten cohorts were correct in stating that rebellion led to the Lord's anger. The problem with their logic was that they had already decided that they were to be the ones who would execute the Lord's wrath. Joshua had instructed them to go find the truth before acting too hastily, but they had assumed that they were right and the Eastern tribes were wrong. They accused them of rebellion.

The proper way to have conducted an investigation would have been to ask, without accusation, for an explanation. Instead, I can imagine Phinehas or one of the others would put his hands to his hips and point his fingers at the eastern tribes with an accusing voice: *"How could you break faith with the God of Israel like this? How could you ..."* (Josh 22:16). Does the self-righteous attitude come through? They had become the judge without listening to the facts or the Lord.

It is a dangerous situation to put oneself in, thinking that doing God's will includes doing God's wrath. We are not God. This is the problem with pride: if we take on the appearance of God, we can become a false god, and demons can flock to that false god.

Some people refer to righteous anger as a means of justifying their actions. They may refer to Jesus with the money changers at the temple. Some use the quote: *"In your anger do not sin"* (Eph 4:26). Should we be upset with spiritual complacency, abortion, deceit, etc.? Yes, but how we respond is crucial.

> **The problem with self-righteousness is that it causes us to assume a God-like importance.**

A Spirit of Integrity

At the end of the seven years of conquering the land, the Eastern tribes were identified by Joshua as having been an obedient people. Joshua stated: *"You have done all that Moses the servant of the LORD commanded, and you have obeyed me in everything I commanded"* (Josh 22:2). Their obedience allowed them to be released to return to their own land.

In addition, their integrity is revealed in the next inner tier chiasm, which begins the response to the allegations. Truth has a way of revealing itself. The A – A' level of this chiasm assures the Israelites that this is not rebellion. The Eastern tribes invite God's wrath by allowing the Lord's wrath to come upon them if it is rebellion.

Level	First presentation	Inversion	Theme
A - A'	The Lord knows the truth: if this is rebellion, let His wrath be upon us (Josh 22:21-23)	This is not rebellion; we are following the Lord (Josh 22:29a)	Denial of rebellion as a motive
B - B'	Altar is built so your descendents would not say we had no share in the Lord; it is to be a witness between us and you (Josh 22:24-27a)	If they say we have no share in the Lord, we can say to you and your descendents that it is a witness between us and you (Josh 22:27b,28)	Descendents should not say "we have no share in the Lord"; it is a witness between us and you

History showed that they were able to defeat their foes. The territory given to these tribes remained in their hands for many years: *"... God handed the Hagrites and all their allies over to them [the Eastern tribes], because they cried out to him during the battle. He answered their prayers, because they trusted in him"* (1 Chron 5:20). In time, the Eastern tribes fell into the ways of the world, but so did the rest of Israel.

The truth of their response is also shown in the B – B' level. The story that is given in the B verses is the same as the story in the B' verses. This is the way of the chiasms; the stories could have been antithetical (that is, opposites) but they said the same thing instead.

Consistency of the story is a way of identifying truth both in the ancient days and today. When a policeman talks with a suspect, he looks for inconsistencies in his or her story. If, upon repetition, the alibi is different, then the policeman suspects deception is masking the person's involvement in the crime. On the other hand, if there is consistency each time the alibi is repeated, then the suspect is released. The same was true with the Eastern tribes: their truthfulness confirmed their fear that Israel would forget them, which explains why they built a replica of the Lord's altar – it was to be a witness (memorial) between the two sides of the Jordan.

> **Truthfulness can often be revealed when a person's story is consistent and he or she shows a willingness to accept the Lord's consequences.**

A Spirit of Deceit

Phinehas the priest and the other leaders avoided the anger of God by correctly discerning the motive of the Eastern tribes. Let us gather some background regarding Phinehas.

Phinehas was a zealous priest, having avoided the wrath of the Lord before they first crossed the Jordan. When the Moabite women had seduced the Israelite men in Numbers 25, the Lord brought a plague upon the people. Phinehas took a spear and killed a man and woman who were about to commit sexual immorality. The Lord saw Phinehas' action and His anger towards the Israelites went away. The Lord said:

> ... for he was as zealous as I am for my honor among them, so that in my zeal I did not put an end to them (Num 25:11).

In the alleged rebellion by the Eastern tribes, Phinehas again turns away the Lord's anger. He came to understand that the altar that is associated with the tabernacle is not similar to the altar that was built next to the Jordan River. The altar for the tabernacle was intended for regular devotions and sacrifices to the Lord. The altar at the Jordan was intended to be a reminder and was not for daily sacrifices:

Chapter 22 – An Altar to Remember Us By

Level	First presentation	Inversion	Theme
A - A'	The altar at the tabernacle is intended for burnt offerings, grain offerings and sacrifices for the Lord (Josh 22:29b)	The altar at the Jordan is intended as a witness between us that the Lord is God (Josh 22:34)	Contrasting purposes of the two altars
B - B'	Phinehas and other leaders are pleased with the response of the Eastern tribes (Josh 22:30)	Children of Israel are pleased with what Phinehas and leaders said and stopped talking about war (Josh 22:32,33)	Everybody's pleased
C - C'	Phinehas understands that the Lord is among both the Eastern and Western tribes (Josh 22:31a)	Phinehas understands that the Lord's anger has been avoided (Josh 22:31b)	Phinehas states an understanding that they had been deceived and Lord's anger has been appeased

At the center point of this chiasm (C – C' level), we see how Phinehas came to a new understanding about the motives of the Eastern tribes. They had originally been deceived into believing the altar was constructed out of rebellion. But the spirit of truth had intervened to let him see the error of their ways.

Josephus recorded Phinehas' statement, implying their innocence: "*for we are all the posterity of Abraham, both we that inhabit here, and you that inhabit there.*" [51] That is, the Lord is among the tribes on both sides of the Jordan.

As stated on page 185, it was the spirit of arrogance or pride that had allowed the Western tribes to be deceived. Arrogance led them to believe that the Eastern tribes were inferior to the Western tribes because they had not settled in the Promised Land. So when Phinehas announced that the Eastern tribes "*... have not acted unfaithfully toward the LORD ...*"(Josh 22:31), he was renouncing his prideful error. He gives credit to the integrity of the Eastern tribes and the spirit of truth that was over them.

Phinehas concludes his dialog to the Eastern tribes: "*Now you have rescued the Israelites from the LORD's hand*"(Josh 22:31b). He understands that if Western tribes had warred against the Eastern tribes, it would have exposed them to the Lord's anger and wrath.

---

[51] Josephus, 5.1.25.

Good leaders often become good leaders because of lifetime experiences such as this. Aaron had the golden calf, Eleazar had the unauthorized fire by two of his brothers, and now Phinehas had the lessons of the altar at the Jordan.

Perhaps the most important lesson from this chiasm is the proclamation that Phinehas made. In the sense of spiritual warfare, Phinehas denounced the error of their ways and lifted up the actions of the accused. It takes a great man to admit that he was wrong, but the admission can promote the restoration of his relationship with the Lord.

It is often suggested that we must take authority over the evil spirits in the name of Jesus Christ. However, in the case of Phinehas, his proclamation of the truth and his denunciation of the deception accomplished the same purpose.

> **When a person acknowledges he or she was wrong and publicly proclaims the truth, demonic spirits are defeated.**

Communication

The problem that the Western tribe experienced was not rebellion against the Lord. The problem was that the Eastern tribe didn't send an Email to Joshua about their intentions. Seriously, there was no communication back to the Western tribes telling them what they were about to do. After all, they didn't build the altar on their own property: it was on the west side of the Jordan:

> *When they came to Geliloth near the Jordan in the **land of Canaan**, the Reubenites, the Gadites and the half-tribe of Manasseh built an imposing altar there by the Jordan* (Josh 22:10).

Even a voice message left on their answering service might have avoided this communication problem. If we discuss with people what we are about to do, the element of surprise is averted.

> **Simple communication avoids many problems that otherwise might turn into spiritual warfare.**

Chapters 23 and 24 – Love the Lord, Serving Him Faithfully

> ... *choose for yourselves this day whom you will serve ...*
> (Josh 24:15).

I hope you have enjoyed this chiastic look through the Book of Joshua. The chiastic approach has changed the way I approach Scriptures; now I look for and try to understand the Lord's greater purpose in dealing with spiritual warfare. I may have erred on some analyses, and you my readers are free to point that out. I also may have missed some chiasms as they seem to abound throughout Joshua. But in the end, I trust that this book has opened a new and fresh understanding for reading and presenting the gospels.

Christianity is a choice, not a requirement. Some people never make that choice and they are to be pitied. Others make a choice for the Lord but do nothing or very little with their choice; they too are to be pitied.

The Lord wants to take us from salvation to sanctification. That is, He wants a "sold out, on fire" generation; individuals who walk in the fullness of the Lord and the Holy Spirit. **He wants salt, not saline solution.**

In this chapter, Joshua 23 and 24 are combined to coincide with the last middle tier chiasm. By combining these two chapters, we can see the relationship between the Lord's love for us and our love for Him; and between the Lord's service for us and our serving Him.

After we look at this last middle tier chiasm, we will analyze two rather simply formed inner tier chiasms. At the end of this chapter, we will see three chiasms that are interwoven amongst themselves in a very unique structure.

Structure of Chapters 23 and 24

The middle tier chiasm for Joshua 23 and 24 focuses on the choice to serve or not to serve the Lord. Service, when properly understood, should be based on the covenant relationship between ourselves and the Lord.

As the Joshua generation is drawing to a close (A – A' level), there is the concern that their heart for the Lord must last. The Lord uses covenants to ensure faithfulness (B – B' level). The C – C' level describes the punishment if the commands are not kept, and the D – D' level reviews a number of blessings that the Lord has provided.

Level	First presentation	Inversion	Theme
A - A'	Joshua is old (Josh 23:2)	Joshua dies, Joseph's bones are buried and Eleazar dies (Josh 24:29-33)	The end of an era
B - B'	Deuteronomic covenant commandments are repeated (Josh 23:3-11)	Covenant is confirmed between Joshua and the people (Josh 24:21-28)	Covenant is stated and confirmed
C - C'	Punishment for disobedience (Josh 23:12-16)	Punishment for disobedience (Josh 24:19,20)	Punishment for disobedience
D - D'	Blessings: Abraham to Joshua (Josh 24:1-13)	Egyptian to Amorite blessings (Josh 24:17,18)	History of blessings to the Jewish nation
E - E'	Fear the Lord and serve Him (Josh 24:14,15)	We will not give up the Lord and serve other Gods (Josh 24:16)	Fear the Lord and serve Him

The central point of this chiasm is summarized by Joshua in these often repeated verses:

> *But as for me and my household, we will serve the LORD* (Josh 24:15).

These words have hung on the garage door of our house for years. Possibly you have a similar display of these verses somewhere in your home. Hopefully, by the time you have finished this chapter, you will come to a deeper understanding of these verses.

> **Service to the Lord is far more than doing things for a church or for one another; service should be the outflow from a heart that has turned wholeheartedly to the Lord.**

Deuteronomic Covenant Commands: Once Again

The emphasis on the requirements of the Deuteronomic covenant is again repeated in this inner tier chiasm from Joshua 23:

Level	First presentation	Inversion	Theme
A - A'	The Lord is fighting for you (Josh 23:3,4)	The Lord will fight for you (Josh 23:10)	The Lord fights for us
B - B'	The Lord will drive out the nations (Josh 23:5)	The Lord has driven out great nations in the past (Josh 23:9)	The Lord drives out the nations
C - C'	Repetition of part of the Deuteronomic covenant (Josh 23:6-8)	No inverted verse	Deuteronomic covenant commands

The Deuteronomic covenant, which is on the C – C' level of this chiasm, is similar in content to the list of commandments from Joshua 22:5 (page 184). Here is a comparison of these verses:

Command	Joshua 22	Joshua 23 - 24
Fear the Lord your God	v22:18, 20	v23:12-16
Love the Lord your God	v22:5	v23:11
Walk in His ways	v22:5	v23:6 - 8
Obey His commands	v22:5	v23:8
Listen to the Lord's voice	v22:2, 9	v23:5, 10, 14-16
Cling to the Lord	v22:5	v23:8
Serve the Lord	v22:5	v24:14-24

The chiasm of Joshua 23:3-10, along with verse 11, provides an example of a synthetic parallelism: a way of expanding and completing the original thought. The last verse of the chiasm is Joshua 23:10. The next verse states: *"So be very careful to love the LORD your God"* (Josh 23:11). Its placement after the other commands from the Deuteronomic Covenant emphasizes its importance; hence it is an example of synthetic parallelism.

The message of Joshua 23 and 24 can be summarized in chart form. With this message to *"love the LORD your God,"* the first part of a chart can be entered. As we move through the remainder of Joshua 23 and 24, we will complete other portions of this chart:

	Lord's Part	Our Part
Love		Love the Lord
Service		

Sinful Disobedience

The consequences of disobedience are next covered by Joshua. It answers the person who says "What if I disobey?"

Level	First presentation	Inversion	Theme
A - A'	If you align yourself with other nations, the Lord will become a curse (Josh 23:12,13)	By serving other gods, the Lord will cause you to perish (Josh 23:15b,16)	Consequences of rebellion
B - B'	None of the Lord's promises have failed (Josh 23:14a)	All of the Lord's promises have come true (Josh 23:14b,15a)	The integrity of the Lord's promises

The Lord is saying in the A – A' level of this inner tier chiasm that rebellion against the Lord will bring a curse and punishment. Other gods and other nations represent the temptations we can fall into, which further complicate our spiritual warfare. The consequences will be snares, traps, whips, thorns and eventually death. The B – B' level assures us of these consequences. Therefore, we are to fear the Lord, which is the first of the seven commands from the Deuteronomic covenant.

> If a believer bows down to false gods, expect curses in the form of increased spiritual warfare to follow.

The Lord's Unmerited Favor

Blessings from the Lord fall into two major categories: unmerited favor and merited favor. **Unmerited favor**, which is otherwise known as **grace**, is based on the Lord's compassion rather than on something we have done. Merited favor, which could be called blessings or the reward for **obedience**, is the result of having obeyed.

When we come to Christ and receive salvation, this is not because of anything we have done, and so it is called unmerited favor or grace. Church attendance, various forms of penitence and doing good things for people are all examples of doing work for the Lord; however, they are not the basis for unmerited favor. We receive salvation simply because we choose the Lord to be our personnel Savior.

> *For it is by grace you have been saved, through faith ...*
> (Eph 2:8,9).

The blessings and the curses listed in Deuteronomy 28 were for those that had either obeyed or disobeyed after receiving the Lord's unmerited favor. First the Lord gave unmerited favor. Then the blessings were given because they obeyed, and the curses were given because they disobeyed.

To the Jew prior to Christ, the Lord provided considerable unmerited favor, not because they did something, but simply because they existed. From Joshua 24:2-7, we see a summary of some of the unmerited favors that the Lord brought to Israel before issuing the Ten Commandments:

- Took Abraham to Canaan and gave him many descendants.
- Gave Abraham a son, Isaac.
- Gave Isaac two sons, Esau and Jacob, both of which left the land of Canaan: Esau to Seir and Jacob to Egypt.
- Brought the Israelites out of Egypt by empowering Moses and Aaron to bring them out.
- Put darkness between the Egyptians and Israelites, thereby protecting them.
- Drowned the Egyptians in the Red Sea as they pursued Israel.

Because of their disobedience after these unmerited favors, the Lord punished them with forty years in the desert until all the men twenty and over had died. Near the end of the forty years, the Lord continued His unmerited favor, as listed in Joshua 24:8-10:

- Destroyed the Amorites east of the Jordan so that the Eastern tribes could take possession.
- Refused to listen to Balaam, so the Israelites were delivered out of his hand.

The repetition of the Lord's blessings continued. To the new generation, the Lord again blessed them with unmerited favor, based on Joshua 24:11-13:

- Delivered the Israelites from the people of Jericho, as well as the nations of the Promised Land.
- Sent the hornet before them to drive out the nations.
- Provided His own sword and bow to destroy the nations.
- Gave the Israelites a land that they did not create or develop with cities, homes and farmland.

These twelve examples of unmerited favor are another form of repetition. They emphasize how the Israelites did not deserve any of these blessings because they had done nothing to warrant them. It would be interesting for those of us who call ourselves born-again Christians, to list the many unmerited favors that we have received.

Having now looked at these unmerited favors, we are now ready to fill in the second part of the chart that was started on page 195:

	Lord's Part	Our Part
Love		Love the Lord
Service	The Lord's unmerited favor	

Serving the Lord

A significant problem exists for Christian parents: how do we get our children to serve the Lord once we have passed on? Once we have left our life on this earth, we can no longer pray for our children, take them to church or special Christian events, act as a role model of Christian living, or speak to them about the great things of our Lord. We can only leave a legacy while here on this earth.

In this final and triumphant segment of the life of Joshua, we see his last effort to get the children of Israel to follow in his footsteps. The success of this effort is seen at the end of this dialog:

> *Israel served the LORD throughout the lifetime of Joshua and of the elders who outlived him ...* (Josh 24:31).

The elders were able to witness Israel continuing to serve the Lord. In other words, Israel served the Lord during the time when Joshua led the people and sometime thereafter.

The discussion on serving the Lord begins at Joshua 24:14 and ends with a covenant commitment to serve the Lord at Joshua 24:27. These verses start with the plea to serve the Lord (Josh 24:14), followed by Joshua's statement that he and his household will serve the Lord (Josh 24:15), and then the statement and re-statement by the children of Israel that they will serve the Lord (Josh 24:18, 22, 24).

At this point, we can fill in the next portion of our chart:

	Lord's Part	Our Part
Love		Love the Lord
Service	The Lord's unmerited favor	**Serve the Lord**

From this chart, we can see that our part includes loving the Lord and serving the Lord. The command to love the Lord was given in Joshua 23:11, and now, in Joshua 24:14-24, we see the urging to serve the Lord. Joshua 23 - 24 are linked together to stress the importance of both.

The commands to love the Lord and to serve the Lord are mandatory. If we do not walk in all His ways, we will soon stop serving the Lord. If we forsake the Lord by no longer clinging to Him, our love for the Lord has certainly waned.

Joshua, in stating that he and his household will serve the Lord, is upholding the Deuteronomic covenant. To put this another way, "serving the Lord" includes loving Him, walking with Him, listening to Him, obeying Him, and clinging to Him.

The Lord's Love

It is often stated that the word "love" is a verb, not a noun. That is, love is an action, not an emotion. If a person tells their spouse or their children that they love them but does not show it, that statement of love is deemed hollow and meaningless. Love requires action.

Love also needs to be wholehearted in order to be genuine. That is "... *with all your heart and with all your soul and with all your strength*" (Deut 6:5). In this respect it is similar to an emotion, yet it is at a much deeper level.

Can we slow down enough to experience this love? The Lord's wholehearted love for us shines when we see the sunrise and sunset, the flowers that bloom and the birds that sing. This is the love of a mother who takes her baby to her breast. This is the love that is offered during times of intense worship: Him to us, us to Him. He loves us wholeheartedly.

The Lord is patient with us, He is kind. He does not envy, He does not boast and He is not proud. He is not rude, not self-seeking, not easily angered and keeps no record of wrongs. He rejoices in the truth. He always protects, always trusts, always hopes and always perseveres (Paraphrase of 1 Cor 13:4-7).

The heart of the Lord is unending love. When we see or hear of His grace, it is His service to us. Putting it another way, the Lord's love is demonstrated by His unmerited favor as a way of serving us.

We can now complete this chart:

	Lord's Part	Our Part
Love	**The Lord loves us**	Love the Lord
Service	The Lord's unmerited favor	Serve the Lord

From this chart we can see what the Israelites should have understood: the Lord's unmerited favor was His way of demonstrating His love for them. We love the Lord because He loved us first. We serve the Lord because He served us first.

Consider these verses which refer to God's love for us:

> *Know therefore that the* LORD *your God is God; he is the faithful God, keeping his covenant of* **love** *to a thousand generations of those who love him and keep his commands.* (Deut 7:9)

It is by His actions that we see His love. The Israelites too would be able to say that they love the Lord because He loved them first. When a sign appears that is similar to what is on our garage door: *"As for me and my household, we will serve the LORD"* (Josh 24:15), think of our love for Him, how He has served us, and how He loves us.

Interwoven Chiasms

Joshua's final statement to the people of Israel is given in Joshua 24:14-27. These verses are also a grand example of the divine inspiration of the Book of Joshua: three chiasms are woven together.

Josh 24:	First part	Second part	Refrain
14	Now fear the LORD and serve him with all faithfulness.	Throw away the gods your forefathers worshiped ...	serve the LORD.
15	But if serving the LORD seems undesirable to you,	then choose for yourselves this day whom you will serve, ...	we will serve the LORD.
16-18	Far be it from us to forsake the LORD to serve other gods!	It was the LORD our God himself ... who lived in the land.	We too will serve the LORD ...
19-21	Joshua said ... "You are not able to serve the Lord."	He is a holy God ... he has been good to you."	We will serve the LORD.
22a	Joshua said, "You are witnesses against yourselves	that you have chosen to	serve the LORD."
22b-24	Yes, we are witnesses ...	Throw away the foreign gods among you ...	We will serve the LORD our God ...
25	Joshua made a covenant ...		
26	Joshua recorded these things in the Book of the Law of God.		
27	This stone is a witness against us.		

The Hebrew word **'abad** (aw-bad') means "serve." This word **'abad** appears fourteen times in Joshua 24:14-24. The phrase **'abad 'eth YHWH** (serve the Lord) appears nine times in these verses. We begin to see the interweaving of these three chiasms by noting how these three Hebrew words are presented:

Verses	First Presentation	Second Presentation
14	'eth YHWH 'abad	'abad 'eth YHWH
15	'abad 'eth YHWH	'abad 'eth YHWH
18	'eth YHWH 'abad Elohim	'abad 'eth YHWH
21		'eth YHWH 'abad
22		'eth YHWH 'abad
24		'eth YHWH 'abad Elohim

Even though sometimes the order of these Hebrew words changes, the understanding is the same. Again, repetition is for the purpose of emphasis.

In a similar way to the use of the word "Selah" in the Psalms, the words **'abad 'eth YHWH** (serve the Lord) becomes a refrain, indicating the end of the second chiasm. The diagram on page 200 shows this chiasm / refrain construct – there are three chiasms shown, each with a box around them. In other inner level chiasms in the Book of Joshua, we have seen a chiasm come to its completion and then another one start. In these chiasms, however, two chiasms are presented concurrently. The second chiasm ends with the refrain of **'abad 'eth YHWH**, and then the first or third chiasm continues.

The three chiasms, along with their verses, are summarized below to illustrate how these verses from Joshua 24:14-27 come together:

Chiasm	Title	Verses
First	You Are Not Able To Serve Him	Joshua 24:14a, 15a, 16, 19a
Second	The Insult of Rebellion and Sin	Joshua 24:14b, 15b, 17-18a, 19b-21a, 22b, 23
Third	Covenant Is Confirmed	Joshua 24:22, 25, 26, 27

Here is another way to illustrate these three chiasms:

First Chiasm:	Second Chiasm:
You Are Not Able To Serve Him	The Insult of Rebellion And Sin

Third Chiasm:
Covenant Is Confirmed

As with other chiasms in this book, we will look at each of these three individually. I have no explanation as to why this construct has been chosen except to say that this writing prowess again shows how the Lord must have inspired these Scriptures.

You Are Not Able to Serve Him

Many authors have struggled with the first part of Joshua 24:19.

> Joshua said to the people, "You are not able to serve the LORD. He is a holy God; he is a jealous God" (Josh 24:19).

Some take this verse literally by indicating the inability of the Israelites to serve the Lord. To support this premise, these people cite the Israelite's fall from faith as recorded in Judges. Others suggest that the Israelites were not able to serve the Lord when compared to how the Lord has provided for them.

Both of these interpretations have their merits. However, I would like to propose a third interpretation for consideration based on the use of this chiasm from Joshua 24:14a, 15a, 16 and 19a:

Level	First presentation	Inversion	Theme
A - A'	Serve the Lord faithfully (Josh 24:14a)	You cannot serve the Lord (Josh 24:19a)	Can / cannot serve the Lord
B - B'	Joshua: If serving the Lord is undesirable (Josh 24:15a)	Response: Serving other gods is undesirable (Josh 24:16)	Joshua's testing and the people's response

The A – A' level is an apparent contradiction. First Joshua says to serve the Lord faithfully, and then he boldly states that they cannot do that. But remember Joshua's heart: he wants his spiritual children to faithfully serve the Lord.

Let me try to explain this with an example. We have wasps that build nests under the eaves of our house. My wife, God bless her, could ask me to remove their nests. Because I can have an independent spirit, I would then choose when and if I would tackle that problem.

But what if my wife poses that problem as a challenge?

> "That wasp nest is too high for you; you can't possibly get that one."

In that case, she is more likely to see me rise up to the challenge. Some people call this "reverse psychology."

The B – B' level reveals this challenge. Joshua challenges them with his statement *"If serving the LORD seems undesirable to you ..."* (Josh 24:15), and their response is a hearty "No!"

The people that Joshua was speaking to in these verses were the leaders of Israel: the elders, leaders, judges, officers, etc. (Josh 24:1). Because of their position, they would potentially influence the Israelites with their actions. Joshua was looking for consistency.

The result is that the *"not able to serve"* (Josh 24:19) wording is not a statement of defeat or disgust; it is a challenge to give up their foreign gods and become faithful servants like Joshua.

> **Commit to live a life for the Lord in this battle for our minds.**

The Insult of Rebellion and Sin

We are studying the three interwoven chiasms that comprise Joshua 24:14-27. This second chiasm covers Joshua 24:14b, 15b, 17,18a, 19b, 20, 22b and 23.

Level	First presentation	Inversion	Theme
A - A'	Throw away the gods your forefathers worshipped (Josh 24:14b)	Throw away the foreign gods among you; turn your hearts to the Lord (Josh 24:23)	Get rid of the worship of the foreign gods
B - B'	Choose who you will serve (Josh 24:15b)	You have chosen to serve the Lord (Josh 24:22b)	Choose between the Lord and the other gods
C - C'	Unmerited favor in removing them from Egypt and in conquering the Promised Land (Josh 24:17,18a)	Curses will occur if the result of the unmerited favor is serving other gods (Josh 24:19b,20)	Considering the Lord's unmerited favor, sin and rebellion is an insult that will bring curses

The A – A' level identifies that some Israelites were still worshipping false gods from Mesopotamia, Egypt or the Amorite gods of the Promised Land. Joshua urged them to give up these false gods.

The B – B' level identifies the choice that was before the Israelites, just as we are given a choice today. We are not born into faith and the

Israelites were not born into the faith. The Lord grants unmerited favor, but we still have to walk in that faith.

The center point of this chiasm is presented on the C – C' level; it is a major theme of the entire Bible. The Lord shows in these verses how severely He responds to sin and rebellion.

> ... he will turn and bring **disaster** on you and **make an end of you** ... (Josh 24:20).

If the Lord has granted the grace (unmerited favor) of salvation, then rebellion and sin are a severe insult to the Lord who loves us and serves us. The Lord's unmerited favor gave His son Jesus Christ to suffer and die on our behalf. Sin and rebellion turn His suffering into a mockery.

> **If we fall into sin and rebellion, we must be prepared for the consequences because we have insulted the Lord.**

Covenant Is Confirmed

The third of the interwoven chiasms is presented in Joshua 24:22b, 25, 26a and 26b,27. For a covenant to be personally binding, two witnesses are essential. When a man and woman become married, two people attend the event but a judge or clergyman is an outside and personal witness. Notice in the following chiasm how the rock becomes the other witness:

Level	First presentation	Inversion	Theme
A - A'	You are your own witnesses (Josh 24:22b)	This stone shall be a witness (Josh 24:26b,27)	Two witnesses
B - B'	Joshua made a covenant with the laws and decrees (Josh 24:25)	Covenant is recorded in the Book of the Law of the Lord (Josh 24:26a)	Covenant is made and recorded

With the confirmation of this covenant (A – A' level), which may have been the commands of the Deuteronomic covenant, the first witnesses were the leaders of Israel. The second witness is the rock. There is a kind of permanence in the rock, just as there is permanence in Jesus Christ. The first set of witnesses may die, but the second witness is lasting.

On the B – B' level, Joshua confirms their pledge to serve the Lord with a covenant. This covenant was first spoken and then written for posterity.

In Joshua's first message at Shechem, he had the Law of Moses copied onto the stones (Josh 8:30-35). Joshua's final message to the Israelites was also delivered at Shechem, presumably at the same location.

I wonder: Was Christ in that rock? I'm just speculating and I have no proof. Only the inference from 1 Corinthians 10:4 would seem to support the idea that Christ could be in a rock:

> *They all ate the same spiritual food and drank the same spiritual drink; for they drank from the spiritual rock that accompanied them, and that* **rock was Christ** (1 Cor 10:3,4).

If Christ was in the rock in Shechem, then when Joshua culminated the covenant between the Lord and the people, he had Christ as a witness.

Jesus Christ, the Rock of all Ages, is our witness and our strength in spiritual warfare.

Concluding Remarks

Josephus concluded his writing about Joshua with these words:

> *He was a man that wanted not wisdom nor eloquence to declare his intentions to the people, but very eminent on both accounts. He was of great courage and magnanimity in action and in dangers, and very sagacious in procuring the peace of the people, and of great virtue at all proper seasons.* [52]

The writings of Josephus are admittedly difficult to read. The sentences are long, the sentence structure is awkward and the choice of words can be obscure. Yet within these writings is a wealth of information that compliments the Bible very well. The statements about Joshua which are shown above are such an example.

The above quote identifies seven characteristics of Joshua:

- Eminent in wisdom (he was wise).
- Eminent in eloquence (he was expressive and articulate).
- Wanted neither wisdom nor eloquence (he was humble).
- Of great courage (he was courageous).
- Of great magnanimity (he was noble and generous of spirit).
- Very sagacious (he knew how to obtain peace).
- Of great virtue (he had high integrity).

These are the characteristics of the people we should look for in our elected officials, pastors and spouses. Hopefully our President is a person like this. I hope you can say that your Pastor has these characteristics. If you or your children look for a spouse, I hope that this person resembles Joshua in these areas.

Regarding **wisdom**, we have repeatedly seen in this book where Joshua was able to use the spirit of wisdom that was passed on from Moses. Four of these examples include knowing when and how to cross the Jordan; knowing how to destroy Jericho, Ai and the many other cities; taking the people to Shechem for a time of commitment; and knowing to speak to the Lord that the sun and moon would stand still.

Joshua's **eloquence** is most apparent in Joshua 23 - 24. In this lengthy discourse, Joshua speaks to the leaders of Israel and obtains their commitment to continue what has been started in this conquered

---

[52] Josephus, 5.1.29.

land. Also, if Joshua was the author of the Book of Joshua, then his frequent use of chiasms would also be an example of his language skills.

When Joshua fell to the ground upon learning of the defeat at Ai, he showed true **humility**. Also, when the officers gave orders to be separate when the ark goes by, Joshua does not dispute the officers; instead, he told the people to *"consecrate yourselves"* (Josh 3:2-5).

I believe it took a great deal of **courage** to send the priests to the edge of the Jordan with the expectation that the water would stop. This was because both Moses and the Lord had instructed Joshua to be *"strong and courageous"* (Deut 31:6,7, 23).

Joshua was both **obedient** and **generous** in distributing the land to each of the tribes. The Lord indicated the land by the drawing of the lot, and Joshua gave without selfish motives.

Regarding **peace**, Joshua handled the determination of innocence or guilt regarding the Eastern tribes with discretion. Moses had promised peace to these tribes if they helped conquer the land. Joshua assured this by sending Phinehas and ten tribal leaders to investigate the alleged rebellion.

Joshua's **integrity** is best seen by how the people reacted to his commands. If he did not have the necessary upright character, a spirit of rebellion would likely have crept in during the invasion. But instead, every evil spirit that manifested itself was subdued in one way or another because of his righteous ways.

Following the Deuteronomic Covenant

Another measure of how Joshua performed is to look at how well he carried out the Deuteronomic Covenant:

- Fear the Lord your God (Deut 10:12).
- Love the Lord your God with all your heart and all your soul (Deut 10:12; 30:6, 16, 20).
- Obey the Lord your God (Deut 10:13; 30:2, 8, 10, 14).
- Walk in the ways of the Lord (Deut 10:12; 30:16).
- Listen to the Lord's voice (**rhema**) (Deut 30:20).
- Hold fast to the Lord (Deut 10:12; 30:20).
- Serve the Lord (Deut 10:12).

Joshua was successful in spiritual warfare because he closely followed these seven principles.

At the conclusion of the Jordan River crossing, Joshua lets the people know that the Lord stopped the water so that they would always **fear of the Lord** (Josh 4:24). Joshua knew this fear when the army was defeated at Ai, causing him to fall on his face in reverence to his

Lord (Josh 7:6). In his final discourse to the people, Joshua instructed them to *"fear the Lord"* (Josh 24:14).

Joshua never stated that he **loved the Lord his God**, but words can be cheap. On the other hand, he did tell the leaders of Israel to *"be very careful to love the LORD your God"* (Josh 23:11). It was Joshua's actions that showed how he loved his Lord. When there was sin in the camp, he acted swiftly to remove it (Josh 7:25). When repentance was needed, he took the Israelites to Shechem to encounter the Lord (Josh 8:30). When mercy was needed, he granted it to the Gibeonites, and he did not retract when the ruse was uncovered (Josh 9:26).

Whenever the Lord gave direction to Joshua, he **obeyed**. The Lord had said that circumcision was required, so Joshua had the men circumcised (Josh 5:3). In the same way, the Lord had said that celebrating the Passover was required, so Joshua had the people celebrate the Passover (Josh 5:10). The Lord said to purge the land of the Amorites, so he did his best. Obedience was a key component to Joshua's virtue.

Joshua **walked in the ways of the Lord** throughout the Book of Joshua. When the law was read to the people at Shechem, it was Joshua, not the high priest, who read the law (Josh 8:34). Joshua had lived with Moses as his understudy; he knew the ways of the Lord because Moses, his mentor, had taught him. So it is natural that Joshua would repeat the commands of the Deuteronomic Covenant to the people (Josh 22:5).

The Lord spoke to Joshua and he **listened**. In the first verse of the first chapter of the Book of Joshua, the Lord spoke to Joshua (Josh 1:1). This is a pattern that had started in the time of Moses: the Lord spoke to Moses face to face in the Tent of Meeting in the presence of Joshua. When the Lord was done speaking, Moses left the tent but Joshua remained (Ex 33:11). Throughout the Book of Joshua, the Lord spoke to him; this was the rhema word of the Lord.

False gods were shown to Israel during their entire campaign to conquer the Land. Each king and kingdom had their own gods, but Joshua **held fast to his Lord**. In his warning to the leaders of Israel, Joshua warned that if they served other gods and bowed down to them, the Lord's anger would cause them to quickly perish (Josh 23:16). Joshua saw the evil spirits manifest themselves: discouragement, criticism, pride, obsession, complacency, lust, deception and so on. Joshua was able to overcome these spirits by holding tightly to his Lord, the one true God.

Finally, Joshua **served** the Lord with all of his heart, mind and strength. Being a leader is a difficult assignment. For Joshua, he never complained but just kept on being the Lord's servant. He saw many battles and his army triumphed most of the time. His greatest success was not the victory of the Promised Land, but his servant relationship with his Lord. What a tremendous man of God!

As a result of Joshua's leadership in obedience to the Deuteronomic Covenant, the Lord gave Israel the following:

> *So the LORD gave Israel all the land he had sworn to give their forefathers, and they took possession of it and settled there. The LORD gave them rest on every side, just as he had sworn to their forefathers. Not one of their enemies withstood them; the LORD handed all their enemies over to them. Not one of all the LORD's good promises to the house of Israel failed; every one was fulfilled* (Josh 21:43-45).

They took possession, they were given rest and their enemies were defeated. That was successful spiritual warfare. Amen.

But as for me and my household, we will serve the LORD (Josh 24:15).

Like Joshua, I love the Lord and I fully commit to live my life for Him. I want a relationship with the Lord as Joshua had and I desire complete victory in this spiritual warfare.

_____   _____
Date   **Signature**

Spiritual Principles

Authority of Christ

Page	Principle	Reference
19	Do not fear the sword, but welcome its ability to remove causes of disobedience, thereby bringing greater holiness in our lives.	Lev 26:3-8
94	As with the angel and the hornet, Jesus Christ and the Holy Spirit have the authority and power to protect us, lead us and destroy demonic spirits that are tormenting us.	Ex 23:20-28
15	Christ provides the spirit of authority to believers; authority includes the ability to encounter the evil spirits and defeat them.	Num 27:15-20
76	The power of the Lord sets the captives free and causes the enemies of the Lord to fear Him.	Josh 4:3-9
115	Speak with the authority of Jesus Christ when engaging in spiritual warfare.	Luke 10:19
118	Christ, through His death and resurrection, wants to remove any curses that have been placed on us.	Josh 6:26

Deliverance

Page	Principle	Reference
109	As we deliver a person from demonic spirits, surround the individual with people and prayer so that Christ is in our midst.	Josh 6:3,4
111	All deliverances are unique; what worked previously may not work again.	Josh 6:4-13
134	The removal of the ruling spirit (king) brings deliverance to an individual.	Josh 8:1, 29
137	When attempting to liberate an individual, the demons must be removed from their place of safety.	Josh 8:5, 6
138	When attempting to intentionally deliver a person of demonic spirits, be well prepared.	Josh 8:14
150	When dealing with demonic spirits, understanding the name of the spirit or spirits will often identify how to deal with that spirit.	Josh 9:8
154	The demons must be brought under control before removing the ruling spirit.	Josh 10:7-15
158	Have strength and courage when going after the ruling spirits because the power of the Lord accompanies us.	Josh 10:22-25
160	Deliverance requires the total removal of the demonic forces.	Josh 10:35, 37, 39, 40

Dependence on the Lord

Page	Principle	Reference
13	To become better at spiritual warfare, be eager to be taught and be receptive to correction.	Deut 4:1
57	The more we allow the Lord to be our strength, the more fear we put in the devil and his demons.	Josh 2:11
74	Open hearts are needed to understand spiritual warfare; hardened hearts block the truth.	Josh 3:8, 9
162	In spiritual warfare, thank the Lord that we are able to witness His successes; do not give any credit to ourselves.	Num 20:12
205	Jesus Christ, the Rock of all Ages, is our witness and our strength in spiritual warfare.	Josh 24:22-27

Evil Spirits

Page	Principle	Reference
86	When we come across a spirit of rebellion, deal firmly and directly with that spirit.	Josh 5:2-8
91	If we want success in our spiritual warfare, stop complaining.	Josh 5:11, 12
124	Overindulgence, even when done in the name of the Lord, can leave a curse that lasts for generations.	2 Chron 7:5
140	Through the death and resurrection of Christ, He took authority over all principalities, powers, ruling spirits and demons.	Josh 8:29
178	Test the motives: if there is a spirit of discontentedness, deal with those issues in the presence of the Lord.	Josh 17:16
180	Test the motives: if there is a spirit of complacency, allow the presence of the Lord to help deal with those issues.	Josh 18:3-10
187	If we see a sudden change of attitude, suspect that the devil may be using a spirit of arrogance or pride to pull us down: gather the facts first.	Josh 22:10-14
188	Obsessive and compulsive behaviors can cause us to loose our relationship with the Lord.	Josh 22:17-20

Fighting the Battle

Page	Principle	Reference
48	After an intense spiritual battle, the Lord gives us His rest.	Josh 1:15
82	Put on the full armor of God (Eph 6:11, 13).	Josh 4:12, 13
114	Protect the presence of the Lord that is in our hearts, for we are in battle every day.	Josh 6:9
116	Spiritual warfare ultimately ends at the judgment seat of Christ; the Lord watches how the short term battles are handled for their long term consequence.	Josh 6:20-23
139	When preparing to be freed from demonic spirits, each and every area of our lives must be strong in the Lord so that we can withstand any attacks.	Josh 8:21
151	When a large spiritual battle is on the horizon, a humble heart will often save the day and no battle will need to be fought.	Josh 9:21-23
155	Be aware of potentially strong demonic attacks coming shortly after times of spiritual victory.	Josh 10:6
174	The Lord is looking for consistent, faithful servants who will do their part wholeheartedly in spiritual warfare.	Josh 15:14-17
203	Commit to live a life for the Lord in this battle for our minds.	Josh 24:14-19

Spiritual Principles

Lord's Methods and Plans

Page	**Principle**	**Reference**
16	If we are called by the Lord to a particular ministry, the Lord will provide the necessary spirit(s) to supplement our needs.	Deut 34:9
45	What we see in the physical is often a representation of what is happening in the spiritual.	Num 25:1, 2
59	Effective spiritual warfare can not only defeat the enemy's stronghold; it can lead people to Christ.	Josh 2:9-11
106	Be willing and available to conduct spiritual warfare on all seven days of the week, including the Sabbath.	Lev 23:5-8
166	In spiritual warfare, we may not be able to see what the Lord is doing with our natural eyes.	Josh 24:12
169	The Lord wants the whole assembly to show up when He appears in His glory.	Josh 18:1
175	We should each step into the full anointing that is available through the Holy Spirit.	Josh 15:1; 16:1

Our Walk

Page	**Principle**	**Reference**
11	In our pursuit for increased holiness, we must be successful at spiritual warfare.	Lev 22:31, 32
42	Salvation is available to many but few will find it.	Josh 6:22
52	We are to honor our commitments so we don't inadvertently increase the spiritual warfare in ourselves or others.	Josh 2:8-14
64	With effective spiritual warfare, we are to fear the Lord, love the Lord, obey the Lord, walk in His ways, listen to His voice, hold fast to the Lord and serve the Lord.	Deut 30:6-20
80	Transformed lives should understand the Lord's might, power and love, and His requirements for righteousness and holiness.	Josh 3:1 - 4:24
113	When looking for a release from demonic attacks, develop a strong and sincere practice of worship.	Heb 11:30
144	Success in spiritual warfare requires Christ to be at the center of our lives.	Josh 8:33
167	The Lord is not interested in the external; He is interested in our hearts.	Josh 12:6-8
190	Truthfulness can often be revealed when a person's story is consistent and he or she shows a willingness to accept the Lord's consequences.	Josh 22:24-28
194	Service to the Lord is far more than doing things for a church or for one another; service should be the outflow from a heart that has turned wholeheartedly to the Lord.	Josh 24:16

Spiritual Principles

Overcoming Oppression

Page	Principle	Reference
25	Having a deep love for the Lord and one another is a key to obtaining victory in spiritual warfare.	Mark 11:12, 22
79	Issues of spiritual warfare should be dealt with quickly.	Num 16:1-49
44	When we are told that a spiritual promise is ours, then possess that which was promised.	Josh 1:10
60	Be desperate for freedom from demonic oppression for ourselves and for others.	Josh 2:13
68	In seeking freedom from demonic attacks, remember that our enemy the devil can be filled with fear, and demons can tremble and shutter.	Josh 2:24
73	Stand firm against the devil's schemes. (Eph 6:11)	Josh 3:8,17
157	The Lord is waiting for us to take our stand first.	Josh 10:7-15
173	No matter how large the enemy appears, the Lord is to be our strength in overcoming obstacles.	Josh 14:10-12
192	Simple communication avoids many problems that otherwise might turn into spiritual warfare.	Josh 22:10

Rhema (Word from the Lord)

Page	Principle	Reference
21	Without a rhema word, the battle is much more difficult and can sometimes be impossible.	Deut 8:1-3
47	Keep the words of the Lord alive in our spirit.	Josh 1:8
98	Ask the Lord for a Word and be ready to receive.	Josh 5:14
108	When we hear the rhema Word, we are to be obedient to it.	Josh 6:2-16
113	Patiently seek discernment from the Lord to distinguish between demonic attacks and the hand of the Lord.	Prov 14:29
125	If the Lord is quiet about whatever direction we are to take, setting out on our own can give opportunities for the devil to advance.	Josh 7:4, 5
135	As we are about to take authority over the devil, we need to be sure we have heard correctly from the Lord.	Josh 8:13
147	Allow our thoughts to wander and dreams to be dreamt so that we can hear from the Lord, and truly see and understand the spiritual warfare that is taking place.	Josh 9:23, 24

Sin

Page	Principle	Reference
70	As we come to understand our own sinfulness, do not be separate from the Lord, but draw near to Him in cleansing and purification.	Josh 3:5
99	Sin can cause the presence of the Lord to disappear.	Josh 7:1
127	Sin, both overt and hidden, eventually breaks the covenant promise of protection.	Josh 7:11, 12
129	By confessing and turning from our sins, we prevent the footholds from becoming strongholds.	Josh 7:22, 23
163	Total obedience is a prerequisite for the complete defeat of the enemy's powers and rulers in our lives.	Josh 11:12-23
189	The problem with self-righteousness is that it causes us to assume a God-like importance.	Josh 22:18, 19
192	When a person acknowledges he or she was wrong and publicly proclaims the truth, demonic spirits are defeated.	Josh 22:31
196	If a believer bows down to false gods, expect curses in the form of increased spiritual warfare to follow.	Josh 23:12-16
204	If we fall into sin and rebellion, we must be prepared for the consequences because we have insulted the Lord.	Josh 24:17-20

The seven commands of the Deuteronomic Covenant:
- Fear the Lord your God
- Love the Lord your God with all your heart and all your soul
- Obey the Lord your God
- Walk in the ways of the Lord
- Listen to the Lord's voice (rhema)
- Hold fast to the Lord
- Serve the Lord

www.ingramcontent.com/pod-product-compliance
Lightning Source LLC
Chambersburg PA
CBHW071700090426
42738CB00009B/1604